MW00453896

Reverse Integration

Helping White America
Join the Village

Jay Klusky, Ph.D.

Foreword by Joy DeGruy, Ph.D.

U   E
P T O N
Press
Portland, Oregon

Reverse Integration
Helping White America Join the Village

by
Jay Klusky, Ph.D.

Published by:
Uptone Press
P.O. Box 66844
Portland, OR. 97290

Klusky, Jay
Reverse Integration: Helping White America Join the Village

ISBN: 978-0-9634011-4-4
LCCN: 2017917340

$19.95 Paperback
Printed in the United States of America

*This book is dedicated to
my dear, dear friend Ron Narode, a husband,
father, friend, and educator par-excellence.
Throughout his life he showed us all how to live . . .
and, most unfortunately and untimely, how to die.
This work would be much better if he were
around during its writing.*

.
.
.

Reverse Integration

Helping White America
Join the Village

.
.
.

Table of Contents

·
·
·

Foreword

In this timely and important work, Dr. Jay Klusky challenges the growing divisive trends that are threatening the integrity of American freedom and justice with the possibility of co-existing in a collective unified village. Hailing from New York, but embracing Portland, Oregon as his home, he describes his journey as a white man seeking to be a part of a broader community as a humble and life changing discovery.

There is no white savior complex to be found here, no claims to be the new expert on the experience of African Americans, Latino Americans, Native Americans, or people of color in general; poor people, people struggling at the bottom, or people occupying limited space at the top. In fact, he asserts no special or magical understanding of any other "other" for that matter.

Dr. Klusky does however, provide us with a rare glimpse into an outsider's journey to the inside of a culture and community reeling from multiple displacements, racial terrorism, and policies designed to economically marginalize its residents. This book is not just about the people that are living under the historical yoke of oppression, it is more a book about their heightened capacity and skill, beauty, strength and resilience. This book is for people wanting to join the 'village' to connect and grow themselves in the company of individuals, families, and groups that are different from themselves.

He invites white Americans to re-examine what they have been taught about American history and what they have come to believe about what it means to live in a multicultural and multiethnic environment. He discusses the etiology of our society's cultural divisions along the color lines and what the future holds, considering the majority non-white world that we have inherited.

Mostly, Dr. Klusky shares his experience and what he has learned about how to be and connect with people, presenting a sound argument for the social, economic, political, and personal benefit of making such connections. Beyond this, he asserts that to 'connect' is more than a grand social gesture, it is the moral and spiritual imperative of our day.

Dr. Joy DeGruy

Reverse Integration

Helping White America
Join the Village

.
.
.

Prologue

The Community That Was

The year is 2017. The African-American community in my city is no more. What was once a thriving, vital cultural enclave in my predominantly white city has been dismantled. Barbershops, barbecue joints, nightclubs, bookstores, and any number of black-owned businesses serving the community have been replaced by upscale grocery stores, coffee shops, high-end restaurants, boutiques, and any number of white-owned businesses serving the new residents. You can still find barbecue, but not like the old traditional.

Twenty years ago, numerous African-American grassroots and religious organizations serving the African-American residents who made this community their home did abound. These organizations were responsible for programming aimed at helping youth excel, seeing to the health needs of the elders, and providing employment services, to name but a few. Over the past two decades, these organizations have been in decline as those they were tasked to serve have left.

Did I say left? Actually, the former residents were systematically moved out to make way for the more affluent. Realtors descended on the community, literally knocking on doors offering the homeowners a fraction of their home's actual value in cash if they would sell immediately. Some homeowners, particularly those in financial distress, took the money. One of the reasons for their distress was the unwillingness of the local banks to allow them to borrow money against the value of their homes. Where realtors couldn't get homeowners to sell, the city raised their property taxes, making living in their homes unaffordable. To top all of this off, statutes were put on the books allowing landlords to evict their tenants without cause by giving them a simple 90 day notice.

In the 1990s, this dismantling went unnoticed by all but a few, though all the necessary systems and conditions were in place. Today, the community is unrecognizable to those of us who knew it a mere 15 years ago. The community that sprung up during World War II when African Americans, mostly from the South, moved here to work in the ship yards, was torn asunder and its denizens moved to the less desirable outskirts of the city, to an area dubbed "the numbers."

Did this happen in a city in a 'Red' state? Were these the machinations of your run-of-the-mill, stereotypical conservatives? Hardly. All this took place in one of the most progressively liberal cities in America, in one of the 'Bluest' states in our country. Portland, Oregon.

In a city that has a national reputation for being on the social cutting-edge, the powers that be continue to work to culturally isolate themselves, and hardly any of Portland's white citizens act as if they are aware that this is happening. At the same time that these citizens pat themselves on the back for creating one of the most 'livable' cities in America, they have made it, and continue making it, more and more unlivable for citizens of color.

Of course, this movement has not been without its consequences. Black students no longer had their old neighborhood schools to attend. The schools in their new neighborhoods, schools that have historically served their white constituents, have been ill-equipped to work with their African-American students and their families, and certainly not up to the task of addressing their needs. Few teachers and administrators understand the mores and nuances of African American culture. Most do not understand the role relationship building plays in the culture, and so do not identify the need to connect. Consequently, most are at a loss when it comes to building connections in a manner that resonates with those they are trying to serve. As a result, discord as well as dropout rates have increased, while at the same time the quality of education black students receive has declined.

Like the local schools, social service agencies in these areas are also unfamiliar with addressing the needs of African-American families. Many of their workers, the great majority of whom are white, have little experience working with families of color. Worse still, some of those workers are fearful of those families. Very often this results in well-meaning workers inadvertently angering and alienating those they are genuinely trying to help. In such instances, everyone loses.

And we haven't even begun to discuss the psychological, emotional, and spiritual impacts on a people who have lost their community. I can only imagine what it must be like to not have a familiar place to go; where I can feel connected to my roots; where I can be with people who look as I do, have similar sensibilities and reference points. Today, in Portland, if you are black, no such place exists.

White Americans who do not think about this may be excused, for it is our privilege to not have to go anywhere that we do not feel a part. Likely, Portlanders did not think about this, and Portlanders are decent people, right? We are progressive. We are forward-looking. We are socially enlightened. We certainly are not racist . . . Yet, we destroyed a community.

This is the big disconnect. On the one hand, Portlanders believe themselves to be good, inclusive, progressive, tolerant people . . . and I believe we are. On the other hand, most Portlanders remain unaware of our state's racist beginnings and how our state's historic racism plays a part in our institutions. And Portlanders are not unique in this respect. Most white Americans remain unaware of how our country's history of racism has been baked into the institutions of our society, how those institutions benefit even the poorest of white citizens, how those institutions continue to impact our fellow citizens of color, and how they contribute to the separation between white Americans and everyone else. So, we remain unaware of how those institutions can encourage us to view each other through the lens of 'us versus them,' and how that lens promotes disharmony and isolation.

Perhaps of greatest import, we remain unaware of how that lens diminishes us.

As America rapidly evolves into a society in which Americans of color outnumber white Americans, it is becoming increasingly important for us to learn how to act as one, how to make choices for the greater good, how to truly be a village. At the end of the day, this is the only approach that makes sense if we are all to thrive. Doing so first requires that we understand and respect each other, for understanding and respect are the roots of connection.

Until now, our sisters and brothers of color have had to develop an understanding of white America simply in order to survive. They have a much deeper understanding of white America than most of us know. They have had to work to integrate into the dominant culture. They've had to develop an understanding of our value structure, the manner in which we communicate, how we view fundamental concepts such as time and space, in order to be able to adapt. At the same time, those who have been most successful have kept their identity, strengthened their roots, and passed their legacy on to their children, while at the same time making significant contributions to our society.

It is time for white America to return the favor. It is time for us to open ourselves up to understanding the ways of others, to begin to explore how we can best integrate into their cultures, and how we can work together for the greater good. It is time for us to connect, join the village, and fight for justice for us all.

.
.
.

Part I:

Laying the Foundation

Carefully watch your thoughts, for they become your words. Manage and watch your words, for they will become your actions. Consider and judge your actions for they have become your habits. Acknowledge and watch your habits, for they shall become your values. Understand and embrace your values, for they become your destiny.

Mohandas Gandhi

.
.
.

Chapter I

The Challenges

This book is ostensibly about building greater connection and unity across cultures, particularly between white America and Americans of color. Yes, throughout our history there have been white Americans working to end the oppression of our brothers and sisters of color in all its manifestations, and those efforts continue to this day. From the abolitionists of the 18th and 19th centuries to the civil rights workers of the 20th century to the social justice warriors of today, these sung and unsung heroes need to be acknowledged and applauded. Many of you, who have picked up this book are among them.

Reverse Integration

I believe it is important to note that in many of these struggles a critical piece has often been lacking, that of truly understanding those we were and are fighting for and struggling with. Most abolitionists fought against slavery because they believed it was inherently wrong for obvious reasons. Many, if not the large majority of white abolitionists, never had a personal relationship with a black man or woman on equal terms. They were clear as to *what* they were fighting for yet had little understanding of *who* they were fighting for. Things on this account improved some during the civil rights era, as numerous, mostly young, white Americans fought on the front lines with their black and brown compatriots. These fighters notwithstanding, most white Americans who supported the expansion of civil rights, akin to their abolitionist progenitors, knew what they were fighting for yet far less about their brothers and sisters for whom they were fighting. A similar story can be told as to our current struggle for social justice.

Abolition, civil rights, social justice. These have been long, difficult struggles. The abolition of slavery in America was a fight that took 150 years and needed a Civil War to bring it to an end, though slavery in different forms continued for decades after. It took our citizens of color 100 more years to obtain a modicum of civil rights, rights that are today under attack. How long will it take for our society to become one in which equal opportunity and equal justice is the rule?

Contrast these struggles with America's rapidly changing views on gay rights these past 20 years. In this relatively short period of time, we have gone from 'Don't ask don't tell,' to the acceptance of gay marriage throughout much of the country. And heaven help you if you attempt to pass a law limiting gay rights –

North Carolina in 2016 comes to mind. We are likely only a decade or two away from sexual orientation becoming a non-issue.

What has been the difference? I maintain the difference is one of connection. The vast majority of Americans have a personal relationship with a person who identifies as LGBT and/or Q. We have a daughter, son, brother, sister, parent, aunt, uncle, cousin, or close friend who identifies as such. If we don't have a direct connection, we are closely related to someone who does. Heck, even Dick Cheney is pro-gay rights. Would be so if he didn't have a lesbian daughter? I maintain that one of the dynamics holding America back from becoming a nation that lives up to its creed is the lack of connection between white Americans and their fellow citizens of color.

The overarching purpose of this book is to suggest a path white folks can walk to build personal connections with their sisters and brothers of color. I believe that establishing personal connections is the key to bringing people together and making manifest the just society so many of us desire. Unfair treatment of others is unfortunate; unfair treatment of our friends and loved ones is intolerable. I believe that manifesting that just society is the only way to ensure our survival, as injustice has been at the root of so much misunderstanding, discord, suffering, and misery throughout history. Now, more than ever, as the challenges we face threaten to overwhelm us, developing our understanding of, affinity for, and empathy with those different from ourselves will be crucial. I believe doing so begins with establishing real personal connections.

Attempts at connection have been going on for over 50 years. In the 1960s, these often took the form of encounter groups focusing on racism and racial differences. The 1970s saw the beginning of 'fruit and festival' recitations in our schools where racial difference was described by indigenous foods, celebrations, and religious practices. By the late 1980's through the early 2000's, diversity education evolved into somewhat more academic presentations on multi-cultural difference and cultural sensitivity, whereby participants became more cognizant of the diverse ways people express themselves through the lenses of their culture. Over the past decade, cultural sensitivity has been rebranded as cultural humility, with the goals of training being very similar – helping participants view the world from viewpoints other than the one with which they are most familiar. More recently, the focus of diversity education has shifted to understanding white privilege. These are the more forward-looking approaches. However, it should be noted that all the training in the world, even with the best of intentions will only be as valuable as an organization's commitment to change.

On the other hand, there are numerous organizations who view diversity training as something they must do to meet some tacit or written requirement. A few of these organizations have been mandated to provide such training as a result of negative publicity and/or lawsuits. Very often, these trainings amount to little more than an hour or two lecture focused on political correctness – how not to offend others.

Forward-looking or not, rarely, if ever did these attempts require participants to truly build personal connections. Whatever the approach, whether they be presentations genuinely aimed at promoting understanding and change, or presentations intended to simply meet some obligation, it is very common for a number of white participants to feel as if they are under personal attack. The result has been numerous well-intentioned people being put on the defensive and becoming inhibited to engage.

The Challenge of Connection

Working to help white Americans connect with those of color in such a way that promotes greater understanding and unity has posed, and continues to pose many challenges. Chief of which is how can we have discussions about cultural difference in such a way that doesn't put us white folks on the defensive?

Recently, I was teaching a class on educational strategies for physical therapists to graduate students at a local university. Approximately, 85% of my students were white. The focus of a portion of the class was on building relationships with those they will serve. To this end I was presenting a talk on cultural difference and the importance of being aware of the cultural norms of the patients the students would be seeing. I used as an example the value in many Latino cultures of paying respects to the male head of the household upon your introduction to the family, especially if you yourself are a man. In an effort to verify this, I asked one of the students who was from South America if this was actually the case. He confirmed that it was.

I must say, I was not all that surprised as I read the class feedback some weeks later, that one of the white students, (the student identified herself as such) referring to this event, accused me of being racist. As both a presenter and a participant, I have been involved in similar discussions at which a participant, most often white, takes offense at any mention of differences among groups of people. Deeper discussions of race, racism, privilege and injustice are far more likely to trigger stronger defensive responses.

Most white Americans, like folks all over the world are good people. We mean well and are sensitive to the trials and tribulations of our fellow humans. Witness how so many of us respond to disasters at home and around the world – we give our time and our money to help those in need, regardless of race, creed, or color. So, when we are presented with information that challenges our beliefs about who we are and what we do, some of us can get defensive.

This can be particularly salient for those of us who work to help others. Whether we are a professional or a volunteer in service to others, it can be difficult to learn that some of the things we have done have been more harmful than beneficial. Failed help can be an awful feeling. I don't know anybody who enjoys hearing that their best efforts were not good enough – worse still, that their efforts contributed to making matters worse for those they believed they were helping.

An awful tragedy occurred at a Portland elementary school in the late 1980s. A young Thai boy, not feeling well in class, was sent to the school nurse. Upon examination, the nurse noticed what she believed to be a bruise on the boy's lower back. The nurse, a mandatory reporter, called the child abuse hotline and filed a report. An investigation was triggered and when the father found out he was being looked at as his son's abuser, he took his own life in shame and embarrassment. Subsequently, it was found that the mark on the boys back was a birthmark typically found on boys from Thailand.

Certainly, this was an extreme and unusual event, one which most likely traumatized all involved. The depth of the family's calamity was without measure. As someone who has worked on the front lines serving people for over 40 years, I can only imagine what the nurse had to endure. Was the nurse a racist? Certainly not. Did the nurse believe she was helping? Almost certainly. Was she a good person? Now, I never met her but I would say a person devoting her professional life to ministering to the health needs of children is highly likely to be worthy of admiration.

On a much less consequential scale, events in which white people believe themselves to be helping people of color, though actually getting in their way abound. Good, well-meaning, inclusive, progressive folks behave in ways that are regularly perceived as insensitive and at times even racist by those they are working to aid. Being anything but helpful is the farthest thing from our mind, yet our efforts are at times perceived otherwise. I find it sad that some people, having too many experiences in which their efforts to help have failed, can come to resent those they were attempting to assist. What a far cry from the original intent. Without the means to connect with those who are different from us, the good we can do, the good we want to do, the good we intend to do will be limited. If we are to be the best we can be and do the most good we can do, we need to build our capacity to connect more deeply with those around us.

In order to do so we need to make these difficult discussions inviting and respectful of all. We need to help people open their hearts and minds to the differential treatment their fellows of color receive at the hands of our society's institutions. We need to support well-meaning people doing good work in organizations and institutions that traditionally disadvantage those of color in their efforts to do even better work and perhaps to change the culture of their workplace.

Well intentioned outcomes that go awry are but one of the challenges of this work. There are others. A number of white Americans are not even aware differences between the treatment of white Americans and Americans of color even exist. Just the other day, I was having dinner with some friends when the topic of gentrification came up. As I was relating the plight of the African-American community in Portland one of my friends, a commercial banker, responded somewhat incredulously, "Bankers can't treat people differently because of race. That's illegal." He had no idea that his industry has been doing so since its inception over 200 years ago.

Of course there are those who are clearly aware of such differential treatment throughout the fabric of our society and believe this is how things ought to be. My hope, nay my expectation, is that over the ensuing decades these people will be marginalized and wield less and less power as we become a more inclusive, healthier society.

The Challenges of Writing This Book

After reading the first draft of the manuscript my close friend, Dr. Joy DeGruy, a woman who has been working the past 30 years in the fields of diversity education, trans-generational trauma, and social justice told me succinctly that she understood what I was trying to do, that the effort had merit, and that my book would mostly piss people off. A lengthy discussion ensued.

The challenge of tackling this subject in such a manner that, rather than being off-putting, will invite thoughtful consideration has not been insignificant. My purpose is to present what many have found to be difficult material in a manner that may invite both reflection and discussion, and so inspire folks to connect more meaningfully with each other. My hope is that this work will invite readers, white readers in particular, to take a more critical look at the injustices inherent in our systems. My hope is that this work will invite readers to further examine their own behaviors, attitudes, and beliefs towards those different from themselves. And my hope is that such an examination will encourage my white brothers and sisters who have not done so already, to work to genuinely connect with their sisters and brothers of color.

Another challenge in writing a book of this nature is the wide disparity of experience that readers bring to it. Many of us have been involved in this work for the better portion of our lives – some for much longer than I. At the same time, there are many others who are just beginning. I am well aware that for a number of readers some of this material, perhaps much of it, will be familiar. I have struggled with this throughout the process of writing. At times I have thought this work trite and so put it down and prepared to move on to my next project. Then I speak with somebody about it and they tell me how beneficial they believe this work can be. Hence, I write on. So, for those readers for whom parts of this work is old hat I ask your forbearance. For those for whom these discussions are relatively fresh, all I ask is that you address them with an open mind and open heart.

Why Me?

Good question. One that I often ask myself. Personally, I rail at injustice. My heart aches when I see people treated unfairly. Though I have tried to maintain my perspective and optimism, I have been both angered and dismayed at the politics of divisiveness that has taken hold in our nation, for these are antithetical to our creed. I believe white America has yet to play its part in making America a truly just, unified, and yes, great society. To this end, I would like to make a contribution before I die. So, here's a little background before we begin in earnest.

I am a short, bald-headed, goateed, 62 year-old white man. I was raised in an orthodox Jewish home in the Bronx, though I am neither observant, nor do I really identify as Jewish. (That said, if they take to killing Jews again, I know whose side I'm on.) I am also well aware that there are still those white folks who, due to my ethnic background, would not let me into their clubs. I also know that, those people aside, in America I am viewed as a white man and receive most of the benefits and privileges that redound to that status.

I moved to Portland 43 years ago at the age of 19, and with the exception of a three-year hiatus to get my doctorate in cognitive psychology at UCLA in the late 1980s, I have lived here ever since. In the summer of 1990, after completing my graduate studies, I began working in Portland's African-American community. Working with grassroots organizations, I developed and presented leadership programs for middle school students, and life/learning skills programs for high school students. Through one of the most successful organizations, Self Enhancement, Inc.(SEI) I ran their Family Literacy Program and contributed to programs helping youth make the transition out of gangs and into the mainstream. I put an alternative high school in Portland's House of Umoja, a residence facility for African-American youth in lieu of traditional juvenile detention. Most recently, my partner Aaron Bell, Sr. and I founded Guiding Light Family Services. Guiding Light, contracts with Oregon's Department of Human Services to help distressed families at risk of being torn asunder remain intact, and help families reunify after their children have been removed.

While I believe I've done some pretty good work helping youth and their families through the years, in retrospect I can't claim I have done anything earth shattering. I have not been a 'savior,' and I don't expect another movie to be made highlighting a white guy or gal who gets with the disadvantaged kids of color and changes their lives. I have just been a guy who has contributed, and I certainly couldn't have done any of the work without the blessings and support of those African-American leaders who ran the organizations in which I served.

What I can claim though, is that my life has been enriched immeasurably both by the friendships that grew during my time in the community, and through relationships with the colleagues with whom I worked and the students whom I have served. I certainly believe I have received considerably more than I have given.

The opportunity to become part of a community so different from the one with which I was most familiar, provided me with the education of a lifetime. As a result of my friendships I have had the chance to learn about the experiences of African-Americans in Portland Oregon from their perspective. I was able to hear their true views on events current and historical. Through the years, I grew to have a better sense of the different ways we all move through the world. Underpinning all of this, I learned how to simply be part of a community.

I learned all of this and more thanks to the generosity of all my teachers, from the youngest child to the wisest elder, all those who took the time to call me out and pull me up. I am grateful to all of them. Over the years, they came to accept me as part of their community, the African-American community of North-Northeast Portland, a community that has all but ceased to be.

One last item before we dive in. There are two people I would like to introduce you to: my mentor and friend, Dr. Jim Samuels, and my friend and guide, Dr. Joy DeGruy. Lessons I have learned from both of them flow through this book. I would certainly not be the person I am today without their friendship, tutelage, and guidance.

My Mentor and Friend – Dr. Jim Samuels

It was in the midst of my youthful angst at the age of 19 that I contacted Jim and he invited me out to Portland to study with him. He remains my mentor, friend, and ally to this day. He has been one of the most influential people in my adult life, a life that has been blessed by relationships with so many exceptional and wonderful people. It was under Dr. Jim's tutelage that I developed my counseling chops. It was under his tutelage that I began to develop my own philosophical approach to the world. It was under his tutelage that I learned how to maintain my equilibrium in the most stressful of circumstances. It was Dr. Jim who developed many of the training materials that I have been using in my practice the past 35 years.

My Friend and Guide – Dr. Joy DeGruy

We first met in the summer of 1990 at SEI at a lecture Joy was presenting on cultural difference. At that time she was not Dr. Joy, she had not yet written her seminal book, *Post Traumatic Slave Syndrome: America's Legacy of Enduring Injury and Healing*, nor was she yet a nationally, and internationally renowned speaker. She was warm, brilliant, driven to help her people, and one of the most interested, thoughtful, and engaging persons I have had the pleasure to know. We could and would talk for hours about all manner of subjects. There was nothing we wouldn't talk about and not much we couldn't talk about. Of course, the topics of so many of our conversations turned to race, ethnicity, and culture. In short order, she became my chief guide through the African-American community. Today, Joy remains one of my closest friends and confidants. It will not be surprising that she plays a role in so many of the stories told throughout this book.

The seeds for this work were sown by Joy who, on a number of occasions, would tell me of the unique position my journey has put me. She believes, as have I come to see, that my academic training as a cognitive psychologist coupled with my years of experience working on the ground in the African American community in Portland and becoming a part of that community, provides me with a unique perspective. Translating that perspective through this book has been one of my greatest challenges, a challenge I hope to have adequately met.

Now, just to be clear, I am not an 'expert' on African-American culture, on African-American history, and certainly not on the African-American experience. That said, I have had the opportunity to be around many cultural experts and have strived to learn from them all. These experts, my teachers, have been everyone of color with whom I have come in contact. From the youngest to the oldest, I have worked to do my best to understand their experience, see the world as they see it, then do my best to help white folks build connection through understanding.

In part, *Reverse Integration* is the story of my journey and the lessons I learned along the way. In part, it is a discussion of the evolutionary sociological and psychological forces in play as we work to truly connect with each other and build a better world for us all. It is my hope that some of my white brothers and sisters, who have not already done so, will be inspired to set out on their own expedition of discovery.

Chapter 2

Joining the Village:

A Matter of Survival

America is changing. Powerful demographic, economic, social, and technological forces are in play as America morphs into a society barely recognizable from the America that existed as recently as 50 years ago.

America is no longer the white country white Americans have believed it to be for the past 250 years or so. We've had a Black President and have a Latina on the Supreme Court. As of this writing, an African American woman is about to grace the front of the twenty dollar bill. There are a growing number of African, Latin, and Asian American civic leaders and local news people. More and more advertising is being directed at consumers of color. But these are just some of the more visible manifestations of the changing face of our country.

Our Changing Demographics

Numerous demographic studies project America will become a majority minority country by the middle of this century. In 2010, the U.S. minority population was 30 percent; and according to one study it is expected to exceed 50 percent by 2050.[1] Another study projects the white majority to be gone by as early as 2043.[2] In 1960, the population of the United States was 85% white; by 2060 it will be only 43 percent white.[3]

> "In fact, most of America's net population growth will be among its minorities, as well as in a growing mixed-race population. Latino and Asian populations are expected to nearly triple, and the children of immigrants will become more prominent. Today in the United States, 25 percent of children under age 5 are Hispanic; by 2050, that percentage will be almost 40 percent."[4]

Today, in 20 of the 25 most populous American cities, ethnic minorities outnumber whites. Ethnic minorities outnumber whites in New York City, Los Angeles, Chicago, Houston, Philadelphia, Phoenix, San Antonio, San Diego, Dallas, and San Jose, our 10 most populous cities.[5]

Perhaps one of the most telling indicators of our shift in demographics is that more and more advertising is being directed at consumers of color. In early 2014, three iconic American brands, Coke, Chevy, and Cheerios, rolled out ads during the Super Bowl and Olympics that were aimed at what one voice-over called "the new us."[6] Is it any surprise that there are greater and greater numbers of actors of color being used in television advertising? Yes, our society is changing.

Our Changing Economics – In America

Not only is America changing in terms of ethnicity, it has significantly changed when it comes to the distribution of income and wealth. The Congressional Budget Office reported that between 1979 and 2007 the average household income of the top 1% of earners increased by just about 400%. The average income of the top 20% doubled during this time. The average income of the remaining 80% of us has stayed the same, and when you take into account the increase in our cost of living during this time, the functional income of the bottom 80% of Americans has declined.[7]

In 2011, the top 1/10 of 1% of households in America earned just about $24 million a year; the top 1% of households earned just over $1 million per year; the next 9% earned $161,000 per year; and the bottom 90% earned just under $30,000 per year, and these gaps continue to widen.[7]

Economists Emmanuel Saez and Gabriel Zucman reported that over the past three decades the share of household wealth owned by the top 1/10 of 1 percent has more than tripled from 7 to 22 percent.[8] In 2012 the share of wealth owned by the top 1/10 of 1% of families equaled that of the bottom 90%. The last time such disparity existed in our country was almost 100 years ago as we were building toward the Great Depression.[9]

Simply put, the vast majority of us are growing poorer, and we are not alone. Our African, Latino, Native, Asian, Arab, and Island citizens are in the same boat. Unless we make significant changes, our prospects are not looking bright. The American dream has, for the majority of Americans, mostly been more myth than reality and it has become even more so over the past 30 years. The overwhelming majority of those who are born into families occupying the lower rungs of the socio-economic ladder will remain there throughout their lives. The same holds true for those born into wealthy families. Until recently, the overwhelming majority of those born into middle class families were likely to remain there throughout their lives also. Today, a few of those born into the middle class are rising up while many, many more are dropping down.

Since 1982, real median household income in the United States has increased by approximately 10% while, according to the American Institute for Economic Research, our cost of living has almost tripled.[10] With few exceptions, we are all feeling it. Solid, stable jobs that once provided those with a high school education a middle-class lifestyle have all but disappeared, having been replaced by service sector jobs that barely pay a living wage. The cost for higher education, still the most reliable path to economic viability, is through the roof and Americans now have more education debt than credit card debt. In 1982, my last term at Portland State University, I paid $230 for 21 credits worth of courses. Today, for Oregon residents to attend, it costs about $160 a credit!

This decades long downturn in economic fortunes alone, justifiably has many Americans of all ethnicities concerned, even frightened. It wasn't too long ago when Americans with a high school education could find good paying jobs in manufacturing – jobs that allowed them to buy a home, raise their children, send them to college, provide for their family's health needs, take regular family vacations, and secure their retirement. These workers were the backbone of America's middle class. Few such jobs remain.

Couple this with our changing demographics and it is readily understandable how many white Americans have become downright fearful – fearful of losing what little wealth they have, fearful of losing their security, their perceived power, and their believed access to the American dream. It is such fears that those in power use to fuel white anger and direct it against Americans of color. This playing upon our fears by the wealthy and politically powerful have provoked many white Americans to adopt that 'us versus them' mentality. It is such fears that have drawn many of us to the rhetoric of division and isolation. It is such fears that have driven some to violence. And it is a strategy that has been adopted by the rich and powerful for millennia - provoking those on the lower rungs of the socioeconomic ladder to fight each other for the crumbs that remain after the rich and powerful have eaten their fill.

This all might make a sort of sense if Americans of color bore some of the responsibility for our economic misfortunes, but of course they have not. The responsibility lay primarily with the forces of economic globalization and automation, coupled with our government's economic policies.

Economic Changes Around the World – Some Impacts of Globalization

Consider the following from Howard J. Ross's book, *Reinventing Diversity*:[11]

- *If you're one in 1 million in China . . . There are 1300 people just like you. If you're one in 1 million in India, there are 1100 people just like you.*

- *The 25% of the population in China with the highest IQ is greater than the total population of North America. In India it's the top 28%. They have more honor students then we have students.*
- *In 2006 there were 1.3 million college graduates in the United States, 3.1 million in India, and 3.3 million in China.*
- *All of the college graduates in India speak English.*
- *In 10 years, China will become the number one English-speaking country in the world, if it is not already.*
- *In the next eight minutes, 60 babies will be born in the United States, 244 babies will be born in China, and 351 babies will be born in India.*
- *More than half of the 21-year-olds in the United States have already put material on the Internet.*
- *70% of US four-year-olds have used the Internet.*
- *Through radio, it took 38 years to get information out to 50 million people; through television, that number was cut to 13 years; through the Internet it can be a matter of days.*
- *There are now more than 1 billion Internet devices in the world.*
- *More than one in eight married couples last year met online . . . Many met and married people from different countries. (pg.20)*

Our world is changing rapidly. From the time of Columbus' misguided voyage (he was nowhere close to where he thought he was) to World War II, European nations had been the dominant force in the world economy. Soon after World War II, the United States took the lead. We have been the dominant economic force for the past seven decades. While still powerful, our position is being challenged by what we arrogantly used to call the second and third world.

Today, China and India are becoming economic superpowers; Brazil is not too far behind. While English continues to be the language of world business, much business is being done in places other than the English-speaking world. With globalization, Americans are competing for jobs with Kenyans, Iranians, Indians, Koreans, Chileans, Fijians, the Chinese, Egyptians, Nigerians, you get the idea. India's Institutes of Technology are so competitive that some prospective students are using elite American academic institutions such as M.I.T., Cal Tech, Harvard, and Stanford as their "safe" schools.

Perhaps the greatest change we now face is the disempowerment of nation states. Countries, even the most powerful, are losing their influence as business goes global. If an enterprise doesn't like the business climate or tax structure in America, it may move its offices to Ireland or its manufacturing plants to Mexico. If labor becomes too expensive in one country, a company will simply move to another. If a corporation believes regulations to be too onerous in North America, it may very well move to South America.

As recently as 70 years ago, most of us lived and worked within miles of where we were raised. Since the 1970s, many of us have been crisscrossing the country in search of economic opportunities. Soon, we will have to crisscross the world. Once again, if we and our children are to be successful, we will need to be able to fit into a variety of societies.

Fears Real and Imagined

Be afraid – be very afraid! That's been the message since the attacks on 9/11. Be afraid of the Taliban. Be afraid of Al-Qaeda. Be afraid of ISIS. Be afraid of terrorists. Be afraid of Iran and North Korea. Be afraid of Ebola and Zika. Be afraid of Russia and China. Be afraid of Muslims. Be afraid of immigrants and refugees. Be afraid of young black men. Be afraid of the 'Other.' Be afraid that America is changing.

In the Summer of 2014, there was an Ebola outbreak in West Africa. A gentleman traveling in that part of the world arrived in America already infected and despite the best efforts of those caring for him, died a few days later. Seemingly within hours, Americans were losing their minds over the dreaded virus. It turned out Ebola in America was very much ado about very little. The ensuing months saw, I believe, six people in the United States contract the virus. All of them survived.

During that time I was facilitating a father's parenting group when one of the participants came in highly agitated.

"We're all going to die!" he screamed in panic.

Assuming he was not stating a philosophical and biological truth, I asked him why he believed that, to which he responded nearly hyperventilating,

"A woman checked herself into a hospital in Milwaukie (a Portland suburb) with Ebola earlier today."

I knew of the event of which he spoke and informed him and the group that what actually happened was a woman, believing she had unusual symptoms, quite responsibly, went to the hospital to have herself checked out. The resulting examination indicated she had nothing more than a cold. Of course, the local media sensationalized the story leading many to draw a similar conclusion to that of our participant.

Fear is healthy when it is in response to real threats and when it moves us to take actions that will mitigate those threats. Fear is debilitating when the perceived threats are not real or when it either provokes us to take inappropriate actions or leads to a kind of paralysis. Unfortunately, it appears as if efforts have been made over the past 15 to 20 years to turn us into a fearful people. More unfortunate still, is that many Americans have become more concerned with imaginary threats than with real ones. Yes, I believe we are in a state of crisis. The overarching question is whether or not we will act to mitigate the real ones.

Crises Near and (not so) Far

Amadou Diallo. Manuel Loggins Jr. Ronald Madison. Kendra James. Sean Bell. Eric Garner. Michael Brown, Tamir Rice. The list goes on. These are just a few of the unarmed African-American men, women, and boys who have been killed at the hands of police. The summer of 2016 saw Alton Sterling, an African-American father of a 15-year-old son shot and killed by police in Louisiana, as they had him pinned down; Philando Castile, an African-American man was shot and killed by police in Minnesota as he reached into his pocket to provide them with the ID that they had asked for; and an African-American gunman shot down five police officers in Dallas.

Unfortunately, unnecessary fatal shootings of men and women of color by police is nothing new in America. Equally as unfortunate, are attacks on police officers. It seems as if our society is on the verge of war. Not since the 1960s have we seen tensions so high. The good news, such as it is, is that peaceful protests sprung up in response to these tragedies across the country. Perhaps there is a chance for change.

These events are symptomatic of the crises we are facing in our land. Our economy is in crisis. While a handful of Americans have prospered significantly in our economy over the past decades and will continue to prosper for years to come, economic prosperity for the vast majority of Americans during the same time has been on the decline, and prospects are not great.

Our government is in a state of crisis. The entrenchment in Congress of Democrats and Republicans, and the conflict between our legislative and executive branches, have all but paralyzed our government, making it nigh but impossible for them to address the most important issues facing our nation and the world. Heck, many of our representatives will not even accept basic science. In 2016, not a single Republican candidate for president would say publicly that they accept evolution, one of the most fundamental principles of biological science. Fifty-six percent of Republicans in Congress say that they do not accept that humans are partly responsible for our changing climate, a fact accepted by 99.9% of the scientific community.[15] Views on something as basic as science are just one example of the yawning gap between the parties. If the seemingly unbridgeable chasm between the two main parties continues to widen, our democracy no longer will be able to function.

We, the people, are in crisis.
- In 2010, America ranked 27th among industrialized nations as it pertains to infant mortality.[16]
- In 2014, 46.7 million Americans (14.8%) were living in poverty; 15.5 million were children. (That's 21.1% of America's children) [17]

- In 2011, of the 19 OECD nations (Organization for Economic Co-operation and Development) America had a higher poverty rate than all but Mexico and Turkey.[18]
- Since 2000, the number of Americans living in poverty has increased by 24%.
- In the 10 years between 1989 and 1999 the number of billionaires in America quadrupled, from 66 to 268.[19]
- In 1979 top executives earned 27 times the average worker's salary. In 2008, that grew to 275 times. [20]

American children across the country are going hungry. Large numbers of them arrive at school each day on empty stomachs. When they are fed at school, the food is often not terribly nutritious. Many of the selections have been long on empty carbohydrates, sugar, and fat; and short on protein, vegetables, and fruit. In 2011, as part of an agricultural appropriations bill, Congress declared that 1/8 of a cup of tomato paste had as much nutritional value as half a cup of vegetables.[21] As a result, schools were able to declare that they were providing 'vegetables' to their students when they served your basic cheese pizza.

Our water supply is at risk. In Los Angeles, no one who can afford to buy water drinks water out of their tap. In Flint, Michigan the water is downright poisonous. Washington D.C. and New York, all of Southern California and Illinois, and agricultural regions in the Dakotas, Nebraska, Arkansas, North Texas, Ohio, and Minnesota comprise the top 10 areas with the highest risk for water scarcity in our country.[22] The aquifers in in California's Central Valley, the Colorado River basin, and the southern Great Plains are being severely depleted to counter severe drought that has been one of the effects of our changing climate. In the Central Valley, where once farmers had to drill down 500 feet for water, today they have to drill down more than 1000 feet. When the water in these aquifers is gone, it will be gone for good.[23]

Our ability to reason and critically address issues is on the decline. The Internet is rife with folks spouting all manner of foolishness, often with the intent to incite our baser emotions. Yes, all of our mainstream news agencies select their stories based upon some editorial agenda; fair enough, there's a lot of stuff to choose from. However, a small handful of those outlets have demonstrated time and again they are not beneath reporting unvetted stories made up out of whole cloth. This can become a problem when a significant portion of Americans, are either unwilling or unable to critically think about what they are watching and reading. The hoo-ha about President Obama not being an American citizen comes readily to mind.

While our leaders are concerned about Islamic terrorists coming to our shores, they rarely acknowledge long-standing homegrown American terrorism. The KKK and other white supremacist/neo-Nazi groups have been encouraging people towards violence for decades. As more and more of us white males become disaffected and stressed out by our perception of limited opportunities, more will turn to violence. Sandy Hook, Columbine, Emanuel AME, the Oklahoma City bombing, Charlottesville the list goes on, were all perpetrated by white American males. The same is true for those who have attacked clinics and doctors who provide family-planning services, including abortions. Most of the perpetrators had some connection with homegrown terrorist organizations. Organizations that advocate separation from, and hate of, others are terrorist organizations. Those with a microphone that condone and/or insight such violence, aid and abet them. Please, make no mistake, the number of white terrorists in America far outnumber those of any other group.

These are just some of the crises we face here at home. Climate change, a shrinking water supply, terrorism, war, religious extremism, are global crises that impact us all. It is estimated that oceans will rise between 2.5 and 6.5 feet by 2100. Such a rise would swamp many of our East Coast cities impacting tens of millions of Americans living on the eastern seaboard. But that would be a drop in the bucket compared to the hundreds of millions, perhaps billions of people impacted around the world. In addition to threatening our homes and businesses, oceans rising a few feet could wreak havoc with our food supply. Some dire estimates predict that the oceans could rise as much as 23 feet, enough to swamp London.[24]

Six hundred and fifty million people in the world do not have access to safe water; 2.3 billion people do not have access to adequate sanitation; 900 children die every day from diarrheal diseases caused by dirty water and poor sanitation.[25] In December 2015, the Chinese government declared a "red alert" over air pollution in Beijing. The air quality index read 308, rated "hazardous" by United States standards with deadly particulate matter hitting 40 times the exposure limit recommended by the World Health Organization.[26] Breathing air of that quality is the equivalent of smoking two cigarettes at a time without let up.

Religious wars are being fought in Syria, and other parts of the Middle East, displacing tens of thousands. Refugees are fleeing these lands at great risk hoping to find safe haven in European countries. Many countries in Europe are having their own problems providing for these refugees as well as being targeted by terrorists.

Of course, it goes without saying that all these crises impact the lower socio-economic classes disproportionately. In America that used to mean people of color. Today, as greater numbers of what was once the middle class are relegated to the lower rungs of the socio-economic ladder, these crises are affecting white people as well. Once again, as more and more resources are amassed by fewer and fewer people, greater and greater numbers of people, all across the racial/ethnic spectrum are feeling the strain.

Today, like the average Latino or Pacific Islander, the average white American has considerably more debt than wealth. Today, the average white American does not have that much more power than the average Arab or Asian American. And today, the average white American has little more access to the American dream than does the average African or Native American.

While whites in America still remain the privileged class, our economic circumstances have become more similar to those of our non-white brethren than they are different. Together, as a village, we may be able to affect change, and so increase opportunities for all. Apart, the challenges will likely be too great. If we and our families are to all prosper, we would do well to learn how to effectively engage with others towards our common goals.

A Matter of Survival – Successfully Addressing the Crises
The Bigger Picture

If we are to meet these challenges and leave a thriving world for our children and grandchildren, we need a different approach. White folks in general, and white Americans in particular, need to join the rest of the world to address the real crises facing us all. The world needs us and we need the world. The world doesn't need us to show them the way nor does the world need us to take the lead in that paternal manner that has been the European calling card since the scientific and industrial revolutions.

The world needs our entrepreneurial and innovative spirit. The world needs our facility with research and development. The world needs us to be a part of the whole as we work to move us all forward, together. At the same time, we need the world. We need the world to help us understand different ways of being. We need the world to help us open our eyes to other approaches to problem solving. We need the world to help us fill the gaps that we don't even know exist, but that have held us back for centuries. Perhaps of greatest import, we need the world to help us focus our energies towards addressing the real crises that are impacting our sisters and brothers around the globe.

Perhaps a little closer to home, white society is becoming less relevant as the rest of the world evolves. If nothing else, just look at the numbers. Last century, white people accounted for a third of the world's population. It is estimated that by 2050, we will account for a tenth. As the white birthrate declines, as economies around the world grow, as people of all ethnicities intermarry, it is likely the world's white population will continue to shrink. If for no other reason than to avoid our coming irrelevancy, we need to expand our capacity to understand and interact with others.

As our manufacturing base has moved overseas we are becoming marginalized economically. The world no longer relies on us to make much. "Made in America" used to be prized all over the globe. No longer. The result has been fewer and fewer good paying jobs. Today it seems the primary two aspects of our society that the world now looks to are our pop culture and our military. The former provides few economic opportunities for those of us at home; the latter makes a poor basis for an economy.

Americans have always been innovators and entrepreneurs. It has been these innovators and entrepreneurs who, since the Industrial Revolution, have formed the backbone of our economy. Unfortunately, there have been times that American business has been perceived by some as more exploitive than supportive. Today, if we are to develop good paying jobs and help our economy, as well as the world's economy, grow for the many rather than as it has been for the few, it will be necessary for American business to have a greater and greater understanding of the needs of people around the world. American business would do well to demonstrate their interest in working to help communities around the world grow - joining the village. If they fail to do so, there are many others who would happily take their place.

I am an optimist. I believe, working together, we can resolve the crises we are facing. I am certainly no expert on any of these matters. I am neither ecologist, economist, biologist, political scientist, nor theologian. As such, proposing solutions to these crises on a macro scale is way above my pay grade. However, I believe the prerequisites to addressing these issues successfully are our ability to connect with people different than ourselves, understand as best we can the world as they see it, and join together for the common good. Given America's great cultural diversity, starting at home makes a lot of sense.

Much, Much Closer to Home

Yes, we are facing significant crises both nationally and globally, the addressing of which will take large communities working in tandem to resolve. Yet, there may be more immediate concerns that require our personal attention and willingness to unite - our more short-term well-being.

As our nation's wealth gets more and more unevenly distributed, as gentrification in our cities becomes more and more the norm, and as more and more of the middle class is sent down the ladder, the great majority of us will have a better chance of surviving and thriving together than apart. In my city, as in a number of cities across the country those Whites, Natives, Blacks, Latinos, Asians, Islanders of the lower socioeconomic classes are living amongst each other. Ethnic enclaves are shrinking and will likely by and large disappear in the coming decades to be replaced by socioeconomic enclaves.

Throughout America's history, ethnic groups built communities in which the members provided social and economic supports for each other. When my Jewish grandparents, who lived in a Jewish ghetto in New York City, had a little extra money, and knew one of their neighbors was hurting, they would anonymously leave a bag of groceries at their neighbor's door. Small kindnesses such as this occurred daily in tens of thousands of ethnic communities across the country.

As these communities go by the wayside new communities need to take their place, communities of people from all backgrounds living in close proximity to one another working to help each other make it in a society in which costs continue to rise and incomes continue to stagnate. We need to help each other get jobs. We need to help each other raise our children. We need to help each other start businesses. We need to help each other make it through hard times.

Building such communities will require all involved to connect with each other and in so doing grow to understand each other. As mentioned earlier, I believe our brothers and sisters of color have a head start on this process. If we are to survive and thrive, it is imperative that many of our white sisters and brothers catch up.

Reverse Integration: Joining the Village

I know we Americans are a tougher people than the fear mongers would have us believe. We are far stronger, more optimistic, more compassionate, and have greater moral courage than those who preach xenophobia and hate understand. Again and again, throughout our 240 year history, we have risen up to face our challenges and flourish.

As the look of our people change, we are presented with our next great challenge – truly living up to our nation's creed of equality – equality of treatment and equality of opportunity. Since our beginning, America has been the grandest of social experiments. We are the most diverse populace in the world. The question is, will we embrace our diversity and forge a society that can change with the times and work for all?

For those first 240 years we have been a white dominated society. In order to avail themselves of the benefits of our society, our citizens of color who were able, (those who were neither enslaved, falsely imprisoned, nor otherwise bound) had to learn how to interact with us. They had to learn how to navigate our educational/social systems, engage in our economic systems, adapt to our society's mores. In short they had to integrate. In many communities of color this is known as 'Code Switching,' behaving one's traditional way in one's own community and adopting the behaviors of the dominant culture when engaging in the larger community. This is how so many Americans of color have gotten by since our inception. Where whites have been able to tolerate those of color, it has been the expectation. Cries against the expanding use of Spanish and for immigrants to "learn our language," is just one example of this oft assumed expectation.

Most of the white people I know are clearly uncomfortable around people of color on their home turf. How many of us have attended a Black or Latino church? How many who are not Muslim have ever participated in services inside a mosque? How many have joined a Native American sweat? How many of us have been part of a Thai family celebration? How about an Indian wedding? The funeral of a Chinese friend? Thanksgiving in the home of an African American friend? And if we did do any of these, how many of us felt comfortable, like we belonged?

More to the point, how many of us made efforts to become part of communities other than our own? How many of us have strived to understand, and adapt to, the socio-economic, educational, and social norms of a community other than our own or those with which we are very familiar? How many of us have been accepted by communities other than our own?

For centuries, since settlers from England first began arriving on these shores and establishing permanent colonies, new immigrants had to figure out how to adapt and fit in with the growing white culture. This was not too arduous a task, as most of these immigrant groups enjoyed some fundamental similarities with the whites already here. These similarities also made it relatively easy for the established white society to accept the newcomers. Typically, it would only take a generation or two.

For those who would not be so readily accepted, those of non-European ancestry, it has been considerably more difficult to become a recognized part of the whole. While the dominant society has worked to keep people of color at some distance, those people have had to learn how to adapt in order to survive and even thrive. Through the years we have called this integration: people of color having to learn our ways in order to fit in as best they could. As a consequence of being dominant for so long, white folks have never really needed to understand the ways of others. As Bob Dylan wrote, "the times they are a changin'." As our country browns and as the world shrinks, over the coming decades the tables will turn. It is becoming more important for us white folks to learn and understand those different from us and adapt to their ways so we all can thrive, together.

Up till now efforts towards integration have been uni-directional, from communities of color to white society. In the coming years, as the white majority in America dwindles, we would do well to learn how to reverse this direction and integrate with communities of people different than our own. We need more than inclusion and diversity training as they are currently presented; we need to learn how to be. It is time we, white Americans, learn how to truly join the global village.

The Value of Reverse Integration to Professionals

As an educator working in communities of color, I can attest that the benefits for such 'reverse integration' are great. Although our population has been browning, our teaching force does not come close to reflecting the student population. In 2011, 84% of public school teachers in America were white,[27] and in 2014, 50.3% of public school students were not.[28] More and more students of color will be attending our schools. In Portland, Oregon, demographically the whitest city in America, there are elementary schools at which over 40 languages are spoken by students.

Some view this as an opportunity; others, not so much. I have worked with a number of very good white teachers, who are uncomfortable around some of their students of color and those students' families. At times such discomfort is manifested as fear, at other times resentment, and sometimes even animosity. In most instances these feelings are indicative of a lack of understanding and connection, for every community has their own nuanced way of interacting. The most effective teachers are those who understand the nuances of the families and communities of their students. It takes intentional efforts on the part of teachers to make a connection and develop such an understanding, and so gain acceptance by those they serve.

The same can be said for those who provide medical and social services where there are like disproportionalities between service providers and those whom they serve. As with teachers, I have worked with a number of white social service providers who are uncomfortable around their clients and their families of color. How can such social service providers help them effectively?

This disproportionality between service providers and clients holds especially true for law enforcement where life and death decisions are made routinely. How can an officer do his duty effectively, if he is not comfortable and at ease with those he is sworn to protect? How can an officer do her duty without the understanding of, and the acceptance by, the community she is tasked to serve?

While there certainly are many teachers, social service providers, and law enforcement officers who do not feel uncomfortable around those of color and their families, still, our schools, social service organizations, and law enforcement are routinely under attack. While they might not be uncomfortable, many professionals often lack a nuanced understanding of the cultures of those they serve. The result is dedicated, well-meaning teachers, social workers, police officers, business owners, and others working with the best of intentions, inadvertently angering and turning off those they are working to assist. As a result, as their well-intentioned efforts go unrecognized and unappreciated, many become jaded and resentful towards those they believe they have been serving. Is it any wonder so many of them become frustrated, demoralized, and burned out? Imagine how much more effective they would be with greater understanding and connection? Imagine how much more effective they would be if they were accepted by those they serve?

The Value of Reverse Integration to Corporate America

As of 2014, 35% of the workforce was comprised of workers of color.[29] This will only continue to climb. Add to that the increasing globalization of our economy, and the value of being able to integrate with communities of color to white Americans becomes clear.

Fifteen years ago, a gentleman (a white American) I knew was working to start an import-export business, focusing on trade with China. He had the financing arranged and all that remained was receiving the blessings from the powers that be in the Chinese company with whom he was about to partner. With this company's sign off, his financiers would be capitalizing his company to the tune of $4 million. He went to meet with those whose favor he sought and was invited to dinner. At dinner, the evening before contracts were to be signed, his hosts had live eels brought out, slit open, and their blood drained into glasses. The glasses were passed around and a toast was made. The gentleman could not bring himself to drink. The next day he was sent home sans contract and his business never got off the ground.

Was his refusal to partake in the toast the reason he failed? I am not integrated to any significant degree in Chinese culture, so

I do not know. (A Chinese friend of mine believed that very well might have been the case.) I do know he did not have enough understanding of their ways. He was just your run-of-the-mill American businessman seeking opportunity. He was a nice guy; sharp and not particularly arrogant or full of himself. He was affable and a good family man. It was not enough in this instance.

Yes, business gets done on a daily basis between folks from different cultures, and no, one doesn't have to understand the finer points of those with whom one deals in order to have success. However, as the people of the world become more interconnected, those who can relate, those who can comfortably be with, and be accepted by those with whom they engage, will find themselves at great advantage.

Here on our shores, a number of my African American friends routinely discuss the stress that they experience working in predominantly white organizations. This stress is above and beyond the stress inherent in their work. It is the stress that comes with working in an environment that seems to care little for their well-being and that holds them to higher standards than their white co-workers. Now, stress in all its manifestations leads to illness and illness leads to lost productivity. A study by the Integrated Benefits Institute, as reported in Forbes, found that businesses in America loose over half a billion dollars per year due to illness.[30] Certainly, a portion of that cost could be mitigated by creating work environments that are more thoughtful, understanding, and accepting of the needs of employees from differing ethnic backgrounds.

From a bottom-line perspective, companies that foster such environments are more likely to be more profitable. "Diversity Matters," a research study published by McKinsey & Company in 2015 found that,

"Companies in the top quartile of racial/ethnic diversity were 35 percent more likely to have financial returns above their national industry median." and *"Companies with 10 percent higher gender and ethnic/racial diversity on management teams and boards in the US, for instance, had EBIT (earnings before interest and taxes) that was 1.1 percent higher."* [31]

The authors make it clear that having a diverse workforce alone is not what drives these results. In addition to a diverse workforce, they discuss the need for commitment from those in leadership to creating an understanding and inclusive environment in which all may be heard and have opportunity for advancement.

The Value of Reverse Integration to the Non-Profit Sector

Grassroots, nonprofit organizations rely on charitable foundations, corporate gift giving, contributions from individuals, and grants from government agencies to raise the resources they need in order to serve their communities. The majority of those disbursing funds are well-intentioned white women and men, often on the upper rungs of the socioeconomic ladder, with only limited connections to the communities they seek to support. Similarly, those tasked in government agencies to develop programming for which they will allot funds are also, for the most part, from the same demographic with the same limited connections. In this manner much money is raised and many programs are created by white folks based upon their own sensibilities, believing they understand the needs of those they are attempting to support.

46

Often, the result is effective grassroots organizations, who clearly understand the needs of their community, attempting to provide for those they serve while at the same time working to meet the different requirements of their funders. Such efforts demands that organizations use a portion of their funds on activities not directly beneficial to their communities. How much more valuable would these funds be if those responsible for disbursing them were more closely connected to those they are funding? How much more valuable would these funds be if those responsible for disbursing them had a deeper understanding of the communities they wish to support?

The same questions may be asked with regard to cultural institutions, institutions that have a mandate to provide the communities in which they reside cultural/educational exposure and opportunities. Art museums, natural history museums, historical societies, theaters, concert halls all across the country are, more often than not, administered by predominantly upper-middle-class white men and women with their own sensibilities.

In 2017, the American Alliance of Museums reported that "93% of museum directors are white, as are 92.6% of board chairs and 89.3% of board members." This even though "museum directors and board chairs believe board diversity and inclusion are important to advance their missions." [32] When they wish to create programming for their patrons of color, they typically look through their lens of what they believe patrons of color would enjoy and find beneficial. How much more successful would they be if they had the understanding necessary to look through the lenses of their patrons? And, of course, how much more likely would this be to happen if their boards were more diverse?

The Value of Reverse Integration to Entrepreneurs

In the summer of 2017, a former corporate tax attorney from Toronto, Canada opened up what she envisioned would be an upscale bar and sandwich shop in the Crown Heights neighborhood of Brooklyn, New York. She called her eatery, 'Summerhill,' after an affluent neighborhood in her hometown. For decades, Crown Heights had been home to lower income African-Americans, Hasidic Jews, and somewhat more recently, West Indians. Today, like many such neighborhoods, it has been targeted for gentrification, hence her decision to locate her restaurant there.

In a press release introducing her establishment she touted its "bullet hole-ridden wall," 40-ounce bottles of rosé, and the space's alleged history as an "illegal gun shop," seemingly as an effort to connect her restaurant with its 'history.' What she was unaware of at the time of her press release, though was that rather than connecting with history, the Crown Heights community saw her description as an attempt to capitalize on stereotypes of black violence and poverty. Needless to say, the community was none too happy with her presence. It was further antagonized when, a few days later, it was revealed that the bullet holes were not real and that there has yet to be presented any evidence that the building she is in was ever an illegal gun shop. Her initial responses to the early criticism were glib and dismissive. After a few days she took a more apologetic tone.

For its part, the community (residents of all ethnicities) staged protests in front of her restaurant, put up flyers throughout the community labeling her a "racist," "colonialist," and 'gentrifier,' and issued a series of demands. It remains to be seen whether or not Summerhill survives. How different circumstances would be if she had been aware of the value of connecting to the community in which she wished to place her business.

Helping White America Join the Village

Summerhill is not an isolated event. Good, well-meaning entrepreneurs have entered into communities not their own, with little to no connection or understanding of that community's history and customs, thereby engendering distrust and animosity. Done correctly, these businesses could have received the community's support, helped address some of the community's needs, and provided jobs for the community's residents. Everyone could have won.

Whether we are entrepreneurs, teachers, social workers, or law enforcement officers, whether we are counselors, salespersons, service workers, attorneys, or engineers, regardless of our occupation or station, if we engage with others, we can benefit from increasing our capacity to be with others. At its core, joining the village is about becoming more understanding, more empathetic, more connected . . . more human. Becoming a part of a different community can enrich your life in ways you have to experience to understand. Reverse integration is not an academic exercise. It is an exercise of heart, mind, and soul.

It begins with deepening our understanding of the social and psychological forces that have brought us to where we are today, forces that are the roots from which the trees of disconnection and injustice have grown. Race and racism, oppression and genocide, white privilege and white guilt are some of the fruits. Particularly as it relates to our brothers and sisters of color in America, it is imperative that we, who have not already done so, become cognizant of the injustices great and small that have been visited upon our fellow citizens of colors, many of which continue to this day. More than cognizant, it will behoove us to feel the injustices as best we can., imagining what it must be like to be on the receiving end.

Reverse Integration

Reverse Integration continues with increasing our capacity to engage in what for many can be very difficult discussions about these subjects. We would do well to acknowledge the difficulty of addressing these subjects. Some readers may find themselves angered, others saddened, still others may find feelings of guilt are aroused. Such feelings are to be expected and embraced for they are feelings that often come with expanding awareness. If we are to truly integrate, it will behoove us to do our best to see the world as others see and experience it. Please know that whatever emotions are awakened in us as we strive to do so, they pale in comparison to the emotions experienced by those who experienced events firsthand . . . not unlike men and childbirth.

Once we are more comfortable having these discussions and become more readily open about our experiences and our world views, we can better explore the ways those different from ourselves view and approach the world. Then we can begin to establish more and more meaningful connections with each other which will lead to an even greater understanding of each other, which will result in even deeper connection. And so we may come to accept, appreciate, and revel in both our similarities and our differences. For it is our similarities that make us human and our differences that make us valuable.

Part II:

Understanding:
The Psychological and Sociological Forces Behind Disconnection

... I have some very sad news for all of you ... and that is that Martin Luther King was shot and was killed tonight in Memphis, Tennessee. ...

For those of you who are black and are tempted to be filled with hatred and mistrust of the injustice of such an act, against all white people, I would only say that I can also feel in my own heart the same kind of feeling. I had a member of my family killed, but he was killed by a white man. But we have to make an effort, make an effort to understand, to get beyond these rather difficult times ...

So I ask you tonight to return home, to say a prayer for the family of Martin Luther King ... We can do well in this country. We will have difficult times. We've had difficult times in the past. And we will have difficult times in the future. It is not the end of violence; it is not the end of lawlessness; and it's not the end of disorder.

But the vast majority of white people and the vast majority of black people in this country want to live together, want to improve the quality of our life, and want justice for all human beings. Let us dedicate ourselves to what the Greeks wrote so many years ago: to tame the savageness of man and make gentle the life of this world. Let us dedicate ourselves to that, and say a prayer for our country and for our people.

Robert Kennedy addressing the crowd in
Memphis hours after MLK's assassination

.
.
.

Chapter 3

The Psychological
Underpinnings of Disconnection

It was Thanksgiving 2002, and has had become my custom I was celebrating with Joy's family. Many years I was the only white person at the festivities. Like many families, Joy's celebrated with copious amounts of food followed by an evening of interactive, interpersonal games. Most Thanksgivings we played games like Taboo, Charades, and Pictionary. This year they introduced me to Killers.

For those of you who haven't had the pleasure, Killers is a game of imagination in which all players get to be members of a town. There is a narrator who oversees and directs the game. Before the game begins, the narrator takes a deck of cards, removes a couple of kings, a red jack, a black jack, a queen, and an amount of numbered cards all equal to the number of players. The narrator would then shuffle up those cards and distribute them amongst the participants. Then the game would begin.

The narrator asks everybody to close their eyes, then asks the two people who received the kings to open up their eyes. They are the Killers and their assignment is to silently, between the two of them, pick someone in the town they want to kill. They then close their eyes and the narrator has the queen, who is the doctor, open his or her eyes and select someone in the town they would like to save. (If the person they chose to save was the same person the Killers chose to kill, that person remains alive when the game continues.) Next, the narrator asks the red jack, the red detective, to open his or her eyes and take a guess at who the Killers might be, the narrator confirms or dis-affirms their choice. The narrator then has the black detective do the same thing, thus ensuring that two players have a little more information than the other players.

Once all is done, and everybody's eyes are closed again, the narrator has everyone open up their eyes and tells the village in whatever elaborate manner they wish, that a murder has been committed in our fair town, points out the person the Killers chose to kill, and removes that person from the game. Now, the real game begins, for it is up to the townsfolk to try to figure out who the killers are. With a good group of players, this leads to an animated debate over 'who done it,' culminating in a vote. The person who receives the most votes, is taken out by the vigilante townsfolk and is out of the game. This cycle is repeated until either the townsfolk get the Killers or the Killers get all the townsfolk.

The very first time I played the game with Joy's family that Thanksgiving, I was a simple townsman. In the very first round, during a heated discussion about the perpetrators, Joy's daughter said she thought it was me. I, jokingly said, "Sure go after the white guy." When it came time to vote shortly thereafter, the vote went around the room, "Jay," "Jay," "Jay," "Jay," "Jay," and so on. It was almost unanimous; I was out of the game.

A few years later, Joy was hanging out with my family at my nephew's Bar Mitzvah. Like Joy's family, my family loves games. So, after the reception, 15 to 20 of us gathered in a hotel room and I introduced them to Killers. I played the role of the narrator. As fortune would have it, Joy was one of the killers. Before the first round when the Killers were choosing who to eliminate from the game, one of my cousins, and if you're reading this you know who you are, peaked to see if he could learn something. Joy had him killed immediately.

In the second round, while the townsfolk were debating who the killers might be, one of my cousins suggested it might be Joy. Joy jokingly said, "Sure go after the black woman." No one called her name again; she took out the entire town.

 Driving her to her hotel later that evening I said, "Joy, you pulled the race card!"

"I didn't mean to." she said as we both laughed uproariously.

I have a wonderful extended family on my mother's side. We love each other, we have each other's backs, and for the most part we are very accepting of all manner of people. We are funny, opinionated, and certainly loud. We are educated, at least a little enlightened, and with a few exceptions, progressive,. I know I am biased, but I am proud that as a group we are good, well-meaning people, a number of whom are on the front lines in the fight for social justice.

That said, their response to Joy during that game is just one very small demonstration of why the effort of white folks to truly connect with others can be so difficult. I think it's fair to say that Joy's joking remark triggered feelings of white guilt among my family.

From the white perspective, I believe fear of accusation and the resulting defensiveness often precludes any real connection. Make one mistake and you may be called a racist. So instead, we play it safe. We talk about work, the weather, sports, the gossip of the day. And this is as it pertains to white folks who are interested in making the effort. There are others who have difficulty seeing this disconnection at all or, if they see it, see little value in working to connect.

White guilt, white privilege, efforts at political correctness, and our inability to move beyond our dichotomous thinking, are just a few of the dynamics that often preclude the serious, in-depth discussions of such difficult subject matter; discussions that are necessary if we are to increase our understanding of each other. Discussions such as these are necessary for us as individuals to move forward and for White America to join the rest of our country and the world.

Why Four Hundred Years of Disconnection

In 1992, Andrew Hacker's *Two Nations: Black and White, Separate, Hostile, Unequal* [33] was released. His book is a comprehensive statistical study of the differences between black and white America. In the first chapter, he presents an excellent discussion about 'whiteness' through American history. What follows is brief synopsis.

Helping White America Join the Village

The first white people to establish permanent roots on these shores were from England. As the story goes, Englishmen seeking greater economic opportunities and/or freedom from religious persecution brought their families to the New World, establishing their first settlements in the 1600s. From their perspective English and White were synonymous.

In the 1700s, folks from Scotland and Ireland began immigrating to the colonies. It might surprise some to learn that from the original settlers viewpoint those Scotch-Irish were not really white. They were often viewed as low, mean, dirty, less than. While the majority of these new immigrants settled and farmed in the backcountry of the Carolinas, Virginia, Maryland, and Pennsylvania, many of those that remained in the cities took jobs that were beneath the 'White' people, some becoming no more than indentured servants. Decades after the first wave of Scotch-Irish immigration, they played a significant role in George Washington's army. With the success of the Revolutionary War coupled with their service to the cause, in time they were accepted as 'White.'

In the early 19th century, the next wave of immigration, folks from Germany and Scandinavia, began reaching our shores. At the time of their arrival, they too were not considered 'White." Like immigrants that came before, they took jobs that the more established citizens did not wish to do, they were looked down upon as being 'different,' and they began to settle lands farther to the West. With the coming of the Civil War and their service in the Union Army, they too, eventually became accepted as 'White.'

As the 19th century turned to the 20th century, new waves of immigrants arrived from Eastern and Southern Europe. Italians, Greeks, Hungarians, Slavs, Polish and Russian Jews all seeking better lives for themselves and their families arrived in America.

And like their immigrant predecessors, they, too, were certainly not 'White.' They, too, were viewed by 'White' America as 'other.' They were thought to be low, less intelligent, unsanitary, the list goes on. They too, took those jobs that 'White' Americans considered beneath them. In time, in part as a result of their service alongside 'White' Americans in two world wars they graduated to 'White.'

Twenty-five years ago, as Hacker was writing his book, another trend began to take root. "Brown" people in America were gaining in numbers over 'White' people. What to do? In the 1970s, people from Eastern Asia began immigrating to America in larger numbers. They too, had been considered the 'other.' They too, took the jobs' White' Americans did not want. Only this time, those jobs were in high-tech and paid six-figure salaries. You see, 'White' American youth did not particularly like studying math and science. Hacker proposed that in an effort to increase their numbers, 'White' America has put our Asian immigrants on 'Probationary White' status. Perhaps, they too, in time will be considered 'White.'

The most recent wave of immigration is coming from Central and South America, as well as the Middle East. Will these immigrants ever be accepted as 'White'? Time will tell, though for now acceptance does not seem to be in the offing. Our brethren from south of the border, tending to be of darker complexion, often get lumped in with African Americans, and those from the Middle East are being made targets of our xenophobic compatriots.

These two recent groups aside, why, after 400 years, haven't Native and African Americans ever been accepted into the dominant culture? Like their German and Scandinavian brethren, African Americans made significant contributions during the Civil

War. Both Native and African American served with distinction in World War II. Native, African, and Latin Americans have all served with distinction in Korea and Vietnam, Afghanistan and Iraq. Nevertheless, they have yet to be accepted by white America.

So, why have White and Native, White and African, and more recently White and Latin Americans remained so disconnected? Why has the divide between those Americans of European descent and African descent remained so pronounced? Why has the divide between those Americans of European descent and those indigenous to these lands remained so deep? Why are so many Latin Americans finding themselves in the same boat? Why has it been so difficult for 'White' America to embrace these peoples?

The Nature of Criticism

Natives are uncivilized, alcoholic, lazy, and undisciplined. Blacks are lazy, shiftless, unintelligent, and criminal. Latinos are ill-tempered, lazy, and are suited only for menial jobs. These are just a few of the derogatory stereotypes we have all heard before. There are many others that are even more disparaging. Simply put, they are all criticisms – criticisms meant to demean, denigrate, and dehumanize – criticisms that continue to be reinforced in our television, music, movies, literature, and news. It goes without saying, they are all untrue. So why have we continued to give voice to them through the centuries? The answer lies in understanding what conditions give rise to such criticism and the role such criticism plays in the psychological dynamic of cognitive dissonance.

Criticism falls into three general categories: accurate criticism, inaccurate criticism, and undermining criticism. The first two are usually very simply addressed; the last one is the crux of the issue.

Accurate Criticism

You are a carpenter. You're on the job and your foreman comes to you and tells you the window frame you just cut is too large. You believe it isn't and you both go to the blueprints. It turns out your foreman is correct, so you simply acknowledge the mistake and fix it. Accurate criticism. We have all experienced this many times in our lives. No big deal. We accept our mistakes, apologize where appropriate, correct them, and move on.

Inaccurate Criticism

Same situation. Your foreman tells you that the frame you just cut is too large, you believe you got it right, and you both go to the blueprints. This time, it turns out that you were right, so the foreman acknowledges her mistake, makes an apology to you, and we move on. Inaccurate criticism. No big deal. Events such as this also are regular occurrences in our lives. Someone believes they are right, finds out they are wrong, apologizes, and move on.

Undermining Criticism

In the cases of both accurate and inaccurate criticism, direct truthful communication usually is all that is needed to resolve an issue. Sometimes though, our actions, either intentionally or unintentionally harm another person, put a person at a disadvantage. When we were children, we may have mercilessly teased our brother or sister. As students, we may have cheated on a test. Perhaps we stole money from an employer, cheated on our wives or husbands. Bigger deals? Yes? Most of us have done things we are not proud of. Some of us have taken responsibility, apologized, and done what we could to make amends. Others . . .

Here's how it works. Many of us have siblings. Just about all of us who have younger sisters and brothers were taught by our parents, not to hit them. Those of you who are parents have almost certainly taught your older children not to hit their baby brothers or sisters. Despite their parents' best efforts, every so often the younger son or daughter comes crying to mom or dad, telling them big sister or brother hit them. Being good parents, they sit their older son or daughter down and ask them what happened?

"He started it. He came into my room and started playing with my toys and he messed up the game I was playing. He wouldn't leave me alone. He's stupid. He wouldn't get out. And last week, when I was trying to do my homework, he wouldn't stop bothering me. Remember my birthday party, when he just kept getting in the middle of me and my friends? He never leaves me alone. He's always bothering me."

Sound familiar? Reason, reason, reason, justification, reason, justification. All in an effort to convince mom and dad that punching kid brother was the right thing to do. Allowed to go on, older brother would submit more and more 'evidence' as to why his younger brother's deserved a beating. Among the dynamics at play here as older brother seeks to demean and diminish his younger sibling is the effort to convince his parents that his younger brother is insignificant, and therefore so was his aggressive behavior towards him. In essence older brother is trying to reduce his younger brother to the status of something that is okay to punch or kick . . . say a rock.

Of course, no good parent will buy any of this. They will mete out an appropriate punishment that addresses both the act of hitting brother as well as the effort to demean brother and justify his actions. At the same time, they will work to teach both children how best to interact with each other.

This is what undermining criticism looks and sounds like. At the root of such criticism is an act that harms another, an act that puts another at a disadvantage. The greater the harm - the greater the criticism. The greater the harm, the greater the effort to co-opt others to accept their view of the one harmed. Undermining criticism is almost always an effort to reduce the target of the criticism to a status so small that the attacks on that person become seemingly meaningless, and even justifiable. Let me repeat that, undermining criticism is almost always an effort to reduce the target of the criticism to a status so small that the attacks on that person become seemingly meaningless, and even justifiable. And each of those efforts are themselves harms that invite, nay demands, further undermining criticism.

Now, as an alternative approach, the older boy, rather than attempting to reduce his brother to the status of some inanimate object, could simply tell his parent, "I hit my younger brother, I know it was wrong, and I will apologize." Assuming he is being genuine, this then can revert to an accurate criticism event. Yes, a price still will need to be paid, however the likelihood of this happening again will be greatly diminished.

Remember junior high school and high school? These are some of the most common of activities among many youth. In my day it was called teasing. Today it's called bullying. By any name, these behaviors are inappropriate. Now, I've worked around a lot of young teenagers, and when kids get wrapped up in these kind of events, one of the first questions asked is what did the victim do to deserve such treatment? What did Johnny do to provoke being bullied? What did Susan do to get all those kids to post those nasty comments on Facebook?

A much more insightful question, one that will lead to a much more accurate analysis and greater understanding of the situation would be, "What harm was done to Johnny and Susan that provoked the subsequent undermining criticism?"

Does this make sense? When someone comes to you speaking critically of another person, the most important question to ask is, 'What has the person who has come to you done, or perhaps what is the person planning to do, to the person who is the target of their criticism?' Similarly, when you find yourself being critical of a person, what is your motivation for your attempts to diminish that person?

Again, this is undermining criticism. Many of us see this regularly. Some of us are its targets. Some of us its perpetrators. Far too many of us, unengaged bystanders. Far too often we simply either allow this to continue, or go farther and cosign the behavior.

Please remember, at the foundation of undermining criticism is a harm, a putting another at a disadvantage. Once again, the greater the harm - the greater the need for undermining criticism. Over the years, I have found this to be one of the most difficult concepts for folks to wrap their wits around. I wonder if this might be because so many of us are guilty of such behavior and would rather not confront our own mistakes. Whatever the reason, undermining criticism is one of the great challenges to connection.

Cognitive Dissonance

Humans seek to maintain a general consistency among their beliefs, attitudes, and behaviors. This consistency goes a long way to contributing to our peace of mind and sense of well-being. Cognitive dissonance is a psychological state, usually discomfort or anxiety, that results when a person holds conflicting beliefs or attitudes simultaneously. For example, a person may believe alcohol is bad for them while at the same time drink to excess.

Cognitive dissonance is also the anxiety or discomfort that results when a person's behaviors are in conflict with their beliefs or attitudes about themselves. A person who believes exercise will do them good yet does not go out and exercise, likely will experience a certain amount of anxiety or discomfort as a result of the cognitive dissonance between his belief and his inactivity. Generally speaking, the greater the dissonance the greater the discomfort.

Now, we humans do not like such dissonance, so we work to mitigate and resolve it. Rationalization and justification, are two of the tools we frequently use. The alcoholic who works to persuade herself that one drink won't make a difference and the couch potato who works to convince himself that he earned a day of relaxing, watching television, eating chips and drinking beer are such examples. Certainly, choosing to remain sober or go out and get some exercise would be much better ways to resolve such dissonance.

Undermining criticism, with its concomitant rationalizations and justifications, is the chief tool we use to resolve the dissonance that arises when we, believing ourselves to be good people, harm others. That is assuming we do not wish to step up and do the right things - owning our behavior, making amends, and moving on. Of course, as one might expect, the greater the dissonance (the more we believe ourselves to be good and the greater the harms we commit) the greater the undermining criticisms we will need in order to bring the dissonance into harmony.

America's Two Great Injuries and Our Moral Illness

And so we come to the answer to the questions I posed a few pages prior: Why has the divide between those Americans of European descent and African descent remained so pronounced? Why has the divide between those Americans of European descent and those indigenous to these lands remained so deep? Why has it been so difficult for 'White' America to embrace our African and Native American brothers and sisters?

White America has been responsible for two of the most heinous injuries one group of humans can inflict upon another: the systematic genocide of the indigenous peoples of this land and the systematic enslavement and subsequent continued abuse of those brought here from Africa and their descendants. Both genocide and slavery had only one purpose: the creation and expansion of wealth. (Yes I know, few if any of you reading this book had anything to do with our Country's history of genocide and slavery. Neither did I. My ancestors came from Poland in the early 1900s. I promise we will address this soon.)

There is a Buddhist saying, "As in the beginning, so in the middle, so in the end." Our nation was founded on two immoralities, the crimes against humanity of slavery and genocide. The latter was tacitly agreed to, the former codified in our Constitution. The resulting cognitive dissonance white America has had to manage has impacted us from our founding to our present. These immoralities along with the resulting cognitive dissonance are at the heart of so many of the struggles we are faced with today. Rather than face up to our history, acknowledge our mistakes, be remorseful, make amends, and move on, much of white America has chosen to continue to criticize, rationalize, and justify.

From Thomas Jefferson, one of America's most eminent scholars who wrote in an effort to rationalize the practice of slavery:

> *They smelled bad and were physically unattractive, required less sleep, were dumb, cowardly and incapable of feeling grief.*

Finally concluding:

> *. . . advance it therefore as a suspicion only, that blacks, whether originally a distinct race, or made distinct by time and circumstances, are inferior to the whites in the endowments of body and mind.* [34]

. . . to William Bennett, former Secretary of Education under George H.W. Bush, in a 'reasoned' argument that could justify the mass incarceration of men of color, who pronounced on a radio broadcast on Sept 28, 2005:

> *But I do know that it's true that if you wanted to reduce crime, you could -- if that were your sole purpose, you could abort every black baby in this country, and your crime rate would go down. That would be an impossible, ridiculous, and morally reprehensible thing to do, but your crime rate would go down. So these far-out, these far-reaching, extensive extrapolations are, I think, tricky.* [35]

If it were Rush Limbaugh who made this assertion, we might pass it off as his shtick which few take seriously. However, this was put forward by a man who has walked the halls of power and who had the ear of some of our most prominent political leaders. More concerning, is that I'm sure he has had this discussion with others of those in power who hold the very same, patently ludicrous belief.

Those in power have attempted to palm off such erroneous and fallacious assertions as 'scientific', 'rational', 'reasonable' on a populace, too many of whom neither has the time nor the inclination to think critically about what they see and hear. Throughout our history, there have been those who have used all manner of argument to justify all manner of outrageous acts against our own citizens of color as well as those in other 'undeveloped' countries.

"Slavery was an accepted practice in the Bible." "Africans were put on earth to be enslaved." "They are natural slaves." "Unlike us, Indians are uncivilized." " They are savages." "They are like children." "In the context of the times it was appropriate." On and on and on and on.

Through the centuries there have been those who have used religious, philosophical, logical, and scientific rationalizations to mitigate the dissonance resulting from their crimes and the crimes of their ancestors.

The effort to systematically, 'scientifically' critically undermine the targets of slavery and genocide began with the work of the taxonomist Carl von Linnaeus. (The biological classification system, Domain, Kingdom, Phylum, Class, etc. was his brainchild.) After classifying plant and animal life, he took to classifying people, and with this classification, in the 18th century, came to be considered the father of anthropology. Linnaeus described:

Homo Americanus as reddish, choleric, obstinate,
contented, and regulated by custom; Homo Europaeus as
white, fickle, sanguine, blue-eyed, gentle and governed by

*laws; Homo Asiaticus as sallow, grave dignified, avari-
cious, and ruled by opinion; and Homo Afer as black,
phlegmatic, cunning, lazy, lustful, careless, and governed
by caprice.* [36]

Linnaeus's work laid the groundwork for many who would follow. Fredrick Blumenbach, considered by many to be another eminent anthropologist, in the early 19th century, argued that Whites were superior because their skulls were white.[37] In 1858 *An Inquiry into the Law of Negro Slavery in the United States of America,* T. R. R. Cobb asserted,

*This inquiry into the physical, mental, and moral
development of the Negro race seems to point them
clearly, as peculiarly fitted for a laborious class. Their
physical frame is capable of great and long exertion.
Their mental capacity renders them incapable of
successful self-development, and yet adapts them for the
direction of wiser race. Their moral character renders
them happy, peaceful, contented, and cheerful in a status
that would break the spirit and destroy the energies of the
Caucasian or the native American.* [38]

In the mid-19th century, J. Marion Sims, who is credited as the father of gynecology, did much of his barbaric surgical experiments on countless un-anesthetized enslaved women, believing that. "slave women were able to bear great pain because their 'race' made them more durable, and thus they were well-suited for painful medical experimentation."[39] (And there is a statue of him in New York City's Central Park.)

In 1904, a number of Mbuti tribesmen from what is today, the Democratic Republic of Congo were brought to America to be exhibited at the world's fair in St. Louis. White folks called them Pygmies. Two years later, Ota Benga, one of those tribesmen, was placed in a cage in the monkey house of the Bronx zoo and exhibited with an orangutan. Similar exhibits continued in Europe into the 1950s. Those of European descent have a long history of working to dehumanize others by words and deeds in the name of 'science.'

Efforts to diminish and dehumanize are continued by many to this day and each of these efforts is another harmful act, an act that puts others at disadvantage. "Welfare moms are just trying to live off our tax dollars." "Black teens are thugs." "Natives are lazy and alcoholic." "Mexico is sending us their rapists and drug dealers." Need I go on? Criticism, piled upon criticism, piled upon criticism. Harm upon harm, upon harm, upon harm.

Today, new efforts to simply rewrite more of America's history are afoot. In some states it is getting more difficult for students to even learn about America's past. In 2010, Texas adopted new guidelines that would downplay slavery as a cause of the Civil War and highlight the upside of the slave experience. A geography textbook in Texas, has described the Atlantic slave trade as bringing 'millions of workers' to plantations in the south.[40]

Unfortunately, by dint of their skin tone and foreign language, many immigrants of color coming from south of the border seem to have been artificially lumped in with African and Native Americans to some degree.

Let me be as clear as I can be. There can be no justification, no acceptable rationale, no adequately reasoned argument that would mitigate the high crimes of genocide and slavery. Like the older brother who attempts to reduce his younger brother to insignificance in order to make his act of punching him equally insignificant, centuries of abuse of our Native and African-American brothers and sisters and the resulting undermining criticism against these targets of slavery and genocide, must be viewed as inexcusable. I know for many of you I am restating the obvious. However, it continues to amaze me how many people I speak with who seemingly do not understand this.

As a society we can choose to either face up to our history, acknowledge our crimes, and make amends as best we can, or continue to rationalize, justify, and criticize. Since America's inception, our society seems to have chosen the latter.

The result is our society's moral illness, an illness that impacts us all. Our illness is evidenced by the growing number of our children that go to school hungry. Our illness is evidenced by the number of our brethren who do not have access to adequate healthcare. Our illness is evidenced by the few who have grown obscenely rich and the many who have entered the roles of the impoverished over the past 20 years. From Confucius to Lincoln to Gandhi numerous people have expressed the axiom that a society's greatness is measured by how it treats its weakest members. Given our efforts, we could and should do much, much better. It is evidence of our moral illness that we choose not to.

Of course there are serious economic consequences resulting from our nation's illness. The costs of hunger, poverty, ill health, lack of access to healthcare, addiction, under- education, un- and under-employment, are considerable. Holzer, Whitmore-Schanzenbach, Duncan, and Ludwig writing for the Center for American Progress, estimate that childhood poverty alone costs our country approximately $700 billion a year in reduced economic output, increased crime costs, and increased health costs.[41]

According to the Congressional Budget Office, jobless Americans collected about $100 billion a year of unemployment insurance from 2008 to 2012. Constance Brinkley-Badgett writing for the Atlanta Journal-Constitution estimated that drug and alcohol addiction costs Americans $276 billion a year.[42] The Kaiser Family Foundation estimated the cost of treating uninsured patients in 2012 at almost $79 billion.[43] It is not unreasonable to put the economic costs associated with our moral infirmity to be upwards of $1 trillion a year.

But more significant than the cost in dollars is the human cost. The cost in needless suffering, pain, and distress to Americans of color should be obvious. The cost to white America, particularly those who are economically stable, may be less so. One of the human consequences of our illness is white America's disconnection from America of color and more recently wealthy America's growing disconnection from almost everyone else. From an emotional perspective, such disconnection can contribute to the loneliness and isolation a number of us have experienced. Such disconnection has played, and continues to play a significant role in the anger many feel toward, and the violence some perpetrate upon our brethren of color. Such disconnection helps fuel the general anxiety so many experience regularly. Such disconnection underpins so many of our misunderstandings, our feelings of white guilt, and our lack of understanding of white privilege.

Remember the older brother? He had a choice. Either critically undermine his brother in an attempt to justify his behavior or acknowledge the inappropriateness of his behavior, show remorse, make amends, and move on. If we as a society are to fulfill the promise of our nation, and actually become the land of truly equal opportunity that we imagine ourselves to be, America must heal from the moral illness that has been festering these past four centuries. More fully acknowledging the less savory aspects of our history, I believe, is a good place to begin the healing process.

Chapter 4

Acknowledging Our History :
Tales From the Dark Side

We Americans are an exceptional people; we are a great people who have much to be proud of. We are the first people to have broken the bonds that held us to an empire and built a thriving land for ourselves, teaching the lesson that a foreign power cannot triumph over a highly motivated, armed, local populace. (Unfortunately, a lesson we ourselves seem to have forgotten with our escapades in Korea, Vietnam, Iraq, and Afghanistan.) We established and continue to maintain the first modern democracy in the world, setting the example for people everywhere. We saved our Western European allies from their enemies in World War I and we saved the world from the despotic regimes of Germany and Japan in World War II. In postwar America we built one of the strongest middle classes the world has seen. We inaugurated powered air flight culminating with putting men on the moon. We eradicated polio and other infectious diseases. We have made great strides in the treatment of cancer and we have extended our life expectancy. The computer and software I'm using to write this book were pioneered by Americans. Laptops, cell phones, smart phones, video games, were all invented by Americans. And these are but a few of our achievements. Yes, we have much of which to be proud.

If we are to include our European brethren, the list of the achievements of white folks becomes almost endless. From the Renaissance and the evolution of science, through the Enlightenment, to the Industrial Revolution and the Information Age, we are responsible for the continued evolution of humankind. From the discovery of the New World to the civilizing of the indigenous peoples of South and Central America, Africa, Asia, and the Pacific, we of European descent have worked to bring prosperity to the world.

These are the stories we learn in school. To this day, American girls and boys are still taught that Columbus discovered America. They are taught that Vikings were in North America about 500 years before Columbus, though they did not stay long. Then there are things they are not taught. There is now some evidence that Chinese sailors arrived on our Pacific shores about 70 years before Columbus. Ivan van Sertima, in his book, *They Came Before Columbus*, makes a compelling case for African sailors from Mali arriving on the shores of Central America over 2000 years before Columbus made his voyage.[44]

As glorious as is our history, as accomplished as we of European descent have been, there is another side to us, a side that has been given only the slightest of nods in the histories our children learn. It is a side that is rarely addressed and by and large remains unacknowledged. It is this unacknowledged side of us that has allowed an illness to fester in our national soul along with its concomitant effects throughout our history.

Yes, slavery is mentioned in our school history books, (once again with the exception of Texas) though rarely is its brutality. As far as I recall, the word genocide in reference to Native Americans was never used. While most people with whom I speak readily acknowledge slavery and genocide were bad, in the next breath many become apologists. "You have to look at slavery in its historical context. Yes, it was bad, but it was the times." "We are really sorry for the treatment Native Americans received, but where were Americans to go if not to Native American lands. Besides, Indians were 'savages' who brutalized white settlers to a far greater degree than the settlers brutalized them."

A number of years ago, I was visiting my friend in New York City who had just completed her conversion to an ultra-Orthodox version of Judaism. Now, it is not unusual for new converts to any faith to be particularly devoted to their calling. During my visit one of our discussions turned towards geopolitical events in Israel. We were talking about the continued building of Israeli settlements on the West Bank and she, with the blind faith of a true believer, told me she was in favor of more settlements because after all it is our land.

I, being somewhat astonished by the abject certainty of her statement, asked her how she thought the Jewish people came by that land. She told me, "God gave it to us."

Once again, I saw this as an opportunity to teach, suggesting that, biblically speaking, the Hebrew peoples descended upon the lands and went about killing all who opposed them. In a manner of speaking, Hebrews were the first people on written record to attempt to commit genocide in Western history. Not surprisingly, she would not accept this.

This is not unlike a host of my experiences talking with many white people about slavery, genocide, and oppression here in America. Throughout our almost 400 year history there have been those who have been willing to open their hearts, minds, and souls in an effort to empathize with those who have been unjustly and brutally treated by white America, and of greater import, worked to attempt to balance the books. Still, there are far too many who continue to lack the understanding and empathy needed, if we as a nation, are going to be able to resolve the issues that remain at the heart of our society's disease and dysfunction. If we are to develop our capacity to connect with others, at least on an individual level, we must be willing to come to grips with the darker aspects of our nation's past.

Between 2000 and 2004, I had the profound privilege to work with Joy on her book, *Post Traumatic Slave Syndrome: America's Legacy of Enduring Injury and Healing*. My work with Joy remains one of the highlights of my life. My job was to help her organize her book and help it to flow. I also had the opportunity to help with a small part of the research. It is important that I be very clear here: the work in the book is 100% hers. I simply helped it to flow more or less linearly. (I feel the need to write this because of the history of white Americans being credited for the accomplishments of black Americans. Elvis Presley receiving credit as the originator of Rock and Roll comes to mind.)

It was during this work that I received a tremendous grounding in African-American history and it was during this work that I came to be able to talk about the brutality visited upon black Americans by white Americans. It was during this work that my capacity to understand and empathize grew by leaps and bounds. I suppose I am fortunate, having been raised Jewish, I was no stranger to hearing tales of the unspeakable insults one group of people could perpetrate upon another. Still, there were a number of days I went home and cried; and many more days I went home violently angry. What follows are just some of the highlights of the crimes against humanity that white people in America visited upon their black sisters and brothers. This is the other side of our history that we need to acknowledge, accept, and understand if we as a people are to evolve.

Slavery

Six million. Every Jew, and just about everyone who has had any connection with Jewish culture, knows this number. It is indelibly etched in the minds of all Jews, everywhere, since childhood. For those who are not familiar, it is the number of Jews that were slaughtered in the 1930's and 40's during the Holocaust in Nazi Germany.

Thirty million. This is a number with which most of us are far less familiar. It is our best estimate of the number of Africans who died in the Maafa, Kiswahili for "The Great Suffering" also known as the "The Black Holocaust," and "The Middle Passage," the 200 years of the transatlantic slave trade. We have seen estimates ranging from 9 to 100 million. Recent research places the number at upwards of 30 million, half of those who began the journey that often began with a brutal trek from the heart of the African continent to the slave forts on the coast died before they reached the Americas. Half of those who began the journey lived to become enslaved Africans.

As brutal as that trek was, the brutality only got worse upon arrival at the slave forts. It was often the case that the first thing traders and soldiers did to their arriving captives was rape the women and young girls so as to demonstrate to the men their powerlessness. This was followed by being held in captivity for up to a year in the most inhuman of conditions as they awaited the ships that would load them up like bales of cotton to make the journey across the Atlantic.

What was life like for those African men and women aboard those ships?

> These people were loaded onto ships and crammed together with sometimes less than 18 inches between them. Here they would dwell for many weeks to several months in the bowels of the ship. They were deprived of any human comfort and shared in a collective misery. This disgusting place was where they slept, wept, ate, defecated, urinated, menstruated, vomited, gave birth and died.[45]

What did those who survived the Middle Passage have to look forward to.

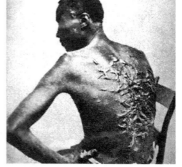

> Being whipped until skin peeled off. Being worked to exhaustion day after day. Being beaten. Being deprived of food and water. Being raped repeatedly. Being considered less than livestock and treated worse. Welcome to the life of a slave. "But most slaves weren't whipped, raped or tortured daily. Most days

*were relatively uneventful," I've heard people argue. Yes,
I'm sure that was often the case. So tell me how many
times does a person have to be brutalized to be traumatized? What is the number of rapes an average woman
must endure before we can assume that she is impacted?*

*And so far we have only considered physical assaults.
Every day of a slave's life was an assault on their dignity,
their humanity, their soul. The simple act of calling another man master is degrading and demeaning. How much
more so saying it to someone for whom you have only hatred and loathing.*[46]

And what must it have been like for the mothers of slave girls
as they reached puberty.

*Imagine that there is a slave mother with young chil-
dren, among them a daughter about 10 or 12 years old.
Like any good mother, she would want to protect her children from harm. Because she is a slave, her children are
also slaves and she must come to grips with the fact that she
is incapable of defending them against assaults from mas-
ters and overseers. This slave mother knows there will be a
day when white men will demand to have access to her
daughter and that these men or boys will use her fragile
young body to satisfy their sexual cravings. That day may
mark the initiation into manhood for the slave master's son,
or perhaps that day she will be offered as an evening gift
for white male visitors. The mother no doubt anguishes
over this fact but still she hopes to lessen the tragic event by
at least acquainting her innocent child with the particulars
of being raped. She tries to help her little girl understand*

what will happen and why it is happening at all. She endeavors to explain how it will feel, how her vagina will tear, burn and bleed. She attempts to tell her how best to prepare and survive the ordeal; tells her to lie still, to not resist and to try to bear the pain. But there are limits to what she can tell her child to better prepare her. She cannot tell her how often they will come, how long it will last, or how many there will be. This mother cannot protect her. Nor can the father, who looks on powerless, defeated and emasculated.[47]

Take a moment and imagine preparing your eleven-year old daughter for such an ordeal. Imagine sitting her down and explaining what would be happening to her very soon.

Such is a small taste, a very small taste, of life in bondage for Africans here in America; in an America in which laws were on the books in many states that allowed for, "the accidental killing of a slave during disciplinary actions," (Virginia's Casual Killing Act of 1705), and 'the killing of a slave who raised his hand against the Christian' (Virginia's Unlawful Assembly Act of 1680). As for rape there were laws that stated,

"no white could ever rape a slave woman" . . ."The regulations of law, as to the white race, on the subject of sexual intercourse do not and cannot, for obvious reasons, apply to slaves; their intercourse is promiscuous". . So black women were perceived to be animal-like. The early English had believed that Black women copulated with chimpanzees or what were thought to be orangutans.[48]

Slavery's Aftermath

With the Emancipation Proclamation in 1863, followed by the ratification of the 13th, 14th, and 15th amendments in 1865, 1868, and 1870 respectively, slavery was abolished and Negroes were acknowledged as full citizens. The oppression of our black citizens by our white brethren had ended. Huzzah!

Well . . .

Soon after the Civil War, states enacted new laws to oppress and subjugate our citizens of color. It began with Exclusionary Acts by which states denied rights to people of color. Here in Oregon in 1859, such an act was written in to our Constitution,

> *Article I Section 35 – No free negro, or mulatto, not residing in this State at the time of the adoption of this Constitution, shall come, reside, or be within this State, or hold any real estate, or make any contracts, or maintain any suit therein; and the Legislative Assembly shall provide by penal laws, for the removal, by public officers, of all such negroes, and mulattoes, and for their effectual exclusion from the State, and for the punishment of persons who shall bring them into the state, or employ, or harbor them.*[49]

> *Article 11 Section 6 – No Negro, Chinaman, or Mulatto shall have the right of suffrage.*[50]

Exclusionary laws were followed by Peonage a system whereby newly freed and impoverished Blacks would be allowed to work the lands they worked while enslaved. Landowners would charge them unfair rent and local merchants would sell them grain and tools at exorbitantly high interest rates ensuring their de facto re-enslavement. This system lasted through 1955.

During the same time the Convict Lease System was established in many southern states. The Convict Lease System allowed prisons to rent their prisoners to businessman in search of cheap labor. Surprising to no one, this system led to the filling up of prisons with black men, usually on false, trumped up charges. Whatever it took to imprison a black man was fair game. Convict Lease became another tool in the effort to re-enslave black men. It was so successful that in 1898, fully 75% of Alabama's state revenue came from their leasing of convicts. Convict Lease was eventually ended in 1928 then rapidly replaced by chain gangs, just another form of brutal forced labor that lasted into the 1950s. However, with the mass incarceration of people of color that is taking place as I write, the idea of convict lease lives on.

Add to this Jim Crow, America's version of apartheid, and voting laws which denied the right to vote to many of our citizens of color, and the codified oppression of African-Americans lasted well into the 1960s.

Lynching

Between 1877 and 1950 a reported 4,000 African-American men, women, and children were lynched by white mobs.[51] This neither takes into account those lynched before and after those dates or those lynchings that went unreported. I believe it is reasonable to put the number between 4,500 and 5,000. Almost all of these horrific acts of terrorism by white Americans on black Americans went unpunished. Horrific though they may have been, they were often viewed by the white community as entertainment.

Lynchings could be quite the party

Once again, Joy DeGruy in her book *Post Traumatic Slave Syndrome*, presents descriptions of these events. Here's a description by Ida B Wells,

Whenever a burning is advertised to take place, the railroads run excursions, photographs are taken, and the same jubilee is indulged in that characterized the public hangings of one hundred years ago. There is, however, this difference: in those old days the multitude that stood by was permitted only to guy or jeer. The nineteenth

Notice the smiling girl looking on

83

century lynching mob cuts off ears, toes, and fingers, strips off flesh, and distributes portions of the body as souvenirs among the crowd. If the leaders of the mob are so minded, coal-oil is poured over the body and the victim is then roasted to death

This has been done in Texarkana and Paris, Tex., in Bardswell, Ky., and in Newman, Ga. In Paris the officers of the law delivered the prisoner to the mob. The mayor gave the school children a holiday and the railroads ran excursion trains so that the people might see a human being burned to death. In Texarkana, the year before, men and boys amused themselves by cutting off strips of flesh and thrusting knives into their helpless victim. At Newman, Ga., of the present year, the mob tried every conceivable torture to compel the victim to cry out and confess, before they set fire to the faggots that burned him. But their trouble was all in vain—he never uttered a cry, and they could not make him confess.[52]

(I included these pictures to illustrate that lynchings were not perpetrated solely by extreme terrorist organizations such as the KKK. Look at the crowds in these pictures. They were every day, often well-heeled, upstanding local citizens. Lynchings were often normalized as part and parcel of life in those communities. Many lynchings became so normalized, that many of the photographs were turned into postcards attendees could send to their friends and relatives who missed the festivities.) Both images were taken from *"Without Sanctuary: Lynching Photography in America"* by James Allen and John Lewis

Joy continues,

> While black men made up the majority of those lynched, as mentioned earlier, black women did not escape this form of execution. In 1918, a pregnant black woman named Mary Turner was hanged, covered with oil and gasoline and burned.

> *As she dangled from the rope, a man stepped forward with a pocketknife and ripped open her abdomen in a crude caesarean operation. Out tumbled the prematurely born child . . .Two feeble cries it gave-and received for answer the heel of a stalwart man, as life was ground out of its tiny form.*[53]

The typical official account of such atrocities read *"Death at the hands of parties unknown."* It is difficult to imagine anything more deplorable than these senseless acts of violence that usually went unpunished. However the following *Weekly Republican* newspaper accounting from Springfield, Massachusetts, on April 28, 1899, reveals a level of barbarism by whites rarely, if ever, acknowledged in American history books.

> *Before the torch was applied to the pyre, the negro was deprived of his ears, fingers and genital parts of his body. He pleaded pitifully for his life while the mutilation was going on, but stood the ordeal of fire with surprising fortitude. Before the body was cool, it was cut to pieces, the bones were crushed into small bits, and even the tree upon which the wretch met his fate was torn up and disposed of as "souvenirs." The negro's heart was cut into several pieces, as was also his liver. Those unable to obtain the ghastly relics direct paid their more fortunate possessors*

extravagant sums for them. Small pieces of bones went for 25 cents, and a bit of the liver crisply cooked sold for 10 cents. As soon as the negro was seen to be dead there was a tremendous struggle among the crowd to secure the souvenirs . . . Knives were quickly produced and soon the body was dismembered.[54]

Between 1882 and 1967 200 bills were presented before congress to outlaw lynching. Additionally, seven presidents urged congress to end the practice. Each and every time these efforts were rejected by the congress and lynchings continued unabated and unpunished. It was not until 2005 that the U. S. Senate offered an apology for what it termed 'domestic terrorism' against mostly black people.[55]

Medical Experimentation

Throughout the 19th and 20th centuries African-Americans have been unknowingly used as subjects in medical experiments. The most notorious of these was the Tuskegee syphilis experiment. From 1932 through 1972, 600 hundred African-American males in Alabama who had contracted syphilis were left untreated so researchers could observe the natural progression of the disease. Even after penicillin was determined to be an efficacious treatment of the disease in 1947, subjects in the Tuskegee experiments remained untreated and unaware that a viable treatment existed.

Tuskegee is only the most infamous of these experiments. As mentioned earlier, J. Marion Sims, the doctor considered to be the father of American gynecology, gained much of his reputation and wealth performing experimental surgeries on slave women. These women remained unanesthetized during these procedures due to Dr. Sims' belief that "slave women were able to bear great pain because their 'race' made them more durable." This absurd belief was commonly held among many who performed experiments on black men and women. Sims' experiments were not limited to slave women. He repeatedly attempted to treat what we know today as neonatal tetanus by prying the bones in the skulls of tiny infants into alignment using a shoemaker's awl. All of his infant subjects died as a result of his experimentation.

These are only three of many. In her book, *Medical Apartheid*, Harriet Washington details the long and sordid history of experimentation on unknowing African-Americans. A number of the experiments like those described above put those who performed them in the same class as the Nazi doctors who experimented on Jews in Germany 70 to 80 years ago.

It is ironic that while many have justified such cruel medical experimentation by asserting how valuable these experiments are for the health of the greater community, few if any of those experimented upon were able to have access to the treatments developed. It should go without saying that these experiments were conducted without knowledge or consent of the subjects, who often were people of color, and almost always poor.

Post-Civil Rights

With the passage of the Civil Rights Act of 1964 and the Voting Rights Act the following year, the playing field was supposed to have been leveled. No longer could employers, schools, or government agencies discriminate based on race, color, creed, or national origin. No longer would municipalities be able to impose requirements that would keep their citizens of color from voting. There can be little question, conditions have improved for our sisters and brothers of color over the ensuing 50 years.

However, the past 20 years have seen concerted efforts to halt and reverse our progress. Efforts to roll back affirmative action began in the 1970s and have picked up momentum after the turn of this century. State after state, predominantly in the south, have passed legislation aimed at disenfranchising hundreds of thousands of people of color. And the brutality and differential treatment of black and brown Americans has continued. We have already mentioned mass incarceration, a subject we will address at length in the next chapter. There are others.

In 2013, the Flint, Michigan's drinking water was switched from a safe source to that of the highly contaminated Flint river in an effort to cut costs. A little over a year later, the General Motors plant in Flint stopped using Flint river water due to concerns about the water corroding engine parts. As Flint citizens, 60% of whom are people of color, and almost all of them poor, continued receiving the contaminated water, General Motors struck a deal with the city to switch their water supply from the Flint river to a cleaner source at a cost to the city of $400,000.[56]

That the city was willing to pay for General Motors' engine parts to have suitable water and not their citizens was unconscionable. The results of the decision to allow the residents of Flint to continue using contaminated water has been, among other health effects, the lead poisoning of numerous children, putting them severely at risk of permanent developmental disability. That an administration would knowingly put its citizens at risk of permanent damage to their health in an effort to save money is beyond the pale. One wonders what decisions would have been made if the majority of the citizens of Flint were white.

The "War on Drugs," was inaugurated in 1971. This too, was used differentially to continue our attack on our citizens of color, and was one of the driving forces that led to their mass incarceration. In the 1980s, crack cocaine became the drug of choice amongst people of color in our inner cities. Powder cocaine had been, and continues to be, used by their predominantly white, suburban, and affluent peers. Under the penalty structure established during the 1980s, possession of crack could carry the same sentence as the possession of a quantity of cocaine that is 100 times larger! The Controlled Substances Act of 1970 established a minimum mandatory sentence of five years for a first-time trafficking offense involving over five grams of crack, as opposed to the same minimum mandatory sentence for 500 grams of powder cocaine. The law imposed the same ratio for larger amounts: a minimum sentence of 10 years for amounts of crack over 50 grams, versus 5 kilograms of cocaine.[57]

You can imagine the results. Since the 1980s, no class of drug has been this racially skewed. According to the U.S. sentencing commission, in 2009, 79% of the 5669 sentenced crack offenders were black, 10% were Hispanic, and 10% were white. Sentenced cocaine offenders that year, while still skewed relative to our nation's demographics, were less so. Of those sentenced, 17% were black, 28% were white, and 53% were Hispanic. Combined with a 115-month average imprisonment for crack offenses versus an average of 87 months for cocaine offenses, this makes for more African-Americans spending more time in the prison system. [58]

Shockingly, in 2016 lynching is once again on the rise. A number of young black men in the state of Florida have been found hanging from trees. Joy DeGruy was giving a talk in the state when, during a break, five police officers who were attending her presentation went up to her with pictures of young black male bodies in various states of decomposition hanging from trees. One of the officers told Joy his superiors have demanded that these murders be reported as suicides. To make their point, one of the officers drew to her attention a picture of one of the young men dressed in a white T-shirt, beige pants, and white shoes hanging from a tree. There was not a spot of dirt on him.

Even more troubling, the New York Times reported that on August 28, 2017, in Claremont, New Hampshire a group of young, white teenagers attempted to 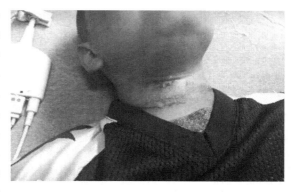 Lynch an eight-year-old biracial boy. Please note, that the black-and-white image on the right does not convey the true impact of the assault on this young boy. If you would like to see this image in color, go to:

http://www.theroot.com/new-hampshire-police-refuse-to-release-information-on-c-1803054596

Genocide

This has been just a small sampling of the atrocities and differential treatment white America has visited upon black America. The atrocities have been equally horrific when it comes to the whites' treatment of Native Americans over the past 400 years. I regret to say I have done nowhere near the amount of study regarding any other community than I have done regarding the African-American community. That said, I am marginally cognizant of some of the outrages our Native American brethren have experienced at the hands of us white people.

At the time Columbus was inadvertently landing on Hispaniola, there were an estimated 10 million native people living in what is today United States territory. By 1900, they were reduced to a mere 300,000, approximately 3%. White immigrants and settlers were responsible for the deaths of 97% of the indigenous peoples.

Disease was the primary killer, responsible for eradicating 90% of the native peoples. For the most part, disease was spread unintentionally, however at times the spread of disease was premeditated.

In 1763, a particularly serious uprising threatened British garrisons in Pennsylvania. Worried about limited resources, and driven by atrocities committed by some Native Americans (in response the their treatment by British settlers) Sir Jeffrey Amherst, commander-in-chief of British forces in North America, wrote to Colonel Henry Bouquet at Fort Pitt:

"You will do well to try to inoculate the Indians [with smallpox] by means of blankets, as well as to try every other method, that can serve to extirpate this execrable race."

Consequently, settlers spread smallpox to the Native Americans by distributing blankets previously owned by contagious patients.[59]

Beyond disease, the list of crimes whites perpetrated against natives is long. In the late 18th century, Massachusetts colonists were paid for each Penobscot Native they killed – men, women, and children. In the 1830s, our government, to support our cotton growers, forced 100,000 Natives out of their homelands. Four thousand people died on the Trail of Tears, the journey from southern states to "Indian Territory" in Oklahoma.

In 1850, the California state government passed the Act for the Government and Protection of Indians that,

. . . addressed the punishment and protection of Native Americans, and helped to facilitate the removal of their culture and land. It also legalized slavery and was referenced for the buying and selling of Native children.[60]

A year later, California Governor Peter H. Burnett proclaimed,

A war of extermination will continue to be waged between the two races until the Indian race becomes extinct."[61]

The Wounded Knee massacre and countless others; court decisions allowing for the overrunning of Native law and overturning of treaties; the establishment of reservations; the providing of alcohol to a people known to be susceptible to addiction; the cultural genocide that resulted from efforts to remove children from their families and send them to boarding schools in order to destroy their language and customs, and assimilate them into ours; our depiction of them as savages, drunkards, and servants throughout our media; have all served white America's efforts to erase the Native presence from this land as well as the history of white America's crimes.

Brutally using Chinese American labor in the building of our railroads in the 19th century, the dispossession and internment of Japanese Americans in the 20th century, the continued underpaying and overworking of Latino migrants which continues to this day – this is our dark side, the side that only grudgingly gets addressed and rarely fully acknowledged. We need to be as readily able to understand and accept the darker angels of our collective nature as we are to understand and celebrate the better angels of our collective souls. Yes, there were the Quakers and the abolitionists, as well as those who marched, were beaten, and at times died for the ideals of the Civil Rights Movement. There are those today who are out there, taking to the streets and the halls of influence and power working for the cause of social justice. White Americans have been, and are, good, and sometimes even great people. Rejoicing in their accomplishments is all to the good, though not at the expense of losing sight of our whole story.

Once again, I relate these stories in an effort to build understanding. I'm not suggesting white Americans feel sorry for their black and brown brethren. I certainly don't recommend that we immerse ourselves in guilt for the sins of those who came before us. It is rather for us to deepen our understanding of the history and experiences of others. Doing so will help us to better build connections with those who have very different experiences from our own.

The Past Is Present — Trans-Generational Trauma

Post Traumatic Slave Syndrome

Once again, I hear a number of people say,

"Slavery, genocide, most of those events of which you speak happened decades, even centuries in the past. What does it matter today? Isn't it time for those people to quit their whining, get over it, and move on?" And of course, "Post Traumatic Slave Syndrome? Give me a break. It's just another excuse for poor choices and bad behaviors."

Would that it were so simple. To their great credit, a number of people have moved on and have had success, though not without their struggles, struggles we white Americans, thankfully, do not have to address.

The impacts, both for ill and for good, experienced by our ancestors influence all of us today. Mind you, they influence us to varying degrees, they do not necessarily rule us. At the same time, we all have the capacity to mitigate our pasts and create the futures we choose.

I will do my best to explain how traumas experienced by our ancestors can impact us in the present. My chief source is, of course, *Post Traumatic Slave Syndrome.* For the best discussion of this, I highly recommend reading Dr. Joy's book. Here goes.

I am going to assume that you have all heard of Post-Traumatic Stress Disorder. (PTSD) PTSD encompasses a number of symptoms that arise as the result of trauma. Soldiers who have been at war, victims of assaults, children living in high stress homes are often diagnosed with this disorder. One can acquire PTSD a number of ways. A person can be a victim of a traumatic event, a person can witness a traumatic event, a person can even hear about a traumatic event and develop PTSD. We all

94

respond to trauma differently; the same event will not affect those involved equally. It can very well be the case that the direct recipient of the trauma may not experience the impact at all, while someone witnessing the traumatic event may be impacted greatly. Similarly, a person experiencing multiple events may be impacted less than a person experiencing a single event. We are all different.

Those who have acquired PTSD may exhibit a number of symptoms including agitation, irritability, hostility, hyper-vigilance, self-destructive behavior, social isolation, insomnia, guilt, emotional detachment, to name a few. The good news is PTSD is treatable. Whether one is a combat veteran, a survivor of domestic abuse, or a witness to tragedy, counseling is available and recovery certainly achievable. But what happens if a person suffering from PTSD does not pursue treatment?

Let's imagine we have a father of two children ages two and seven coming home from war. This man was on the front lines for much of his tour. He was injured by a bullet wound and was able to recover and, in a short time, return to action. During his service he saw two of his mates blown up by IED's and two others shot and killed at close range as they entered a home they believed to be unoccupied. He witnessed a number of other of his troop injured to varying degrees.

When he arrives home his wife notices him exhibit many of the symptoms of PTSD. But he's an old school strong man, and refuses to talk about his time in Iraq. He believes, as many old-school veterans often do, that counseling is a sign of weakness, so he just 'deals with it.' As time passes, he becomes more symptomatic. He startles easily, yelling at his children when they make a sudden noise. He becomes more sullen and less engaged with his children, spending a fair amount of time keeping to himself.

As he becomes more distant and irritable, he also becomes quicker and quicker to discipline his children, often physically. His children and his wife begin to walk on egg shells, doing their best not to disturb dad. It is not too long before his children begin to fear him. Living in such a home, his children developed their own cases of PTSD which, if left unaddressed will impact their families when the time comes for them to marry and raise children. This pattern will very likely continue until someone up the ancestral line addresses and resolves their issues. This is one of the ways trauma can be passed from generation to generation.

So I ask you, did slaves in America experienced traumas? Did slaves in America witness traumas? Did slaves in America hear about traumas? Of course they did. Some experienced hundreds perhaps thousands of traumas across their lives. At the beginning of the Civil War, 90% of all black people in America were enslaved. To paraphrase Joy, "I don't recall counseling and therapy coming along with emancipation." And after emancipation the traumas continued up until this day. Do you think a number of slaves experience PTSD? I think it's fair to say many of them did, most of whom passed it down to their children, who passed it down to their children, on and on.

PTSD wasn't the only thing that got passed down through the generations. Great resilience, endurance, adaptability, all attributes that made survival during their enslavement possible were also passed on to future generations. These have been the cornerstones of the African-American community's ability to thrive through the ensuing century and a half of continued abuses. In every group of people that have been subjugated and/or brutalized, a significant portion of them will suffer from

PTSD to one degree or another, and if left untreated, they will pass these effects down through the generations. Similarly, in every group of people that have been subjugated and/or brutalized, positive attributes and adaptations will also be passed on to future generations.

Post Traumatic Slave Syndrome refers to the adaptive and maladaptive behaviors that were passed on as a result of the slave experience and the brutality that continued long after. Looking through such a historical lens can help us understand much of what we see. It is Dr. Joy's work to help her people recover from centuries of injury by helping them look at their thoughts, feelings, and actions through this lens, and so understand the roots of their behavior that bring them both failure and success.

Let's take an example from a relatively recent event. Some of you may remember, a few years ago Adrian Peterson, running back for the Minnesota Vikings, pled 'no contest' after being indicted on charges of child abuse for using a wooden switch to discipline his four-year-old son. Mr. Peterson was remorseful and apologized for his actions. In an interview following, Mr. Peterson said he was disciplining his son in the same way he was disciplined growing up in East Texas. The public nature of this event sparked a nationwide discussion on the use of corporal punishment.

Simply looking at the use of corporal punishment by African-American parents in the context of today's society is not enough. If we truly want to understand the behavior, it will behoove us to view corporal punishment through the lens of African-American history. For generations, in many parts of the South, a black boy or young man could put themselves at serious risk for being 'uppity.' Black parents worked diligently to ensure that their children, particularly their sons had enough self-control so as not to antagonize slave owners and, once slavery was abolished, any white person, for such antagonism could, and sometimes did, result in death. It was not uncommon for black parents to believe it was better that they strongly discipline their children rather than risk the consequences of inappropriate behavior outside the home. (Today, black parents believe they have to be similarly diligent to ensure that their children have enough self-control so as not to put themselves at risk of being shot by law-enforcement.)

During the centuries of slavery and the times that followed, such efforts by parents were pro-survival; I'm sure the lives of many children were saved as a result of their parents' disciplining. Over the course of centuries, such behavior can become ingrained in a community, so much so that it goes unexamined, hence Adrian Peterson disciplining his child the way he was disciplined by his parents, who in turn were disciplined in the same way by their parents, so on and so forth.

Every community of people that has been oppressed over long periods of time exhibit behaviors that were one time pro-survival and at some point have become counter-survival. This, is one of the lessons of Dr. Joy's work.

I believe the chief value for her work, as it relates to white America, is that it can give us pause to allow us to examine events more fully before we pass judgment on a person or group of people. I present Dr. Joy's work not to make excuses, but rather to explain. There is a fine, though very distinct, difference between excuses and explanations. Simply put, excuses do not move us forward; they do not promote learning. Explanations can point the way to education and growth. Dr. Joy's work serves to provide us with explanations that encourages us to re-examine how we look at others and their actions.

Epigenetics

Evidence is mounting in support of the hypothesis that our environment can impact our DNA and so the traumas a person experiences can be genetically passed on to their children. Scientists in the field of epigenetics are exploring the profound ways environment affects our very chromosomes. They do not believe our environment changes our DNA directly, they believe that our environment changes the way our genes express themselves. Our environment seemingly can do this, not by changing genes, but by turning them on or off.

Virginia Hughes, reporting in *Nature*, tells of research by Brian Dias in Kerry Ressler's lab at Emory University in Atlanta, in which they conditioned a male mouse to become fearful of a particular smell. As you might expect, he did this simply by presenting the smell to the mouse along with a small electric shock to its foot. After three days, the mouse would freeze in the presence of the smell without the electric shock. Standard Pavlovian conditioning.

He then mated that mouse with females who had been exposed neither to the smell nor the shock. Surprisingly, he found that when their young grew up many of them exhibited similar fearful reactions to that particular smell, though they had never been previously exposed to it. The same held true for the original male's grandchildren. That effects such as these are real, there is little disagreement. How the trauma is transmitted down through the generations remains unknown at this time.

Of course, these are studies with mice; they only suggest possibilities with humans. That said, there are studies that point to such trans-generational effects in humans. Hughes, reported that in Sweden, historical records showed that men who experience famine before puberty were less likely to have grandsons with heart disease or diabetes than men who had plenty to eat. A similar study in Britain in 2005 reported that fathers who started smoking before the age of 11 had an increased risk of having boys above average weight.[62]

As we learn more, it is becoming more obvious that the impacts of war, poverty, abuse, neglect, and other traumatic experiences can be passed down through the generations. More than the environmental impacts of trauma, it is now looking like there are biological impacts as well.

Coming to Grips With History: One Example

In 1951, Konrad Adenauer, Chancellor of Germany, reached out to the very young state of Israel in order to negotiate a reparations settlement for the Germans atrocities committed upon the Jewish people of Europe during the previous two decades. A settlement was signed the following year. So began Germany's efforts to acknowledge its moral debt and financial obligations for the horrific acts it committed during the 1930s and 40s. In 1963, Chancellor Adenauer and French President Charles de Gaulle signed the Elysee Treaty ending centuries of enmity between the two nations. Between 1963 and 1965, Germany held the Frankfurt Auschwitz trials, the first major Nazi war crimes cases brought by the Germans themselves rather than the Allied nations. In 1970, Chancellor Willy Brandt signed the Treaty of Warsaw committing Germany and Poland to nonviolence and accepting the borders between the two countries imposed by the Allies in 1945. Since, I believe, the 1960s Germany's role in the Holocaust has been taught in schools at every level.

Contrast Germany's approach to addressing their nation's crimes to that of America's. Textbook companies are writing our nation's crimes of slavery and genocide out of our history books. We fight over whether men and women who defended and fought for the institution of slavery should remain immortalized in our public spaces. We demand folks whose ancestors across generations were the victims of our nation's great crimes, who continue to experience the trans-generational impacts of those crimes, and are today being traumatized by America's version of terrorism, to "Get over it."

For these past 66 years the German nation has acknowledged, and continues to acknowledge, their crimes of the 20th century and has worked to pay for them. This is as it pertains to the German nation; the German people can be a somewhat different story. There remain Holocaust deniers. Many others will not readily speak of their family history as it pertains to events around World War II. Ursula Duba, the German-American author of, *Tales From the Child of An Enemy*, speaking at Pennsylvania State University, told of many German youth, when presented with stories of Holocaust survivors, being un-empathetic, defensive, and even angry. After 70 years, some Germans feel as if they are victims. She attributes these responses in large part to the silence within families regarding past events.[63] Of course, many more Germans have made their peace with their history, some working to help those their nation victimized and their descendants improve their lives.

The varied responses of German individuals is little different from the responses of individual Americans to the darker aspects of our history. What is markedly different is the response of the German nation. Rather than criticize the victims, rationalize and justify their past actions, they have chosen to acknowledge their crimes, express remorse, make amends as best they can, and move on. Many in German leadership credit their nation's approach to their history as responsible, at least in part, for their nation's rise from the rubble of World War II to the world's fourth largest economy.

Imagine if America responded similarly to its crimes against humanity? How might our history be different? Instead, the way America has responded to the more unsavory aspects of our history (largely by burying. criticizing, justifying, and rationalizing past behaviors), when it chooses to respond at all, has produced sociological forces that promote injustice, misplaced feelings of superiority/inferiority, privilege, and guilt. All contribute to our disconnection. And so our moral illness continues to fester. We can do better. We must do better.

Chapter 5

Sociological Forces Inhibiting Connection: Impacts on Americans of Color

Injustice, misplaced feelings of superiority/inferiority privilege, guilt – these sociological forces are some of the fruits of our reticence to acknowledge the darker angels of our past. These forces serve to promote misunderstanding, widening and deepening our disconnection. Along with the psychological forces discussed earlier, these sociological forces have been great barriers to our becoming the egalitarian and unified society to which we aspire. Examining their impacts can help us gain greater understanding, break down these barriers, and create the society we will then all deserve.

Injustices: Insults and Assaults Large and Small - Micro-aggressions

Micro-aggressions refer to the myriad of person-to-person events that people of color in America are party to on a daily basis. Rarely, is any single event of consequence. In fact, it is one of the privileges of being white that we look upon these events as relatively inconsequential, for we can imagine if they happened to us, we would not consider them to impact our lives substantially. More likely, we would believe these aggressions to be the result of the poor behavior of the perpetrator. This is, in large part, due to the fact that most of us experience these events infrequently compared to the frequency that they are experienced by our fellow citizens of color.

About 12 years ago, Joy and I were at the hospital where her daughter had just given birth to Joy's first grandchild. Joy wanted a cup of coffee so we went down to the lobby where the coffee kiosk was just opening. We were first in line and waiting patiently as the young white woman was getting ready to serve her customers. I didn't want coffee so I was standing behind Joy and off to the right, clearly not in line. When the young lady was ready, she looked directly at me and asked me what I wanted. Joy and I exchange a knowing look, and Joy proceeded to help her understand her mistake.

Recently, Joy's daughter, a young woman with her master's degree, and soon to receive her doctoral degree, was at a meeting of government representatives and community social service providers. She was there in her role as manager of one of the community programs. Before the start of the meeting, as the participants were introducing themselves and mingling, one of the gentlemen, a white gentleman, to whom she was introduced believed it was appropriate to put his hands on her head to feel her hair. Of course, being Joy's daughter, she corrected him. Do you think he feels comfortable approaching white women in the same way? I don't know. But what I do know is that it is clearly inappropriate for anybody older than a young child to feel someone's hair uninvited.

One day, I was driving five of my students from the House of Umoja (the residence facility for gang involved African American young men who had run afoul of the law) to a celebratory lunch. On the way, as we were waiting at a traffic light, a car pulled up alongside of us and we all heard that car's doors lock. The young men in my car shook their heads and said that happens every time.

A friend of mine went to a lecture at the University of Oregon on Egyptian history presented by an eminent African Egyptologist. The focus of the talk was the movement of peoples in Egypt throughout its history beginning with the migration of the Nubian people from the south into Egypt. Upon finishing his talk, he opened it up for questions and answers. At one point, a white gentleman stood up and said:

"I must say I am offended. So much of your talk was about black people. Everyone knows Egyptians are white."

My only explanation for the gentleman's ignorance is that he learned his Egyptian history from watching movies such as *Cleopatra*, starring Elizabeth Taylor and Richard Burton. And of course Charlton Heston played Moses and Yul Brynner played Rameses in *The Ten Commandments*.

That same friend, was at another talk presented by Dr. James Mason, who at the time was the Dean of the Black Studies department at Portland State University, when upon the completion of his talk a white woman raised her hand and asked,

"Where did you learn to speak so well?" She went on to say how impressed she was with his articulateness and his pronunciation. I have been speaking in public for going on 40 years. No one has ever asked me such a question nor complemented me on the way I pronounce my words.

A very good friend of mine, a highly educated African-American woman who develops museum educational programming for students in New York City, tells me of the countless times her white peers, not believing that she could be as accomplished as she is, ask her if she went to a 'special' school to get her degrees. When she is at conferences with her boss, a white woman, she asks her boss to introduce her with her title, Manager of Teaching and Learning, for without her title most people believe her to be simply her boss' assistant.

Every so often during my time at the House of Umoja, the students would not be in a space to sit in a classroom and focus. Those days we would load them up in a van and get them outdoors. We would take them hiking to places that they had never been before. Many of the young men had never even been in a forest. One of these times, as we were driving to the hiking trail, I asked Tim, one of the staff, if he got out hiking much. He looked at me surprised and told me:

"Heck no! People have accidents out there. You know, sometimes we can be mistaken for deer."

In the same manner, Joy and her sister only half-jokingly voiced similar sentiments when I asked them if they would like to try cross-country skiing.

The number of times I've been with my black friends at a shop where I purchased something with a check and my friend behind me did the same but was asked for two pieces of ID or some such difference are too numerous to count. The number of times I am smiled at while they are looked at suspiciously are almost beyond measure. The number of times I have seen people cross the street to avoid walking past black men are innumerable. If you don't hang out in communities of color, it can be hard to see. Honestly, until I have these discussions with my white friends, most of them say they had no idea.

If you're black or brown in America, events such as these happen throughout your day, just about every day. If you're white, you have the privilege of rarely having to experience such a barrage of insults. Imagine the repeated effect of such insults. Imagine having people look at you and assume you are uneducated, poor, criminal. Imagine having to do all those little things: voice inflection, small movements of your body, putting out numerous signals to demonstrate that you are simply a decent person who deserves the respect anyone of us gives to each other on a regular basis.

Then, there are all those indirect insults and injuries people of color receive secondhand. Watching news footage of black men and sometimes black boys being shot and killed by police. Listening to news stories about your people being disenfranchised. Hearing that George Zimmerman got off after killing Trayvon Martin. Seeing a white man coldcock a young black man who was just walking up the stairs after voicing his protest at a Trump rally, then seeing security take down the victim of the assault. Watching television and going to the movies, and seeing the vast majority of people who look like you portraying criminals and/or caricatures.

Can you begin to imagine what it must've been like for African-Americans witnessing their brothers and sisters starving and thirsty in New Orleans after Hurricane Katrina, as they watched footage of dogs and cats are being flown to safety in commercial airplanes?

These are all insults and assaults. And then there are the physical assaults that can part of daily life. In the Fall of 2016, just after the presidential election, Joy's 11 year old granddaughter and her friends, most of whom were children of color, were walking to the store after school. As they were hanging out in front of the store a white man on a motorcycle stopped and cursed them out. He then proceeded to circle the block, return, and pepper spray the school children. As of this writing, a year later, that man remains unidentified.

Such assaults rarely ever go well for the person of color, though every once in a while justice is served. In May 2016, a woman with whom I work got into an altercation. This woman experiences insults and assaults almost daily from two directions. She is a black woman and she is wheelchair-bound as the result of a brain tumor. That day in May she wanted to go to her daughter's elementary school which was three blocks from her home. She got in her wheelchair and started rolling to school. (She rolls in the street, keeping close to the parked cars, rather than on the sidewalk because in her neighborhood the sidewalks are pretty broken up.)

This day, as she was rolling to school, a school bus filled with middle schoolers slowed down to stop at the corner. As the bus was slowing, some of the children leaned out their windows and started hurling racist epithets at her. Now, this is a woman who faces daily physical challenges and sometimes her medication leaves her a bit raw. So in response to the middle schoolers, she cursed back at them.

The bus driver waited for her to get close to his window, leaned out, put his finger in her face, and started yelling at her. To her credit, she grabbed the man's arm, pulled on it so his head was out of the window, and then popped him in the eye. The bus driver proceeded to get out of the bus, stand over her and point his finger in her face, while admonishing her loudly. She responded by kicking him between his legs, and as he was bending over, she kneed him in his jaw then broke his nose with the palm of her hand.

The night before she had had an emergency with her daughter and called 911. Her physical condition is such that on her medication she will at times slur her speech. The 911 operator told her she was drunk and put her name on the bottom of the list. Help arrived six hours later. Fortunately, by that time, with the help of a friend, the emergency was for the most part resolved.

A person can only take so much.

I wonder how this event would have gone if she was white? Would the children have verbally assaulted her? Would the bus driver have admonished his students rather than the woman? What might have happened if she was not in a wheel chair? Would she have been arrested for assaulting the driver?

"But that's not me," you say. Maybe you're right. But are you sure? And maybe if you are not responsible for any of this, have you witnessed the insults of others and not called them to account?

In the summer of 2011, I was visiting my lifelong friend Gilbert at his timeshare in Vermont. Gilbert and his family picked me up at the airport. In the van were Gil, his wife, their two sons (two of my godson's), and his younger son's friend, Freddie. All three boys were in high school. As we were driving from the airport a car suddenly pulled out in front of Gilbert forcing him to swerve to avoid an accident, which he did expertly. Freddie noticed that the driver of the car was black and made some derogatory comment about him.

Now I had an opportunity to educate. I immediately looked at him and asked him if he knew who he was in the car with? Of course, we had just met, so he didn't. I proceeded to tell him who I was, who some of my extended family members are, that my goddaughter is black, as our some of my closest friends.

Freddie is a really good young guy, as of course are my godson's. This began a discussion, Freddie telling me that he and his friends of color at school throw 'friendly' racial and ethnic epithets at each other regularly. It's part of their banter. My friend and his family live in a pretty small town in western New York; there weren't more than 20 students of color in their high school and only a few of those were black. I told Freddie that one day after they all graduate his black friends will likely make their way to a black community somewhere in America. Then they will learn how uncool their high school experience really was, and it would not surprise me if they hate you and their other white 'friends' for it.

We continued these discussions on and off over the five days of my stay. Gil's wife thanked me for these talks with her sons and their friend. She had been trying to find a way to broach the subject for a few weeks and was very glad I did. I am led to believe their behavior changed. To this day, Freddie and I stay in touch. I last saw him a year ago at my godson's wedding. He has a family of his own and they are doing very well.

Injustices: Insults and Assaults Small and Large – Macro-aggressions

Whereas micro-aggressions are, for the most part, person-to-person aggressions, macro-aggressions refer to aggressions at an institutional level. Yes, they are perpetrated by individuals, but the rules, written and unwritten, of the organizations for which they work encourage them and set them up to treat our citizens of color differentially. All of our fundamental systems: criminal justice, education, social services, employment, finance, the media have unjust treatment based on skin color built into them.

Once again, white Americans have the privilege to remain blissfully ignorant of these injustices as they rarely, if ever impact us. Studies have been done, papers have been published, and books have been written exposing the differential treatment people of color receive. In the following pages, I will highlight just a few, and please believe me, these are just the tip of the iceberg.

Criminal Justice: Guilty Until Proven Innocent
Mass Incarceration

Remember William Bennett's assertion that aborting all black babies in this country would reduce the crime rate? That assertion plays into the myth that our black brethren are more criminal than we are. Let's take a closer look.

Nationally, in 2014, according to the U.S. Census, Blacks were incarcerated five times more than Whites were, and Hispanics were nearly twice as likely to be incarcerated as Whites.[64]

Race/Ethnicity	% of US population	% of incarcerated population
White (non-Hispanic)	64%	39%
Hispanic	16%	19%
Black	13%	40%

The racial and ethnic make-up of incarcerated populations is dramatically different from that of the U.S. as a whole:

So, in 2014, 64% of Americans were white yet they comprised only 39% of our incarcerated population. At the same time, 13% of Americans were black, yet they comprised 40% of our incarcerated population. The simplest way to interpret these statistics is that African-Americans commit more crimes than their white counterparts. However, if one delves a little deeper a different story emerges.

Roughly 75% of all those incarcerated were convicted of drug charges. Certainly, people of color are convicted of drug crimes at a considerably higher rate than their white fellows and a cursory reading of incarceration rates by race/ethnicity might lead one to conclude that people of color use drugs disproportionately when compared to white folks. Would you be surprised to learn that there is a higher frequency of drug use among white Americans than Americans of color?

According to the 2004 publication by the National Institute on Drug Abuse, "Monitoring the Future," white youth in 8th, 10th, and 12th grades use illicit drugs more frequently (11.9%) than their African-American peers (9.3%).[65] A survey done the previous year, found that white youth were a third more likely to have sold drugs than African-American youth.[66] However African-American youth are arrested for drug offenses at about twice the rate of their white peers and African-American youth represent nearly half (48%) the youth incarcerated for drug offenses in the juvenile justice system.[67]

Do you think it is reasonable to assume that drug use and interaction with the justice system changes significantly as these youth transitioned to adulthood?

Deaths During Interactions with Law Enforcement

During the past few years, a number of unarmed African Americans have died at the hands of those sworn to protect and serve. The deaths of Michael Brown, Eric Garner, Freddie Gray, and Tamir Rice are four who garnered much publicity. There have been many, many others. In December 2015, the Washington Post in their article, "A Year of Reckoning: Police Fatally Shoot Nearly 1000," reported that although black men make up only 6% of the U.S. population, they accounted for 40% of the unarmed men shot to death by police that year.[68]

Between 2003 and 2009 the Department of Justice reported that 4815 people died while in the process of arrest or in the custody of law enforcement. As in the above table, though whites make up 64% of the population, they comprise only 40% of those who died while in the process of arrest or in the custody of law enforcement. African-Americans, comprising 13% of our population comprised 32% of those who died.[69]

So why this differential treatment of citizens of color resulting in such terrible consequences? Norm Stamper, former Seattle chief of police and author of *Breaking Rank: A Top Cop's Exposé of the Dark Side of American Policing*, spoke of the unwritten training that gets passed down to young officers: The most dangerous person on the street is a young black man. He writes that police learn to fear these men and that leads, at times, to tragic consequences. His words,

> *"Simply put, white cops are afraid of black men. We don't talk about it, we pretend it doesn't exist, we claim "color blindness," we say white officers treat black men the same way they treat white men. But that's a lie. In fact, the bigger, the darker the black man the greater the fear. The African-American community knows this. Most whites know it. Yet, even though it's a central, if not the defining ingredient in the makeup of police racism, white cops won't admit it to themselves, or to others."* [70]

He goes on to write,

> *"In New York City, twenty-three African-American cops have been shot and eighteen others assaulted by white officers in cases of "mistaken identity." Not one white cop has ever been shot by a black cop. The PBA, while bemoaning these "tragic incidents," has done nothing to help remedy the problem."* [71]

These deaths, while the most tragic of events, do not take into account the exponentially greater number of incidents of police brutality perpetrated disparately on our citizens of color, and these do not take into account the almost daily hassles at the hands of police officers that people of color in this country endure. Just about every African-American man, and many women, I know have been pulled over by police for "driving while black," a term they use when they are stopped for no apparent reason. In

1999, a study in New Jersey found that black drivers on the New Jersey Turnpike are five times more likely than white drivers to be stopped by the New Jersey State police.[72] The powers that be in Arizona attempted to pass a law that would allow the authorities to ask anyone who 'looked' like they might be here illegally to present papers proving otherwise. What group of people do you think might 'look' like they might be here illegally? 'Stop and frisk' policies in New York City resulted in an inordinate amount of people of color having contact with the law.

Add to this the manner in which law enforcement officers who shoot unarmed civilians are treated. It has been reported that in 2015, 104 unarmed African-Americans were shot and killed by police in the United States. In only 14 of these cases were police officers charged with a crime and in only four of these cases were the officers convicted and sentenced. Of the four officers convicted, one officer received no jail time, one officer received three months of jail time, one officer received one year of jail time and was allowed to serve his time on weekends, and one officer received four years of jail time.[73]

Contrast this to the July 2017 fatal shooting of Justine Ruszczyk, a young, middle-class white woman by an African-American police officer in Minneapolis. Rather than letting the process play out as she did in the 2016 police shooting of unarmed Philando Castile (the officer who shot Castile was tried and acquitted on all counts), Mayor Betsy Hodges immediately asked and received police chief, Janeé Harteau's resignation.

Implicit Bias

Implicit bias refers to the biases we have in our brains in the form of associations that are below our awareness. We have implicit biases across many human attributes, e.g.: gender, age, sexual orientation, to name a few. Cognitive psychologists have developed a test that can bring our biases to light, the Implicit Association Test. (IAT) The attribute in question for the purposes of this work is ethnicity. Chris Mooney, writing for *Mother Jones*, describes the test.

> *The test asks you to rapidly categorize images of faces as either "African American" or "European American" while you also categorize words (like "evil," "happy," "awful," and "peace") as either "good" or "bad." Faces and words flash on the screen, and you tap a key, as fast as you can, to indicate which category is appropriate. Sometimes you're asked to sort African American faces and "good" words to one side of the screen. Other times, black faces are to be sorted with "bad" words. As words and faces keep flashing by, you struggle not to make too many sorting mistakes."* [73a]

Biases are revealed by the speed at which a person accomplishes the task and by how well they are able to follow the instructions given the high rate of speed.

A variation of this test was presented to Denver police officers and community members. In the place of the images of faces and words were images of white and black men holding in their hand either a gun or a harmless object. Those participating in this test had to rapidly determine whether or not to shoot the person in the picture by pressing a "shoot" or "don't shoot" button. As one might expect the police were better than the community members at determining whether a person was armed or not. Other results were more troubling. Both groups were four times more likely to shoot if the person in the picture was black. Both groups were also found to be faster at pressing the "don't shoot" button when the person in the picture was white and slower to press the "don't shoot" button when the person in the picture was black. Finally, both groups were found to be faster at pressing the "shoot" button when the person in the picture was black as opposed to when the person was white. [73b] The above results led the researchers to conclude that the participants demonstrated clear biases against African-American men when compared to their white counterparts, and these biases have been playing out on our streets far too regularly.

Myths like 'people of color are more criminal than white people' and 'young black men are more dangerous than anyone else,' play into the significantly differential treatment African-Americans and others of color receive at the hands of the criminal justice system. Is it any wonder those of color view the criminal justice system far differently than most of us do? Is it any wonder that so many African-American parents with whom I speak have told me they live in daily, constant fear for the lives of their sons, children they feel they cannot protect from those who are supposed to be our protectors. Just imagine feeling this way about your children.

Education

Generally speaking, public schools that are in predominantly white neighborhoods are better than public schools in neighborhoods of color. There are a host of reasons for this. White neighborhoods tend to be more affluent so more money can be spent per student. This means that predominantly white schools have more resources, greater variety of class offerings, and better books and facilities. Just about all the communities around Portland Oregon have built new high schools over the past 15 years. Portland Public Schools hasn't built a new high school in over 70 years. Only over the past three years has Portland Public Schools taken to remodeling some of its older high schools.

Greater affluence means fewer students are impoverished, and so fewer students arrive at school ill prepared to focus due to lack of food and high environmental stress. It is more likely that white students have parents who have been through college than students of color. (35% of white parents compared to 20% of black parents.[74]) By the age of three, children of affluent parents, most of whom have been to college, have heard 30 million more words spoken than children of impoverished parents, most of whom have not been to college.[75]

Perhaps of greatest import, white children across all schools get to be taught by people who look like them and understand their culture. In 2012, an analysis of the National Center for Education statistics show that students of color made up more than 45% of the PK-12 population whereas teachers of color made up only 17.5% of the workforce.[76]

Among the effects of this disparity are the implicit biases many teachers bring with them to their classrooms according to research conducted by William Gilliam at the Yale Child Study Center and reported by Corey Turner at NPR.[76a] At an annual conference of pre-K teachers, Gilliam had 135 of them watch a few short videos with the following instructions:

> *"We are interested in learning about how teachers detect challenging behavior in the classroom. Sometimes this involves seeing behavior before it becomes problematic. The video segments you are about to view are of preschoolers engaging in various activities. Some clips may or may not contain challenging behaviors. Your job is to press the enter key on the external keypad every time you see a behavior that could become a potential challenge."*

Each video included four children: a black boy and girl and a white boy and girl. Here was the catch, there were no challenging behaviors in any of the videos. Gilliam used eye-scan technology to track the gaze of the teachers; the question being: When teachers expected bad behavior who did they watch? Gilliam and his team found that black boys were watched most often, correlating with the recent studies from the Department of Education which are found that black children are 3.6 times more likely to be suspended from preschool than white children.

It is difficult to overemphasize how important it is for teachers to understand the cultures of their students. Here is one small example. Amongst many African-American children there is a tradition called, "The Dozens." "The Dozens," is a process whereby children begin to establish their social hierarchy. It's a cultural thing. It's kind of a game in which children call each other out, more or less playfully insulting one another in an effort to get each other to lose their cool. The one who holds him or herself together the longest, is the more dominant. Children will play this game with anyone of any age. (Please note that children of almost all cultures have their methods of establishing their pecking order.)

Now, imagine a child, unbeknownst to the teacher, playing against the teacher. This is a common occurrence in schools across the country. If a teacher loses his or her temper and yells at the child, or sends the child out of the room to the principal, in the child's mind s/he has won and now is likely to behave as if they are senior in that relationship. At the same time, all the children in the class who have established dominance above the child in question, may very well also behave as if they are senior to the teacher. If this occurs, it is likely the teacher will have lost the class, perhaps for the rest of the year. Of course, this is highly likely to be interpreted as students being disrespectful with the concomitant consequences that go along with such behavior. Conversely, a teacher who understands this aspect of black culture will readily handle such a challenge, for it is a poor adult who cannot outthink a 10-year-old.

Every culture has its prerogatives. For teachers to be effective they would do well to strive to understand them. However, it is the nature of having the privilege of being white that often blinds us to the need.

Social Services

In 2012, Aaron Bell and I, as Guiding Light Family Services, began contracting with the Department of Human Services (DHS) in Multnomah County, Oregon to help families whose children have been removed reunify, and help families whose children are at risk of being removed to remain intact. Since that time, we have worked with over 200 families and upwards of 100 caseworkers.

Demographically speaking, in 2014, Multnomah County was just over 81% white. In 2015, 44.5% of the families involved with DHS were families of color. Though I do not have the exact statistic, I believe upwards of 75% of the caseworkers at DHS are white. Of the approximately 30 lawyers with whom I have worked, only two have been people of color and neither of them was African-American. Of the approximately 20 judges and referees before whom I have appeared, one has been Asian, the rest have been white. In Multnomah County, Oregon the social service system is clearly and overwhelmingly white.

I will say that the vast, vast majority of the caseworkers, supervisors, lawyers, referees, and judges with whom we have worked or appeared before have done extremely well at a very,

very difficult job, made considerably more difficult by the fact of being underfunded and understaffed. I do not believe any of those with whom I have worked believe themselves to have treated people of color different from their white clients.

That said, my experience is otherwise. Again, though I do not think the statistics are kept, I believe that it takes longer for people of color, especially African-Americans, to have their families reunited. I also believe that it is more likely for people of color to have their children removed.

In 2014, I was working with an African-American family in which, during an investigation, DHS ran a background check on the father. This is a perfectly normal procedure. The background check turned up nothing, simply due to the fact that the father had had no contact with law enforcement or had had any reports placed on him. The DHS caseworker, unable to accept that the young black father had no criminal past, ran three more background checks, then when they did not find anything, ran three additional federal background checks. I have not heard of this happening to white person.

I know a case in which a child's attorney, interviewing an African-American grandmother, a retired schoolteacher, to ascertain if she would be a good placement for her client, asked the grandmother how she had made it this far in life without a criminal record.

I know of another case in which an African-American mother, working to get her child home, was seeking to receive the services DHS required of her from culturally appropriate providers. Upon finding a group of African-American professionals, establishing an excellent relationship with her counselor, and working with the group for over two years, she was told by DHS that that group was unacceptable because they were biased. As if the white service providers that DHS considered acceptable were not.

Aaron and I had one case in which upon asking the caseworker what she would like us to do for her African-American male client, were told she wanted us to confirm that he was an alcoholic. Given our services, this was a highly unusual request. There are other organizations who address drug and alcohol issues. Both of us left the meeting with the caseworker wondering what was actually going on here.

A few days later we sat down with the father and the caseworker. The father did slur his speech. After listening to him for a couple of minutes, Aaron asked him if he had had any dental work. The father proceeded to take some dental apparatus out of his mouth and told us this is why he slurs his speech. (He did not slur his speech when the apparatus was not in place) Aaron then asked him what he did for a living. He told us he drove trucks for the county. I must say, it is very difficult to be a government truck driver and an alcoholic. They have fairly strict standards.

The father strongly wanted his three-year-old son returned to him. At the time the boy was living with his maternal grandmother. We began working with the father and found out that, like many people, he would drink occasionally on weekends and on nights after visits with his son due to his being so upset at having to return him to another's care. As far as Aaron and I were able to ascertain, there was no reason we were aware of that he should not have been reunited with his son. In this case, and this was the only time I have seen this happen, there seemed to be no way the caseworker was going to return the boy to his father.

At the end of the day, Grandma became the boy's guardian and I am hopeful that father gets to co-parent. Subsequently, I believe this caseworker left the organization.

That particular case, while certainly an outlier, was indicative of the differential treatment families of color receive in the social service system. I suspect that our experiences in Multnomah County are not terribly different than they would be in most other municipalities across America.

Not dissimilar from police, it seems as if far too many white social workers perceive their clients of color, particularly African-Americans, as more dangerous and more likely to harm their children than their white clients, though I know of no evidence to support this belief. Again, and again, as we speak with people of color here in Multnomah County, they strongly believe the system is stacked against them. Even the least privileged, the poorest of white folks receive advantages within the social services system when compared with their non-white peers.

Employment

Look around at your place of employment. What percentage of your fellow workers are people of color? What percentage of those in management are people of color? What about upper management? How many of the jobs that you have had do you think you would've gotten if you were black? Be as objective as you can be. The research shows that the answer is not as many as one might think. Check out this excerpt from *Post Traumatic Slave Syndrome.*

"*In 2002, Marianne Bertrand and Sendlhil Mullainathan, researchers at the University of Chicago and the Massachusetts Institute of Technology, wanted to measure racial dis-*

crimination in the labor market. Their study, "Are Emily and Brendan More Employable than Lakisha and Jamal? A Field Experiment On Labor Market Discrimination," had quite interesting results. Their approach was simple. First, they sent out resumes in response to help wanted ads in Chicago and Boston newspapers. Half of the resumes they sent out had African American sounding first names such as Tremayne or Aisha, and half had white sounding names such as Emily or Brad. All other information was identical. Second, they sent out resumes differing in names as above, and also differing in quality of work experience; half had low quality and half had high quality work experience.

Over the course of their research they sent out approximately 5000 resumes in response to ads for a variety of positions ranging from clerical workers to sales managers. The results surprised some in this country and confirmed what many others already new. White names received 50% more callbacks than black names. As we might expect, white names with high quality work experience received 30% more callbacks than white names with low quality experience. However, black names with high quality experience received no more callbacks than black names with low quality work experience. It did not even matter in ads where the employer advertised, "An equal opportunity employer"; they discriminated just the same."[77]

Once employed, the disparities continue. Valerie Wilson and William Rogers undertaking a study for the Economics Policy Institute found that in 2015, white workers made an average of $25.22 an hour compared to $18.49 for black workers.[78] That almost 27% disparity has been on the rise since 1979 when the disparity was 18%. When broken down by income, this disparity in wages increases as incomes rise. In 2015, white workers in the bottom 10th percentile of wage earners earned 11.8% more than their black coworkers; white workers in the 50th percentile earned 26.2% more than their black coworkers; white workers in the 95th percentile earned 31.2% more than their black coworkers.

Wilson and Rogers also found that these differences could not be accounted for by level of experience. White workers with 11 to 20 years of experience earned 23.5% more than their equally experienced black coworkers, while white workers with 10 or less years of experience earned 18.7% more than their similarly experienced black coworkers.

Nor can this disparity in wages be attributed to the level of education workers attained. Wilson and Rogers found that white men with a bachelor's degree and 11 to 20 years of experience earned 27.2% more than black men with the same level of education and same amount of experience. The disparity in wages was less, though significant, between white and black women in the same circumstances, white women earning 10.6% more than black women. These numbers were also found to be identical among white and black men and women more recently out of college. We can expect to find similar disparities when we compare white wage earners with their Native, Latino, and Islander counterparts.

Home Finance

For those of color in America, it is more difficult to get a mortgage than it is if you're white. In 2014, a study by the Urban Institute found considerable disparities across racial lines as to the percentage of home mortgage denials. In cases in which applicants' credit profiles are equally strong 40% of black applicants and 28% of Hispanic applicants were denied mortgages compared to 12% of white applicants.[79]

For those of color in America who are able to get a mortgage, the interest rate paid on that mortgage will be greater than the interest rate white folks pay on their mortgages.

> *A recent study in the Journal of Real Estate and Finance Economics finds that black home loan borrowers are charged higher interest rates than their white counterparts—and that black women pay the highest rates of all.*
>
> *The three finance professors who authored the study analyzed the mortgages and demographic characteristics of more than 3,500 households during the height of the housing boom—2001, 2004, and 2007—using the Federal Reserve's triennial Survey of Consumer Finances. They found that on average, black borrowers were charged between 0.29 and 0.31 percentage points more in interest than whites, even after controlling for their debt and credit history.*[80]

And we haven't yet spoken about the difficulties people of color have in purchasing homes in neighborhoods that still, to this day, work to preserve their homogeneity. In almost every city in America there are neighborhoods in which people of color are discouraged from buying. As white people, we pretty much have the privilege to live anywhere we can afford, not so much for people of color.

As it becomes more trendy to live closer to our city's cores, gentrification has become the policy in many of our urban areas. In Portland, Oregon this process began ramping up about 15 years ago. Just to review, the North-Northeast Portland neighborhoods had been home to the African-American community since African Americans began moving there as a result of the Vanport Flood of 1948, a flood which destroyed much of the previous African American community. (African Americans began making their way to Portland to work in the shipyards in the 1940s.) Fifteen - twenty years ago, approximately 90% of all the African-Americans living in Oregon lived in this community.

Then came gentrification. Waves of realtors inundated the community, knocking on doors, and offering people cash for their homes. Of course they were offering bottom dollar. Homeowners, some of whom had nothing but their homes saw $50,000 or $60,000 they were being offered as a windfall and accepted. At the time of sale, their homes were actually worth two to three times what they were paid. Today, home prices being what they are in Portland, those homes are worth five and six times as much as the original owners were paid.

Caveat emptor, you may say, and yes you might have a point. But for those readers who are homeowners, how many of you have had someone come to your door and offer you cash for it? What are your options when the city increases the assessed value of your property, thereby increasing your property taxes and making it more difficult for you to pay, while the banks continue their policy of making it more difficult for you to borrow? The realtors that descended on the black community here in Portland were simply taking advantage of an institutionalized system designed to benefit the white community.

The Media

Television, movies, magazines, music, literature, and the news all have historically displayed people of color in such a way as to promote and enhance white society's stereotypes, and these stereotypes are certainly unflattering, to say the least. Until re-

127

cently, with a few notable exceptions over the years African and Latinos Americans have been portrayed predominantly as criminals, often buffoons, or sometimes both on television and on film. Currently, those of Middle Eastern descent are most often portrayed as terrorists. Until recently, Native Americans have been portrayed as savages and/or alcoholics. From *Lawrence of Arabia* to *Dangerous Minds* to *Avatar*, numerous films have been produced depicting a white person in the role of 'savior' of some 'primitive', 'barbaric' peoples. Magazines are notorious for portraying people of color, particularly African and Latino American men as dangerous, people we should be frightened by.

While we can expect artists to have their biases, I suspect most of us would like to believe the fourth estate is, at least somewhat, on the up and up. We believe journalists are doing their best to report sans bias. You know, just the facts. Look at the images on the next page taken in the aftermath of Katrina.

These reports were in the news after Katrina. In the report adjacent to the top image the African-American, the caption by the Associated Press reads, "walks through chest deep flood water after **looting** a grocery store in New Orleans." In the image on the bottom, the two white Americans are described as "two residents wade through chest deep water after **finding** bread and soda from a local grocery store after Hurricane Katrina.

Such disparities in the descriptors many journalists use in depicting behaviors of white Americans and Americans of color can be seen and heard daily throughout our country.

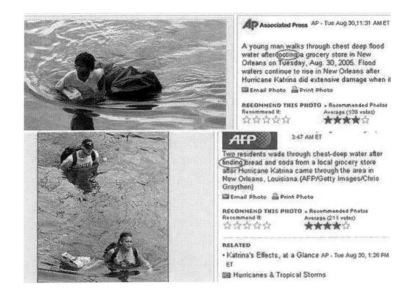

Whether we are considering interactions with the justice system, education, social services, employment, or the purchasing of a home, we white folks have advantages as compared to our neighbors of color at every turn. Given that our advantages have been normalized, it can be hard for us to accept or even see. Be that as it may, if we are to become part of the greater community, it is important that we make sure our eyes are open and we are working to understand the nature of the differential treatment afforded the peoples of our nation.

One last note before we conclude this chapter. I tell of these disparities not to elicit sympathy but to promote understanding. The last thing my friends of color would want is for people to feel sorry for them. This is also the last thing they need. As my mentor once said when describing the difference between sympathy and empathy,

Reverse Integration

"When a person is stuck down a well, a sympathetic person will jump down there with him; an empathetic person will throw him a rope." James Samuels, PhD

We can use our advantages to throw people ropes. We can use our power to help create a more just society with a more fair playing field, thereby allowing everyone to help themselves, their families, their friends, and our community.

Chapter 6

Sociological Forces Inhibiting Connection: Impacts on White Americans

These are just a smattering of the injustices visited upon our citizens of color, the impacts of which affect large swaths of our citizenry economically, emotionally, psychologically, intellectually, and spiritually. But these injustices do not just affect 'them.' They affect 'us' as well.

As a result of the sociological forces that have been evolving over centuries white society has developed, as Shoghi Effendi, Guardian of the Baha'i faith wrote in 1938, "a usually inherent and at times subconscious sense of superiority . . . a tendency towards revealing a patronizing attitude towards the members of the other race."[81]

Today, these forces manifest themselves in our difficulty identifying many of the inequities in our system; in the difficulty many have identifying the privileges that redound to even the poorest of us. These forces manifest themselves in the misplaced guilt many feel for actions of white America over the centuries, actions we ourselves had nothing to do with. These forces manifest themselves in our efforts at political correctness, believing these efforts will close the yawning gap between cultures or perhaps assuage some of our misplaced guilt. These forces manifest themselves in our continuing struggle to understand race, racism, bigotry, and prejudice. Taken together, these forces are part and parcel of the barriers we must overcome if we are to truly understand and connect with our sisters and brothers of color.

Perhaps the greatest impact these sociological forces have had on a number of us, is they have dampened some of our brethren's ability to feel for, and empathize with, others. I refer you to the images of lynchings in the previous chapter, images which depict seemingly average white men, women, and children in their Sunday best unfazed by seeing a fellow human dangling from a tree, kicking and choking as he died.

As of 2016, the Southern Poverty Law Center identified 917 hate groups across the United States, 734 of which are anti-people of color, anti-immigrant, anti-Muslim, anti-Jew, and/or anti-LGBTQ. The number of these groups has doubled in the last 18 years. [81a] And while the number of Americans aligning themselves with these groups are still relatively small, the number of Americans who choose to sit idly by, thus giving them their tacit agreement, is not insignificant. Perhaps many of us are simply becoming inured to witnessing some of our fellow citizens carrying tiki torches and signs with swastikas while chanting "Jews will not replace us" as they did at Charlottesville in the summer of 2017. That our President at the time refused to de-nounce these people only served to exemplify how disconnected from humanity some of our leaders have become.

That so many resources were allotted to rescue pets of some of the displaced in New Orleans after Katrina while so many peo-ple were stranded, thirsty, and starving is another example. That many Americans are in support of sending children of undocu-mented immigrants back to their 'ancestral' lands, lands in which they neither understand the language nor have any connection to is another. There are many more.

Are You a Racist? Defining Our Terms

Racist. It is one of the ugliest appellations we hang on peo-ple. It also is often quite misunderstood. A person saying some-thing that our society deems is politically incorrect, does not nec-essarily make that person a racist. Hating a specific group of people, also does not necessarily mean those haters are racists. Expressing one's ignorance and prejudice does not necessarily make one a racist either. Now, I may get some blowback from this, but working in a system that advantages those of the domi-nant culture and puts others at disadvantage also doesn't neces-sarily make one a racist.

Racist. Once that label is attached to an individual, it can be almost impossible to remove. So, before we can address the ques-tion posed above, we need to more fully unpack the term 'racist. To do that we first must have a clear understanding of 'racism.' And before we have a clear understanding of racism, it is helpful to gain a greater understanding of 'race.'

The Illusion of Race

The idea that we can categorize humanity based upon observable physical characteristics turns out to be nonsensical. Whether we attempt to group people by skin color: black, white, yellow, brown, red; or associate skin pigment with the geographical location: European, African, Asian, Native American, Pacific Islander, these attempts turn out to be woefully inadequate. Dr. Joy, in her book, *Post Traumatic Slave Syndrome*, describes it best.

> *Despite our constant everyday use of the term 'race' and our reference to various races, the biology of human beings is such that there are no real differences between humans. Race is frequently characterized by skin color, hair texture, facial features, etc. These differences are offered as examples of how we differ as humans. The underlying assumption is that there is a genetic/biological component to these distinctions that defines the 'races.'*
>
> *This assumption simply is not true. One cannot separate people into racial groups based upon any set of physical characteristics. Attempting to do so is fraught with contradictions. The Bushmen of Southern Africa look as much Asian as they do African. Pacific Islanders have both African and Asian features. The Ainu of Japan look more European than Asian. The Lapps of Scandinavia look as much like Eskimos as they do Europeans. The Aboriginal peoples of Australia, who often look African, commonly have very straight and wavy hair and are frequently blond as children.*
>
> *These are just a few of the problems one runs into when arguing for the existence of biological racial differences. There are many others, among them dark-skinned*

people from India, or Egyptians who run the gamut from European-looking to African. And how do we identify those from the Middle East? There is however, hope for those who must differentiate people by race: Earwax. Yes, earwax. As far as we know it seems that east Asian peoples have dry earwax and the rest of the population has moist earwax. So if it is important to you to group people by physical characteristics, there's something you can hang your hat on. [82]

Earwax? Yep, earwax. That's about all we have to go by if we are to group people up and focus our animosity. Would that make one a 'waxist?' Just wondering.

Even though 'race' is an illusory construct with little objective meaning, it is a construct that has certainly stuck in our collective minds. When discussing matters of cultural difference I prefer to use the term 'ethnicity.' I realize however, I am in the minority on this one, so 'race' it is. That said, while race may be illusory, in America racism is a reality.

Racism, Bigotry, and Prejudice

Racism: "A belief or doctrine that inherent physical differences among racial groups determine cultural and/or individual achievement, usually involving the idea that one's own race is superior and has the right and capacity to dominate other groups that are believed to be inferior. [82]

Racist: "A person who ascribes to the belief or doctrine of racism."

For racism to be present two conditions must be met. The first being one group of people believing they are superior to another group of people based on some physical characteristic (often skin color) coupled with their capacity to dominate the group believed to be inferior, the second. This is a very important distinction. Simply believing that the color of your skin makes you superior is not enough for one to be a racist. There must also be the capacity for your group to significantly impact the group or groups one believes to be inferior.

Think of the myriad of ways white America has been able to limit its citizens of color past and present. Of course there is the history of genocide, slavery, and oppression. The past aside, today our fellow Americans of color are still kept from living in certain neighborhoods, they find it more difficult to get credit, often the schools their children attend are inferior to the schools of more affluent white children, the criminal justice system differentially treats white America and the rest.

Now, can you think of any ways African America, Latin America, Native America has been able to enforce limits on White America? There are few, if any. However, as our demographics change so may this. For the time being, so long as America is dominated by white society, only members of that society can be racist. Blacks, Latinos, Natives, Asians can be just as bigoted, ignorant, and prejudiced as any White person. They just can't be racist. That title, here in America, is reserved for some of us.

Bigotry: Stubborn and complete intolerance of any creed, belief, or opinion that differs from one's own. [83]

Bigot: One who expresses bigotry.

Prejudice:

1. an unfavorable opinion or feeling formed beforehand or without knowledge, thought, or reason.

2. any preconceived opinion or feeling, either favorable or unfavorable.

3. unreasonable feelings, opinions, or attitudes, especially of a hostile nature, regarding an ethnic, racial, social, or religious group.[84]

While all these terms are associated, they are clearly not interchangeable. In almost all cases, racists are bigoted and prejudiced towards the groups they believe to be inferior. Bigots, may or may not be racists, however they are almost always prejudiced regarding the targets of their bigotry. People who are prejudiced towards another group of people are not necessarily bigots or racists. These folks may simply be uneducated, or more likely, uncritical relative to their misunderstandings.

The Three Forms of Racism

Just to reiterate, racism is the belief in one's group being superior to other groups coupled with the capacity to assert that superiority at the expense of the groups deemed to be inferior. Here in America, I have identified three forms that racism takes. Overt racism, academic racism, and unconscious/unintentional racism. Though these are different, it is important to note that many of my friends of color seem to experience these similarly.

Overt Racism

In some respects this is very simple. The KKK. The Aryan Nation. White supremacists. These are all clearly racist organizations whose members are clearly racists. They proudly exhibit their racism and bigotry for all to see. In other respects matters can seem a little less apparent. There are institutions throughout the land in which policy and practice have historically racist roots, while at the same time attempting to work to administer more just treatment to those they serve. Law enforcement, justice, finance, and education in many places in our country are some examples. There are thousands upon thousands of professionals at all levels of these institutions who work daily to treat all those whom they serve equally. Often however, they have to fight upstream against the inherent racism of the organizations for which they toil.

Academic Racism

"You know we care for you. We really want the best for you. We believe all people should be treated fairly, but as it turns out our tests indicate you black folks just aren't as intelligent as us white folks. Nothing personal, but the numbers don't lie."

Welcome to what I call academic racism. Since early in the 20th century, scholars and academicians have been devising various kinds of intelligence tests to continue, in the tradition of Linnaeus, sorting out and categorizing people. This has been and continues to be all done with the patina of science and objective measurement. Books such as *The Bell Curve*, present seemingly incontrovertible evidence as to the intellectual superiority of some groups over others. Of course, the authors of these works moderate their conclusions with various and sundry caveats, however it is their conclusions that people use to assert their believed superiority. Unfortunately for them, this emperor has few, if any, clothes.

The Sordid History of IQ Testing

Stephen Jay Gould, in his book, *The Mismeasure of Man*,[85] tells the story of IQ testing. Here is a not so brief summary of that story.

Once upon a time, (in the late 1800s) there was an educator in France, Alfred Binet. Over the years, he would notice some of his students struggling with math. He wondered if he could devise some kind of test that might catch students who would struggle sooner and so provide support. He did so successfully and published his work. In his writings, he was careful to caution the reader that the test he created was not an intelligence test, it was simply a test to identify students who might have difficulty with math in their future.

A few years later, in the early 1900s, three American social scientists disregarded Binet's warning and proceeded with the development of the early IQ tests. The first of these, H. H. Goddard, working in New Jersey, took Binet's work, tweaked it some and called what he had created an intelligence test. He administered his test to immigrants arriving at Ellis Island from Italy, Greece, Russia, Poland, and other parts of Eastern Europe.

You can imagine the state these people were in. They had just left their life-long homes, crossed the Atlantic Ocean, and landed in a world foreign to them. You can imagine the stress and disorientation many of them were experiencing. Of course, few of them spoke English. Among all the other poking's and prodding's they were subjected to, they had to take this test that was delivered in English. It likely will surprise no one that by and large these people did very poorly on this test.

Goddard concluded that the countries from which these folks emigrated were sending their least capable citizens across the ocean. Goddard called them 'morons,' a word he coined. Some years later, in part as a result of Goddard's work, Jews, Gypsies, and others were denied entry into America as they sought to escape the Nazi regime.

A short time after Goddard did his work, Les Terman, a Stanford psychologist, took Goddard's work, tweaked it further, and developed the Stanford-Binet Intelligence Test, the forerunner of all later IQ tests. This test, as with Goddard's test, and as with Binet's test, was limited to testing one individual at a time. I believe it was in the 1930s, that C. W. Yerkes adapted the Stanford-Binet test so as to be able to administer it to large groups of people at one time. Yerkes sold his group test to the military before World War II and the military used this test on new recruits to make decisions on their placement. Once again, it should surprise no one, that a number of these recruits, being from small rural communities and receiving very minimal formal education, did not do well on this test. In fact, a number of them could neither read nor write. What did this have to do with native intelligence, I cannot say. And neither could administers.

Since those days, a number of IQ tests and other tests that are supposed to measure intellectual capacity have been developed. The Weschler Adult Intelligence Scale and the Weschler Intelligence Scale for children are the two most prominent in use today in America. What do these tests actually measure? Hard to say.

In the social sciences, tests need to demonstrate that they measure what they claim to measure. This is called validation. So, for Binet to be confident his test would actually catch students before they struggle in math, Binet would've had to administer his test to a number of students and then observe them over a number of years. If his test was valid, those students who did poorly on his test would have done poorly in math a few years later, and those who did well on his test would have become good math students down the road. This is the idea of validation.

Herein lies the problem with IQ testing. The Stanford-Binet Intelligence test, so far as we know was never validated. It was never ascertained whether that test measured intelligence or not. But what about the later intelligence tests? Certainly they have been validated. Well, kind of. You see, later intelligence tests have been validated against the original Stanford-Binet intelligence test, which was never validated. So, all we can say about those tests is that they produce similar results to the Stanford-Binet test, however we still do not know what these tests are actually measuring.

I suppose that we can say something as to a person's intellectual capacity at the extreme ends of the scales. Is it likely that a person with 150 IQ has greater intellectual capacity than a person with a 60 IQ? Sure. But can we make any predictions about two people whose IQs are separated by 25 points? I think not. If it helps, think of this in terms of the SAT. Is it reasonable to predict that a student who gets a 2200 (out of a possible 2400) on their test will be more successful in college than a person who gets a 700? Sure it is. But there is no evidence that a student who gets an 1800 will be more successful in college than a person who gets a 1500.

In the 50s and 60s IQ testing was all the rage. IQ testing was used to place students on tracks in public schools. IQ testing was used to assign soldiers to their stations. IQ testing was often used to determine who would get what opportunities. We now know that certain aspects of these tests are biased, these tests primarily being designed by highly educated white males. We now know that these tests advantaged one group of people while putting a number of others at disadvantage.

Relative to my education, I was one of the advantaged ones. I don't recall why, but for some reason, likely the result of a test I took in first grade, I was put in an advanced class with a group of students that would skip fourth grade together. Were there other students in my school capable of doing that work? Certainly. I just did well on some test. In that cohort of 30 students who would skip fourth grade together there was nary a single student of color.

It boggles my mind that even today people put so much significance on IQ, an artificial construct with precious little predictive value. Repeated efforts continue to be made by social 'scientists' to demonstrate one group's superiority over another. Protestations to the contrary, this is a form of racism, After all, it's not the researchers fault that people respond as they do to their tests. Oh, it's not the overt racism you might find at a KKK rally, but in some ways it is more harmful. It is so reasoned. It makes so much sense. Those who are doing the research are unbiased, good people, just trying to get at the truth, 'truth' upon which our policy makers base their decisions.

Unconscious/Unintentional Racism

This is where the going can get very rough. Every day good, well-meaning white folks say and do things unconsciously and/or unintentionally that expose their assumption of their superiority, while at the same time putting people of color at disadvantage. I have witnessed this again and again with teachers, school administrators, social workers, counselors, police officers, bankers, lawyers, professionals of all stripe; all people whose daily decisions have a direct impact on those they serve.

A white sales manager volunteering to help a grassroots Latino organization and in short order comes to believe he knows what's best for the organization, then acts as if he should be in a leadership position, is almost certainly exhibiting a form of unconscious/unintentional racism. A police officer who every so often let's a white motorist who has been speeding off with a warning yet always tickets people of color is likely exhibiting a form of unconscious/unintentional racism. As is a banker who has differential standards for who will and will not qualify for a loan, standards that she is unaware she is applying.

Are these people racists I say likely they are not. Though I have heard people label them so. They certainly are not in the manner of the overt racist.   Unlike overtly racist individuals, these people are well-intentioned, believing they are working to help those they serve. What many of them are unaware of is the differential treatment they and/or their institutions dispense to those they are working to help, despite their good intentions. Also, some remain unaware that their good intentions are sometimes perceived very differently by those they are seeking to serve.

Back in the mid-90s, while I was running my high school in the House of Umoja, I came to work one Monday morning and found a note in my box. The note informed me that Jordan would be coming to the school on Friday to teach writing. Having been out the latter part of the previous week, this was news to me.

Now, please understand I am highly proprietary about the programs I administer. When I read that note, my first thought was, 'No one does anything in my school without first talking with me.' So, I went to the administrative assistant who took the message and asked her,

"What's up?"

" This guy, Jordan, stopped by and said he wants to teach on Friday. H. V. (my partner at the school) spoke with him. He also donated two computers." (Jordan was a 20 something young white man.)

I found H. V. and asked him about this guy.

"I hate him."

"Why?"

"He asked me if we could protect him."

"Really?" I was fairly amazed. It seemed that Jordan knew precious little about those he thought he would be working with.

It was time to call Jordan.

"Hello, is this Jordan? This is Dr. Klusky over at the House of Umoja. I understand you are thinking of teaching here on Friday. Jordan, I just want you to know no one does anything at the school without first speaking with me. So, what is it you're thinking of doing."

"I'm thinking of teaching writing. Will they like that?

"Well, the young men usually like to learn anything from someone they know and trust."

"How do I get them to do that? he asked.

"Show up every Friday for six months, build relationships with them, and they will get that you're for real, that you care about them."

There was quiet on the other end of the phone, so I continued, "Let's do this. Why don't you come here on Friday before school starts, then you and I can sit down and discuss the possibilities." So he agreed to come early on Friday.

When I arrived that Friday morning, I was informed that there was an altercation between two of the residents in the House the previous evening and the staff was trying to get to the bottom of it. The principle method for finding out who was responsible for what at the house was called "lock down." This involved all the residents sitting on couches until the staff finds out what really happened. There would likely not be any school this day. Into this scene Jordan arrived.

"Hi Jordan. I'm Dr. Klusky. Come on in. It seems that last night there was an altercation. All the guys are on lock down and there won't be any school today, but we can certainly talk. Come on back to the classroom."

Once in the classroom I asked him, "Why do you want to teach writing here?"

"I'm looking to apply to the Naturopathic College and I am looking for service work to put on my application. Why are you here?" he asked me.

"This is my life," I told him.

We went on to talk for 15 or 20 minutes about his goals and plans, the House, and various and sundry other topics. Before he left he bought one of my books. I haven't heard from him since. Oh, and as it turned out, the two computers he donated were old and not worth very much.

I had very few feelings about this event one way or another. That Jordan was honest about his intentions I considered a plus. That he was way out of his depth was no surprise to me, nor was I surprised not to hear from him again. I thought I would at least have a good story to tell. At the time of the event, thoughts of race and racism did not cross my mind, and I regret not having the insight to help educate him.

A few days later, I was talking with Joy and told her the story. To my surprise, she was livid.

"How dare he! How dare he think he can teach some of the most difficult youth to work with! How dare he be that arrogant! Maybe if he wanted to go to teach in Lake Oswego (one of the most affluent communities in the Portland area) where the students have been conditioned to politely listen to guest speakers, he might have a chance. But to think that he could just come in and effectively teach broken young black teens is galling!"

Was Jordan a racist? No, he wasn't. He was deeply uneducated, and ignorant as to this community. That he believed he could help was evidence of the unconscious/unintentional racism of which I write. That said, the manifestation of such racism does not make one a racist. Such racism is inextricably bound to the concept of white privilege, a concept many white people struggle to understand, a concept we will address later in this chapter.

This flavor of racism rears its head in so many ways. Lowering expectations for students of color in our schools is one way. Cornell West, the eminent African-American educator, writer, intellectual, Doctor of Philosophy and Christian practice at Union Theological Seminary and Professor Emeritus at Princeton University, was told as a junior high school and high school student he shouldn't pursue college as he didn't have the academic capacity. Malcolm X was similarly advised in high school. There are a number of alternative schools around the country serving youth of color who have been expelled from their home public schools from which 90% and more graduate and move on to university.

(I want to give Dr. West a big shout out and thank you. In the winter, I believe, of 1997, Dr. West came to Portland to give a talk at Lewis and Clark College. H.V. and one of Umoja's board members met him at the airport and asked him if he would visit the House and talk with our young men. He agreed to stop by the next day. That night we brought the young men to his talk at Lewis and Clark. During the question-and-answer portion of his presentation, one of our young men went to the microphone. Dr. West worked with him to answer his questions for 15 minutes. He did not have to do this as there were dozens of other people wishing to engage. The next morning, he came to the House and spent almost 2 hours talking with our young men. He certainly did not have to do this either. For your time, attention, and love of our young brothers, Dr. West, if you're reading this, thank you from the bottom of my heart.)

Another setting in which unconscious/unintentional racism rears up is in Departments of Human Services. Around the country these departments are responsible for child safety. When it comes to their attention that a child is at risk due to abuse or neglect it is their mandate to either help mitigate the risk if they can or move the child to a safe home. In a number of departments across the country, I believe children are removed from families of color sooner than children of white families and I believe it takes longer for children of color to be reunited with their families than it does for white children. I do not know of studies that verify this, however many workers of color in Portland, and I strongly suspect other similar organizations believe this to be the case.

These are just two examples; there are many more. The question before us is, are these folks racist? I would certainly not call them so. Almost all of them would say they do not believe themselves to be superior to any other group of people. Almost all of them would say they work to be fair and just. I certainly believe they believe these to be true. However, some of their colleagues of color might say otherwise, as might some of those they serve. I would say, they might be unaware of how their behaviors imply a belief in their superiority and how their decisions at times may negatively impact those they seek to help, evidence once again of our disconnection.

For my part, there have been a number of times that my behaviors have been called into question by those that I serve. One day, during a session of the Family Literacy Program, I was walking around and heard a young girl reading better than she had read before. Intending to validate her, I patted her on the head and told her she was doing a great job. Then, from across the room I heard one of the mothers shout,

"What did you just do? What did you just do to that child?" she demanded heatedly.

A bit confused, I told her, "I was just telling her what a good job she did."

"What else did you do?" the heat continued.

"I'm not sure."

She eyed me up and down then told me, "You patted her on the head. You pat dogs on the head!"

I immediately got her point and apologized to the girl, her mom, my teacher, and everyone else in the room. Believe me, I was impressed and I have never done anything like that again. More importantly, that event provoked me to examine more of my thoughts and behaviors.

Was I being racist? Certainly not to my mind. But in hindsight I would understand how someone could have pinned that label on me. Are the teachers who dumb down curriculum and lower expectations, or the Departments of Human Services workers who slow down the process of returning children of color to their families racists? No, they are not. Though their actions, as were mine, were manifestations of racism, I do not believe the term 'racist' applies in these cases.

I believe we would all go a long way to moving these discussions forward by clearly delineating these terms. 'Racist' makes reference to individuals. 'Racism' references behaviors. Words have power. So I believe, for the sake of building connection and unity, it is critically important that we all work to severely restrict our use of the term 'racist'. At the same time, I believe it is equally as important that we work to expose racism wherever and whenever it rears its head.

So, are you a racist? I suspect it's highly unlikely. Now, that doesn't mean some of the things you have said or done haven't been manifestations of racism or that those actions may not have been interpreted by people of color as being racist. Given their experience, as I hope you will see, such an assessment could certainly be reasonable. If you are wondering, you might take the time to reflect on your past interactions. Asking your friends, coworkers, and colleagues of color how you were doing on this front might produce some very, very interesting results. It will take courage. Such is the nature of self-examination. At the end of the day this is for each of us to discover for ourselves.

The Realities of White Privilege

I grew up in a small one-bedroom apartment in the Bronx with my mother, father, and younger brother. (My older brother shared the bedroom with me and my kid brother until he left for college when I was five.) My father worked and my mother was a stay-at-home mom. Our family was on the very low end of middle-class. My younger brother and I each received one gift for our birthdays, one gift for Chanukah, and one small gift at Passover.

When I was a young man in my 20s and strapped for cash, I thought about the money I was given by our relatives and friends for my bar mitzvah, money I had never seen. Boy, could I have used it then. So I called up my mother.

"Hi mom. How are you and dad doing?" After exchanging a few traditional pleasantries, I broached the matter at hand. "I was just wondering what happened to my bar mitzvah money?"

My mom laughed. "What bar mitzvah money? We used the money from your bar mitzvah to finance your brother's bar mitzvah. Then we took the money from his bar mitzvah to pay off the money we borrowed from the bank to finance your bar mitzvah." (For those readers not familiar with bar mitzvahs, it is not uncommon for the boy or girl to receive thousands, sometimes tens of thousands of dollars in gifts.)

At no time growing up did I feel privileged, nor do I have a recollection of feeling so as a young man. I found it nigh impossible to borrow money to start a couple of businesses I had in mind; most of the cars I have owned have been well used and I paid for them with cash. No relative has provided me with significant opportunity. The only job I ever got through a family connection was as a messenger on Wall Street during one summer in high school. What little I have, I have worked for. So what is this privilege of which people speak?

The privilege associated with being white in America is one of the more difficult concepts for many white people to comprehend and acknowledge. After all, so many have grown up in families not that unlike mine. So many of us struggled to make ends meet. So many of us have struggled to provide for our families in the manner that we wish. So many of us have pulled ourselves up by our own bootstraps with seemingly little help from the outside world. I suspect most of you, like me, have conceived of privilege in terms of wealth. In my mind, the wealthy were the privileged class, and the privileged class were the class of people who often looked down upon those like me. I only began to become aware of another kind of privilege when I started working in the African-American community in North-Northeast Portland.

White privilege refers to the benefits and advantages that accrue to white people in white dominated societies, privileges that are not available to those of color under the same socio-economic and political circumstances. It can be extremely difficult for those of the dominant culture to notice, and even more difficult to talk about. Francis Kendall, in her 2002 article, "Understanding White Privilege," said it well. I strongly encourage you to read her complete article.

> *White privilege is hard to see for those of us who were born with access to power and resources. It is very visible for those to whom privilege was not granted. Furthermore, the subject is extremely difficult to talk about because many white people don't feel powerful or as if they have privileges others do not. It is sort of like asking fish to notice water or birds to discuss air.* [86]

Was I born with 'access to power and resources'? Not that I ever noticed. That is until I began looking a little closer. If I were black, would I have gotten my academic programs into two of the most affluent communities in Oregon? Very likely not. If I were Native, would Guiding Light have received the contracts it has? Possibly, though I don't really know. Would a Latino with my financial history, which truthfully is not great, have been able to get a mortgage for a home in Portland as I have been able to? I don't think so. The more I look, the more I see. While I am nowhere near as privileged as many white folks in this country, I am clearly more so than most Americans of color.

The Hidden Advantages of Being White

In the 1980s, Peggy McIntosh, worked on identifying some of the daily affects white privilege had in her life. She did her best

151

to choose those effects that she believed had more to do with her skin color privilege than privileges associated with socioeconomic class, religion, geography, etc. Her exploration resulted in in her 1989 article "Unpacking the Invisible Knapsack."[87] Here is a partial list of the eventually 50 privileges she identified:

> *I can if I wish arrange to be in the company of people of my race most of the time.*
>
> *If I should need to move, I can be pretty sure of renting or purchasing housing in an area which I can afford and in which I would want to live.*
>
> *I can go shopping alone most of the time, pretty well assured that I will not be followed or harassed.*
>
> *Whether I use checks, credit cards or cash, I can count on my skin color not to work against the appearance of financial reliability.*
>
> *I can arrange to protect my children most of the time from people who might not like them.*
>
> *I can remain oblivious of the language and customs of persons of color who constitute the world's majority without feeling in my culture any penalty for such oblivion.*
>
> *I can be sure that if I need legal or medical help, my race will not work against me.*
>
> *I can be sure that my children will be given curricular materials that testify to the existence of their race.*
>
> *I am never asked to speak for all the people of my racial group.*
>
> *I can be sure that if I ask to talk to "the person in charge" I will be facing a person of my race.*

She will be the first to tell you that her list is her list. Each individual's list might be different though they will likely bear many similarities. I will add another, we white folks have the privilege to choose whether or not to engage in matters of race. People of color do not. At least for the time being we can ignore such issues, but the time is coming where we will have to engage.

In the 1990s, Joy and I designed the course, "Building Relationships Across Cultures," and taught it at Portland State University. The students that signed up to take the course were one of the more, perhaps the most, diverse group of students in any class at the school. Men and women, Black, White, Islander, and Latino, all represented in a class of about 25 students. Seven or eight of the students played on the school's football team. One of our favorite students was a white football player named David from Stockton, California. What made him so cool was his willingness to assert his views of the world, chief of which, for the purposes of our discussion, was his belief in the myth of equality in America - equality of opportunity and equality of treatment.

In week eight of the class, Joy and I took our students to the Lloyd Center Mall. At that time the Lloyd Center was the most ethnically diverse public space in the city. The assignment we gave our students was simple: pair up, walk around, and see what you see. We would all meet back at the food court in about 45 minutes. David paired up with one his teammates, Will. Will was a 6'7", 300 pound islander/black man with a full cast on his left leg. Will was the most laid-back and easiest going of young men. He was clearly loved by his teammates and had a warm smile for everybody . . . that is until this day.

About an hour later, we were all grouped up at the food court when a mall security guard came up to us and told us we needed to move. Joy and I asked her where she would like us to move to, and she pointed to another part of the food court. No problem. We all got up to move. Except Will.

"I'm not movin', said Will sternly.

"Why?" asked Joy. "What's up?"

"This is the fifth time I've been asked to move in the last hour. I've had enough."

David, having been with Will the whole time, related how disrespectful mall security had been to them, each time telling them. "You can't stand here. You gotta move." He went on to talk about how this never happened to him before and how, for the first time, he got to see unfair, unequal treatment.

Some of us may have had a small taste of this as teenagers when storeowners shooed us away from hanging out in front of their businesses. When we were teenagers, shop owners may have looked at us with a wary eye as we walked through their stores. However, we were teenagers, and being teenagers many of us were likely a little rebellious and mischievous, and may have even taken pride in inviting such attention. As white adults we rarely, if ever, experience it. If David were by himself, he probably would never have been approached by mall security. If you or I were hanging out in the mall, and for some reason mall security needed us to move, I'm sure they would've asked us politely.

After a time, Joy and I were able to help Will calm down. Our group moved to where we were asked, and we had a great discussion about what they all had witnessed during their time walking around the mall.

A few weeks later, as our class was completing, David gave Joy a big hug and thanked her for helping him to open his eyes. The other football players, all young men of color, thanked us for helping David become more understanding and a much cooler teammate.

Herein lies the challenge for us white folks in understanding the concept of white privilege. It is difficult to feel the absence of something that has forever been present. It is hard for us to know what it is like to experience dozens of insults and assaults, large and small, on a daily basis for most of our lives. Some of us may think Will was just being overly sensitive. I can attest, having been part of the black community and having seen many events like these first hand here in Portland, that the disrespects he experienced that afternoon at the mall were only a few of those he likely experienced since he left his home early that morning.

Here's another example to contribute to the discussion that might help us wrap our wits around this concept of white privilege.

The Value of Our Skin

In *Two Nations*, Andrew Hacker writes a parable he would present to his students as a thought experiment. As Hacker would request of his students, "suspend your disbelief for a moment and assume the following might actually happen:"

> *"You will be visited tonight by an official you have never met. He begins by telling you that he is extremely embarrassed. The organization he represents has made a mistake, something that hardly ever happens. According to their records, he goes on, you were to have been born black: to another set of parents far from where you were raised.*

However, the rules being what they are, this error must be rectified, and as soon as possible. So at midnight tonight, you'll become black. And this will mean not simply a darker skin, but the bodily and facial features associated with African ancestry. However, inside you will be the person you always were. Your knowledge and ideas will remain intact. But outwardly you will not be recognizable to anyone you now know.

Your visitor emphasizes that being born to the wrong parents was in no way your fault. Consequently, his organization is prepared to offer you some reasonable recompense. Would you, he asks, care to name a sum of money you might consider appropriate? He adds that his group is by no means poor. It can be quite generous when the circumstances warrant, as they seem to in your case. He finishes by saying that their records show you're scheduled to live another 50 years — as a black man or woman in America.

How much financial recompense would you request?" [88]

Please, if you are so inclined, think about it. Take all the time you would like. His students did. And when they did, it was typical for his white students to request as compensation $50 million, $1 million for each year having to be spent as a black person in America. That is the value that college-age white students at Queens College in New York City at that time put on their whiteness.

Now, Hacker ran this thought experiment in the 1980s when political correctness did not carry the burden of expectation it does today. Today, many of us 'know' how we are supposed to

answer this question. That said, if we are being honest with our-
selves, I believe few, if any of us, would choose to trade in our
European physiognomy for that of African-American, Native
American, or darker skinned Latino American.

I know I wouldn't. I am acutely aware of the many advantages that have redounded to me simply because of my physical characteristics. I am equally aware of the disadvantages that
redound to those of color in this country. To help make this
more real, the disadvantages to which I refer are not too dissimilar from the disadvantages many Jewish people experienced in
Germany before Kristallnacht in 1938. They bear resemblance to
the experiences of adherents of the Druze faith in Syria and
Christians in Lebanon. The advantages of being white and disadvantages of being a person of color in America may be more
difficult for us to see because they have been institutionalized and
normalized since the founding of our country.

To be sure, skin color is not the only determinant of privilege
in our society. The wealthy are more privileged than their less
affluent fellow citizens. Men are more privileged than women.
More attractive women have advantages over less attractive
women. Tall men are more privileged than short. In much of the
country Christians have advantages over those of other religious
orders. Depending on where you reside, members of some ethnic
groups have advantages over others.

While all these privileged classes are real, the advantages and
disadvantages associated with them are dwarfed in comparison to
those associated with skin color. Skin color is a determining factor in an individual's involvement in our justice system, our education system, and our economic system. Skin color plays a significant role in the opportunities available to us. Skin color plays

a part in the predominance of our daily interactions. Americans of color experience these to their detriment on a regular basis. In the same way healthy people take their health for granted until they experience a serious injury or grave illness, we white Americans rarely notice as we take the privileges afforded us by dint of our skin tone for granted.

And there is so much we take for granted. Shopkeepers smiling at you as you enter their store and offering to help. Knowing we can live wherever we have the financial means to do so. Expecting the police to help and protect our children. People, upon meeting us, attributing good, or at least neutral, intentions to our actions; more often than not giving us the benefit of the doubt. Growing up with the belief in our own self efficacy.

And with our privilege there is so much we do not get to experience. We do not get to experience constant looks of suspicion. We do not get to experience not being recognized. We do not get to experience the need to work harder and be smarter than white folks simply in order to grudgingly be considered equally as competent. We do not get to experience the surprise on people's faces when we speak the King's English. We do not get to experience the need to buttress our children against the institutionalized racism they will certainly face. We certainly do not get to experience the barrage of psychic insults and assaults that our peers of color have to address daily.

Perhaps of greatest consequence, we do not get to experience the often uphill struggle to convince our children that they are truly worthwhile. You see, we have the privilege of having a written history of achievement and highly visible examples of efficacy. In schools all across the country students are taught about the great successes of European peoples through the millennia. Accomplishments in engineering, the sciences, politics, finance, warfare, literature, the arts are all highlighted . . . and they should be. We, of European descent, have contributed much to this world, particularly we Americans.

There is also much we have done to detract from it, and these detraction's are also parts of our history, parts that usually receive little, and sometimes no, attention. When they do receive attention, more often than not, they are minimized. (I refer you once again to the textbook writers in Texas.) This selective history, is understandable, for as the saying goes, "The winners write the histories." One of the chief benefits of writing the histories is that the winners develop belief in their own ability to accomplish and pass this belief down to future generations. This is a good thing, for we want our children to believe in themselves.

Though there is great advantage to being part of the privileged class, membership is not without its costs. There is a downside to the privilege of selecting our history and the stories we tell. Taken way too far, we can develop the belief that we are entitled to oppress and subjugate others; the belief that we are entitled to another's resources; the belief that we are entitled to another's labor. But these are the extremes. More typically, without a fuller view of history, the bad as well as the good, a people can develop a belief in their own entitlement. Belief that they are better. Belief that success is automatic.

Back in 2001, during my martial arts training under Andy Gainer, I had the opportunity to witness a manifestation of this entitlement on an individual scale. Two young students were sparring. William and J.T. William was a 17-year-old high school student who came from an upper-middle-class family with whom I was friends. His father was a building contractor and his mother worked for the city. They were good people who demanded William do well in school and raised him to be a good person, which he was. Because he was a good student, William had all the toys and opportunities you would expect: annual ski lift tickets, all the video games he wanted, travel, etc. J.T., two years William's' senior, had a harder life. An equally good young man, he was one of six children raised by loving parents who made ends meet by running a small business. Other than the basics, if J.T. wanted something, he would have to find work and earn it.

Well, this day the two young men were sparring. William was clearly half-assing it. He was unfocused, lackadaisical, and barely making an effort. Our instructor, noticing this, stopped them and had the class pay attention.

"William, what are you doing?"

"Sparring," William replied.

"I don't know what you were doing, but it certainly wasn't sparring," Andy admonished.

Andy, proceeded to take out $100 bill, showed it to William and asked him,

"If I put this bill in J.T.'s belt, and said if you could take this from his belt you could keep it, would you be able to do it?"

"Yeah," William said nonchalantly.

Andy turned to J.T.,

"J.T., if I put this hundred dollar bill in your belt and told you if William didn't get it you would get to keep it, would William get it?"

J.T., typically a very nice, easy-going young guy who had a smile for everybody, changed. His eyes steeled, his body tensed, his smile gone, said forcefully,

"No way." The threat was palpable.

Andy, turned back to William. "William, did you notice the difference in the way you answered my question and the way J.T. answered it.? William, you have no heart. You do not have the heart you will need to be successful in the world. This is your challenge, to develop the heart you will need to fight through the adversities you will certainly face until you succeed."

This, writ small, is one of the downsides of privilege and entitlement. The assumption of success. The assumption that the world will always provide for you. The upside is that William believed in his own efficacy. He was raised to believe in his own capacity to be successful. We often take such belief in ourselves for granted. We white folks in America see example, upon example, upon example of those who look like us being successful. In schools, on film, in books, in our neighborhoods, in our families, we are repeatedly made aware that people who look like us have achieved at a high level. Couple this with our parents reinforcing the idea that we can be anything we want and the result can be great self-efficacy.

Unfortunately, such belief in ourselves can be accompanied by a lack of grit, the inner fortitude that is required if we are to overcome barriers until we succeed. In this way, privilege and its concomitant assumption of success, even superiority, can weaken us. Academically, students around the world are finding more success than their American counterparts. Once again, I refer you to the tech students in India who are using elite American universities as their "safe" schools. Such belief in ourselves can lead to overconfidence and arrogance as it did when Donald Rumsfeld and Dick Cheney predicted the war in Iraq would be over in weeks, certainly no more than six months, cost America only $50 or $60 billion, with only a handful of casualties. (It lasted almost 10 years, cost about $1 trillion, and resulted in approximately 4,400 Americans killed and 32,000 injured.) Such belief in ourselves can result in overestimating our capacities, as when parents spend thousands upon thousands of dollars in an effort to position their children for athletic scholarships when they would be much better off spending that money on their children's academic and cultural edification. These are all manifestations of privilege.

It is also unfortunate that, too often, this belief in ourselves has come at the expense of others. When history is written in terms of winners and losers in a society, the negative impacts can be profound. What must it be like to be part of a group whose historic achievements are written out of the history books? What must the impact be on a child who goes to school and learns only that his people were enslaved, oppressed, or slaughtered. What must the impact be on a child of color who watches people who look like him predominantly play the roles of criminals, buffoons, and caricatures on TV and in film? What must the impact be on a child of color who looks around his neighborhood and sees few examples of people who look like her having economic success?

This is one of the great privileges we have as white people living in America. Yes, it is incumbent upon all parents to teach their children to believe in themselves and their ability to succeed. However, we do not have to work every day to develop and bolster our children's self-efficacy in the face of a mountain of evidence to the contrary. We do not have to work diligently to help our children process the insults and assaults they receive, and can expect to receive, simply as a result of the color of their skin.

Another disadvantage to being in the privileged class is that many can come to believe the hype, and believing the hype we expect others to believe it too. We can come to expect others to want to be like us and when some don't, we may come to view them as inferior.

For centuries, Filipino culture has been one in which men and women shared power within their families equally. As a result of defeating Spain in the Spanish-American war in 1898 we 'won' the Philippines, as well as a number of other Pacific Island territories. When we attempted to democratize the Philippines, the Filipino leaders asked the United States representatives,

"Do your women vote?"

"No," came the short answer.

"Thank you. We'll pass."

You can imagine how this was viewed in Washington.

Perhaps the most significant downside to assumed privilege is the belief that there is no need to connect with others and come to understand their ways. After all, if they want a relationship with us, it is incumbent upon them to do the reaching out. Such belief results in greater disconnection between white America and everyone else, some costs of which have already been enumerated. If we are to connect with others, it will behoove us to not only be aware of the privileges that come with being a member of the dominant culture in America, but to understand the disadvantages and advantages of having those privileges.

Once again, these can be difficult discussions. It has been my experience that in discussions of white privilege, the discussion is sometimes framed in such a way as to couch white privilege in an accusatory context. I, and others with whom I have spoken, sometimes feel like people are attempting to make us wrong for being white. Now, I am quite aware that these discussions are being viewed through our personal lenses and might in no way reflect the intentions of those with whom we are interacting.

That said, I have learned it is my responsibility to put what defensiveness I feel aside. That we have privilege is nothing to be ashamed of nor is it something for which we need to apologize. Having such privilege is simply a fact, neither bad nor good. What matters is what we do with the privilege and power we have. I will suggest some things we can do with these resources in the book's final chapter.

Freeing Oneself From White Guilt

White privilege is one of the sociological forces at play that inhibit our ability to understand and connect with our sisters and brothers of color. Another is white guilt. We experience white guilt when we take on the responsibility for crimes, historical and current, that white America has perpetrated, and continues to perpetrate on Americans of color. It is important to note that most often white guilt is false guilt . . . well-intentioned, good people feeling responsible for crimes that are not their own.

White guilt can manifest itself in a number of ways. When a white person assumes this guilt, they will too readily submit to being labeled a racist, in fact they may live in fear of being so labeled. As a result they may inhibit their interactions with people of color, limiting their conversations to the weather, sports, gossip, and other banalities of the day. As a result of their feelings of guilt a person may work overly much to be politically correct rather than genuine. Also, those of us who experience white guilt may use those feelings of guilt as a substitute for real action, believing that our feelings of guilt alone demonstrate our compassion for, and solidarity with our brothers and sisters of color.

In the 1960s in racial sensitivity encounter groups, a group was considered successful when the white participants had epiphanies as to their racist behaviors. Usually these epiphanies were accompanied by copious tears and heartfelt mea-culpa's. It was assumed that all the white people in the group were guilty of racist and or prejudicial behaviors.

Over the years I have been in a number of such groups in which the facilitators viewed all the participants as having problems, and if a participant didn't admit to their problem they might be badgered until they did. It would not be uncommon for a participant to make something up just to assuage the facilitators. I grew to develop a very strong distaste for such groups and those who lead them.

Contrary to what some might assert, I do not believe all white people are prejudiced, bigoted, and/or racist. Certainly, some are. The large majority of us are not, though we may do things that can lead others to judge that we are. I would rather say there are a great number of people who are uneducated, or under-educated when it comes to matters of cultural difference and interaction, and this is largely due to our lack of true connection to others different from ourselves.

It is too easy for us to become defensive when it comes to these matters and it is our defensiveness that more often than not gets in our way. Few of us wish to be considered in a bad light and being labeled, racist, bigoted, and/or prejudiced can put us in the harshest of glares. All of us are some blend of ill and good. If we are living a moral life, the bad we have done is outweighed by our good deeds. That said, regardless of our pasts, it is what we do moving forward that determines our quality.

So, I ask us to reflect, are we guilty of harming a person, or people of color? Have we put people at disadvantage, or gained advantage at their expense? How would we know if you have? Have we critically undermined a person or group of color? Perhaps we believe we have not done as much as we should have to help those less fortunate than ourselves. Perhaps we have stood on the sidelines as others have been verbally or physically assaulted. Perhaps we have allowed a friend to demean a group of people in a conversation without correcting him or her.

If we have done any of the above intentionally, we have been guilty. If we are so inclined, we can fix what we can, commit to doing better in the future, and move on. If we come to realize we have done any of the above unintentionally, we can also fix what we can and commit to becoming more educated and doing better in the future.

Of course, for most of us this is easier said than done. Take some time to examine your own words and deeds. If you have not done any of the above, to the best of your knowledge, you do not have to accept other's verdicts about you, especially verdicts from others who don't even know you. However that doesn't mean there isn't much to learn. If a friend, family member, or colleague suggests you have made a mistake, got something wrong, or offended someone, be open to a discussion. Even better, invite discussions. Whenever I begin work with the new client, whenever I go to train or present to a new group, I ask for criticism should I do or say anything that might be offensive. Whenever I'm begin a more personal relationship with a person outside my own group, once we are a little ways in, I do the same. I am grateful that people have taken me up on this offer. The discussions that have ensued have helped to make me much better at what I do, and of greater import, a better person.

Please note, a person being offended by something you have said or done does not necessarily mean that you were offensive. That person might simply be oversensitive. That person might be too wrapped up in asserting their own 'rightness.' More than

166

likely, that person is working on themselves, working to make themselves a better person, and in seeking to 'correct' others they are working to correct themselves. Which brings us to another of the sociological forces that inhibit our ability to understand and connect.

Political Correctness: A Poor Substitute for Civility

Kike. Yid. Heeb. Wop, Dago. Mick, Spic, Beaner, Wetback. Raghead, Nip. Gook. Jap. Chink. Redskin, Prairie Nigger. Coon. Nigger.

And these are just a select few. Clearly, they are all venomous and hateful and have no place civil discourse. (I will not here entertain the debate on whether or not a community should or should not use these terms in reference to themselves. It is not my place to voice an opinion.)

From the beginning, political correctness has served as a substitute for civility – and a poor substitute it seems to have been. I suppose the thinking goes, if people won't actually be civil, at least we might be able to get them to act that way. Perhaps, if people act civilly long enough, they may become so. I guess at the end of the day, it's an improvement, though recent events lead me to wonder how much.

That a group of people laud Donald Trump for 'speaking his mind,' and 'telling it like it is,' when he calls women 'bimbos,' Muslims 'terrorists', and Mexicans 'rapists,' is evidence that a portion of our populace remains pretty uncivilized. Due to his rhetoric, a substantial portion of our people (predominantly white males) feel emboldened to once again express their bigotry and animus for people unlike themselves.

Please, I am not advocating doing away with political correctness in order to encourage people to more freely 'speak their mind,' especially when those minds are small and filled with poison. I am advocating using our judgment rather than strict, arbitrary rules when it comes to our efforts to connect with each other.

There have been times, during the course of intense discussions with one of my black friends, I have said something that exposed my lack of education. Rather than take offense, to their credit, my friends would simply correct me. To my credit, I would accept their correction. These are some of the moments I have cherished the most because they have strengthened our relationship. When I have been talking with white folks, and they say something that exposes their ignorance, my first assumption is that they are trying to get it right and so I do my best to educate. Without evidence to the contrary, I assume everyone with whom I converse wants to get things as right as they can.

In the spring of 2016, I was at one of my student's eighth grade basketball tournaments. I was watching a game played by one team wearing light gray uniforms and another, comprised of predominantly African American players, wearing black uniforms. For those readers who are not too familiar with basketball, when a foul or infraction is called, you will typically hear the referee announce something like,

"Foul. Number 23. White team." Or

"Traveling. 31. Red."

Basically, the ref will call out the infraction, the player's number, and the color of the team's jersey.

Well, I was watching this game between the teams in light gray and black, when a players on the black team fouled one of his opponents. This is how the ref called it,

"Foul. Number 8. Blue team."

When the next infraction was committed by the team in black, I heard,

"Illegal defense. Number 51. Dark team."

Shortly thereafter, when the black team committed another infraction, I heard,

"Foul. Number 10. Dark blue team."

This continued the entire game. The referees could not bring themselves to call the team in the black uniforms the black team. Really? This was one of the most absurd examples of 'political correctness' I have witnessed.

If we no longer can use the word 'black' to describe the color of a basketball jersey, how are we to have substantive discussions about race, ethnicity, and culture? If we white folks are so wrapped up in our guilt, both real and imagined, how are we to have the conversations that will allow us to connect.?

Rather than adhering to some arbitrary guidelines for public discourse, I believe genuine, well-meaning conversation would bring us much closer to each other.

"I don't see color. I treat everyone equally. "

"Here in America, there is equal opportunity; anyone who works hard and is persistent will be successful."

"If a person isn't successful, they just didn't work hard enough or smart enough."

"I know slavery and the times that followed were bad, but neither I nor anyone in my family had anything to do with that."

If we have not expressed these views ourselves, it is highly likely we have heard others do so. It has been my experience that many good, caring white people, hold to these ideals whether or not we actually express them, for we have learned that expressing them is in poor taste, i.e.: not politically correct. Poor taste or no, white folks in America have the privilege of adhering to these beliefs, for so many of us have little experience to the contrary.

Unfamiliarity with and/or unwillingness to accept, our past. Resolving the dissonance between our national ethos and our nation's crimes. Racism, individual and institutional. White privilege, white guilt, and political correctness. Defensiveness and the fear of being mislabeled. These are a few of the forces that have been barriers to deepening our understanding of, and connecting with, our sisters and brothers of color in America and around the world. They have inhibited us from truly becoming part of a much greater whole.

These barriers are not natural barriers. They are not eternal barriers. They have been built and maintained by people. They can be overcome and dismantled. This will not require an act of God, simply many acts of will. It begins with understanding and accepting where we are and how we got here. It continues with each of us making more and more genuine connections.

Part III:

Connection:
Reverse Integration
and Joining the Village

"A human being is a part of the whole called by us universe, a part limited in time and space. He experiences himself, his thoughts and feeling as something separated from the rest, a kind of optical delusion of his consciousness. This delusion is a kind of prison for us, restricting us to our personal desires and to affection for a few persons nearest to us. Our task must be to free ourselves from this prison by widening our circle of compassion to embrace all living creatures and the whole of nature in its beauty."

Albert Einstein

.
.
.

Chapter 7

Joining the Village:
The Nature of Connection

As I write this book, America seems to be a nation deeply divided. Liberal and Conservative. Republican and Democrat. Poor and rich. Middle class and rich. Urban and rural. White Americans and Americans of color. It seems as if the fabric of our society is being torn asunder. Certainly this is how our news outlets present it. Television, radio, print, online magazines and blogs, have all found that controversy sells. Hence, it is in their economic interests to present, promote, and even in some instances create, division and disconnection.

I have a different assessment of what is happening in our society, particularly as it pertains to racial/ethnic relations. I believe we are moving toward becoming the more just and egalitarian society most of us would like to have. I truly believe racism and racists are in their final death throes, and clearly, as we evolve, they will not go down without a fight. Today, I believe we are in the midst of that final struggle. Standing on the shoulders of our ancestors and predecessors we, the baby boomers, fought for civil rights and our society advanced. That a number of those advancements are under attack is evidence of that final struggle. Partly as a result of the Civil Rights Movement, Gen Xers have experienced less interracial hostility, and Millennials even less. Though less hostility does not necessarily mean greater connection.

While some signs point in the right direction, we are still not out of the woods. Far from it. The forces of division can still win, though only if we remain disinterested and disconnected. There remains a relatively small, yet vocal and active, segment of our society who struggle to hold on to their White dominance. This is understandable, as many of them do not see how they will have a place in our emerging society; so they attempt to hold on to the illusory power they believe themselves to have. Then there is a significantly smaller segment who are simply haters, the true racists. If all goes well, at the end of the day, they will grow old, die out, and become a footnote to history. Of course, there is the infinitesimally small $1/10^{th}$ of 1%, the wealthiest individuals in our country, many of whom seem to be predominantly concerned with expanding their wealth. Over time, even this group will come to represent the diversity of our country.

This all said, I believe there is a much, much larger segment of our society who are open to, even excited by, the prospects of addressing the psychological and sociological forces of disconnection, and being part of a truly egalitarian and just community. Some, the social justice warriors, are working to bring this about.

These devoted people may be community activists, religious leaders, artists, artisans, educators, academicians, law enforcers, comedians, political leaders, tradesmen and women, musicians, social service and healthcare providers, writers, organizers, public speakers, and many others. Some are rich, some are poor, and most are somewhere in between. They represent every racial/ethnic segment of our society; every profession and every level of academic achievement. Many of these unsung heroes and heroines have worked tirelessly to improve our lives and those of our sisters and brothers.

Many, many others of us are not sure how to contribute. We devote the vast majority of our time to providing for our families, raising our children, and maintaining our friendships. Many of those with whom I speak tell me that they do not have the time to engage in the fight for justice. I truly understand, for it is difficult to take care of others when we and our families are not taken care of. Yet there is something I believe we can all do to contribute to making our the society one in which all members are treated justly and have equal opportunity to make of ourselves what we will. I believe one of the most impactful ways we can all contribute is to keep expanding our ability to understand each other, to connect with each other, to be with each other.

Connection

Individuality. It is at the heart of the American mythos. In America anyone, through hard work and perseverance, ingenuity and gumption can be a success. Great men from humble beginnings have pulled themselves up by their own bootstraps and made America what it is today. If they can do it, you can. Andrew Carnegie, Thomas Edison, the Wright brothers, Eli Whitney, Sam Walton, Steve Jobs, Bill Gates. These are just a small sampling of those we hold up as paragons of the American dream.

We worship the cowboy, the rebel, the lone wolf, those who we view to live life on their own terms, who don't trod the beaten path. Yes, in America we hold the individual in the highest regard. Of course, the America of which I write is white America, and predominantly white male America. Individuality is in our blood; it's in our DNA. This focus on the individual has gotten us far. At the same time, it is held us back. The focus on the individual has blinded us, for as much as we are individuals we are also a collective. Whether we are aware of it or not, we are intimately connected with each other.

We are all intimately connected with each other. We always have been. Believing otherwise can leave us at a disadvantage. The effects of everything we do ripple throughout the world and the effects of the actions of others ripple through us. And, like tossing a pebble in a lake, the closer one is to the actor the greater impacts of the action.

Think otherwise? How do you feel when you hear about a child being abused? Would your feelings change if the child was the daughter of your neighbor? Would your feelings change if the child was your own? Similarly, most of us enjoy human interest stories, stories of others' success. When we watch the Olympics, how much more do we enjoy it when an American wins? How much more do we enjoy it when the winner went to our high school? And how much more would we enjoy it if the winner is our son or daughter?

Think otherwise? I doubt anyone believes there was no connection between the murdering of police officers in Dallas and the killing of black men by police in Minnesota, Louisiana, New York City, Cleveland, Baltimore, and Ferguson. Can anyone think that economic hardship in the Middle East is isolated from the terrorist attacks that have been on the rise in Europe? When a large-scale tragedy hits, whether it be an earthquake in Nepal, a tsunami in Indonesia, or meltdown in Japan, why is it that people around the world pour out their support?

We are all connected and as the world shrinks we are becoming more so. Periodically, events occur obviating our need for connection. Usually these events involve people losing their lives: mass shootings, people of color being murdered by self-styled vigilantes, Americans, usually of color, being needlessly shot and killed by police, police needlessly being shot and killed by those they are sworn to protect and serve. When such tragedies occur the calls go out for connection.

Most often the calls are for white America to connect with the rest of the country. The more I think about it, the more I have come to believe that these calls for connection are slightly misplaced. You see, we are already connected. It's just that much of the time we might not be aware of it. I should say rather that we are not consciously aware of it, for we truly are aware of it deep down. Many of our brethren have a strong need to justify our poor behaviors. Just as we've felt the need to justify slavery and genocide in our nation's past, many white folks continue to have to justify the mistreatment of young men of color by police, attempts at disenfranchisement, and unfair lending practices by financial institutions, to name a few. How come many white folks who claim that they, "do not see color" almost always only say this to people of color? If we were truly unaware of our connection with others, there would be little urge to make excuses for such behavior.

In a similar regard, the title of this book implies that white America is not already part of the global village. We most certainly are, though here too, we may not be consciously aware of our membership. After all, up until now we've been able to get along well enough behaving and believing as if we are not part of the greater whole. So, I think now would be a good time to bring ourselves up to speed and become aware of the connections we all share.

Yes, we are all one . . . and we are also individuals. These are two sides of the same coin. Those who chant the American mantra of hard work and perseverance, ingenuity and gumption only see one side of the coin, and in seeing that single side run the risk of becoming arrogant, solipsistic, and even pathological. Throughout human history, there have been those believing themselves and/or their group separate from everyone else, better/more right than everyone else, who have severely mistreated their fellow humans. Slavery, genocide, exploitation have, in part, been the results of the pathology of disconnection.

There are those who view most of mankind with contempt. Some years ago I read an article in which the author was interviewing the founder of one of our larger chemical companies. This particular company was in the midst of being sued for their contributions to environmental hazards. In response to the journalists suggesting that even if the founder cared little for others, should he at least care whether or not his grandchildren and great-grandchildren have clean water to drink and clean air to breathe. As I recall, he responded by saying something like, "Why should I care. I'll be dead." Such is the impact believing oneself to be just an individual can have.

Here's another way to think about this. Social psychology's Attribution theory addresses the assignation of causal factors of behavior. Simply speaking, we attribute our behavior and the results that follow, as well as others' behavior and their results, to some combination of internal and external factors. Studies have shown that successful people typically attribute their success to internal factors such as motivation, persistence, talent, etc. Unsuccessful people tend to attribute their lack of success to external factors such as lack of opportunity, lack of resources, bad luck, etc.

Of course, the truth is success is the result of both internal and external factors. I have yet to meet the person who has succeeded by him or herself. There is almost always some positive, supportive parent, guardian, teacher, counselor, mentor, or friend who has been there. Some people simply got lucky going to the 'right' schools, meeting the 'right' people. If a successful person is white in America, simply their skin color likely provided them with opportunities they might not otherwise have had. On the flipside, I know a number of people who blame their lack of success on everything other than themselves. Neither of these approaches are accurate. Of course, the successes we have or the lack there of are a result of both internal and external forces.

What It Means to Join the Village

In the early 1990s, one of television's newsmagazines did a piece on a white guy in the Bronx who opened an athletic store in one of the more impoverished neighborhoods, a neighborhood of color. They were doing this piece because he had become a beloved member of the community and they considered that pretty unusual. The piece told the story of how he did it. All his employees came from the neighborhood his store served. He generously donated gear to neighborhood athletic programs. He became friends with a number of his customers from the neighborhood, starting by showing up to their children's basketball and football games. He orchestrated fundraising events for the neighborhood schools. Over time, he became part of the neighborhood. This wasn't simply a one way interaction. All he did for the community was returned to him multiple times over. After all, he was a businessman. He understood that contributing to the community was good for his business as well as his soul.

Contrast this with some of the white owned businesses in the North-Northeast Portland African-American community that once was. There were certainly a number of businessmen and women whose business practices were similar to those of the guy from the Bronx. There were many more whose owners did not see the value of connecting beyond the owner-customer relationship. Many of them were nice enough, decent enough, and personable enough, but they contributed little to the community. Being somewhat distrustful of young African-Americans, they rarely hired people from the community. They infrequently, if ever, contributed to local schools or churches. Understandably, they took the money they earned and brought it back to their communities.

When we are members of a village we act in the interests of the whole. At the same time, a healthy village works to benefit each of its members. For a community to remain healthy, no one person can amass resources at the expense of the other members. Amassing vast resources for the benefit of the community is much more in line with being a good villager. In a strong village each member contributes according to his or her talents and everyone works to take care of each other. In a strong village each member's contributions are valued, honored, and appreciated.

When we are healthy members of a community, we share. We share goals, we share struggles, and most importantly, we share power, and the sharing makes us stronger. From the viewpoint of the individual it is easy to see how we can come to believe life is a zero-sum game, a game of limited resources, winners and losers, us versus them. Understanding the connectedness of us all, there can be only one loser and/or one winner, and they are both us.

This, of course, begs the question, what do you consider to be your community? What do you consider your 'self' interest to be? There are those of us who believe their community to be a community of one. Others believe it to be their family and friends. Still others, their church, mosque, or temple. Some of us define our community in racial terms, some in national terms. The most inclusive of us define our community in global terms. How we define our community matters. If our definition is too limiting, we may all but disappear. (Remember the shrinking white population in the world?) So, if white America is going to take its place as part of the larger America, as part of the global village, we would do well to define ourselves in the largest of terms.

Our Common Bonds

We are much more alike than we are different. Most people around the world share very similar goals. We all want good health. We all want a good life for ourselves and our families. We all want our children to be safe. We all want opportunities for our children and a world in which our grandchildren can thrive. The vast majority of us want peace.

Here in America, much has been made of the great divide between Republicans and Democrats, red states and blue states. Observing the manner in which our political leaders have conducted themselves these past 20 years or so it is easy to see how folks can come to this conclusion. Yet, poll after poll show Americans to be nowhere near as divided on a number of issues.

While we may differ on the degree of gun control we would like, The Hill reported that 88% of Americans favor making background checks mandatory before a person can purchase a gun.[89] In their polling, Pew Research found that 73% of us favor raising the minimum wage.[90] Gallup reports that from 1975 to 2015 on average only 18% of Americans favor making abortion illegal under any circumstances.[91] In 2000, when Gen. Colin Powell was considering running for president, he was asked about his stance on abortion. His response seemed to be that of the great majority of Americans - he would not want anyone in his family to go through that experience, but in the end the choice should be that of the woman and her family.

In the summer of 2016, I was listening to a journalist on NPR discuss her observations as she attended numerous Donald Trump rallies. She reported that the crowds she observed were very friendly and engaged in easy banter with those who attended in protest. She said that it was only after he began speaking that the crowd became more aggressive and at times violent towards those who protested, as he played on their sense of disconnection. Before he started speaking the crowd was more connected.

Do we have differences? Of course we do. While most of my friends and family lean towards the left of our political spectrum, I have a number of friends, and a few family members, who lean strongly in the other direction on some issues. We certainly disagree about a number of things, yet we have always been able to have respectful, and even enlightening discussions. From my perspective, many of their views are kind of nuts. I suspect they feel similarly about many of my views. However, they are all members of my village and they are very supportive of those for whom I care deeply, including myself. Whatever I think about their politics, their value and their loyalty remains unquestioned.

My idea that family should remain close, everyone having each other's back began with my mother's mother. The story has been passed down that among the rules my grandparents had in their home was, 'No one is to go to bed angry at anybody in the family.' My aunt Rita would tell of the time she and her older sister, my aunt Sally, got into an argument over something. Rita no longer remembered what it was, other than it was likely trivial. When it was time for bed, Grandma told them both to settle it. Being headstrong young women, like their mother, both said no. Grandma followed them into their room with a kitchen chair and placed it in between their beds. She waited for her two daughters to take their respective places, turned to Sally, said, "Make up with your sister," waited a few seconds, got up and elbowed her. She then sat back down, turn to Rita, said, "Make up with your sister," waited a few seconds, got up and elbowed her, and sat back down. She repeated this for quite some time. Eventually, Sally, having to go to work in the morning, and Rita, having to go to school, finally had enough. They apologized to each other, gave each other a hug, and went to bed. Everyone in my family is certain Grandma was prepared to stay there all night long.

So many of us are working to meet many of the same challenges every day. We work to find meaningful work that pays well. We work to keep ourselves healthy. We work to maintain good relationships. We work to find love. We work to make ends meet. We work to do what we know is right even when it seems to not be in our best interests at the time.

If we are parents, we work to keep our children healthy and safe, keep them doing well in school, keep them away from the dangers of the street. In our tenuous economy, we work to provide our families with the lives we wish them to have. Parents around the world have to work to keep their children safe on the internet. We work to teach our children to become good people, often in the face of a myriad of messages suggesting they be otherwise. Here in America, the majority of us who work to teach our children to eat healthfully, have to combat a food industry bent on addicting our children to their sugary, salty, and fatty products, willing and able to spend hundreds of millions of dollars on advertising aimed at seducing our children.

In 2010, there was a ballot measure in the state of Washington aimed at eliminating the sales tax on soda pop and other drinks. As you might expect, beverage companies poured tens of millions of dollars into this campaign. One of the commercials produced in favor of this ballot measure showed a very sympathetic young mother of three children expressing dismay at the economic burden her family will face if the tax remains in place. "What will my children drink?' She asked her audience. I was surprised that I did not see a follow-up commercial by those working to defeat the measure suggesting her children could drink water, a vastly healthier alternative. Such is one very small example of what we have been up against.

These challenges are all part and parcel of the human condition. We all work to address them daily. Some form of these challenges exist in every community regardless of ethnicity. The immediacy of these challenges may vary from community to community, yet for the most part they remain ever present. How much better chance would we have of successfully meeting these challenges if we met them as one community?

In my heart I know this is possible. I know we can do this. I truly believe that the better we get at truly connecting with each other, the more readily we will join together and work with each other. For my fellow white Americans, this means becoming comfortable integrating, becoming part of other communities, in particular communities of color.

.
.
.

Chapter 8

Respect:
Taking Another Look at
Ourselves and Others

So where do we go from here? How does one become part of a community different from their own? I believe it all starts with respect, both respecting ourselves and each other. Sounds pretty easy, fairly straightforward, almost trite. "I respect everyone," I hear many people say, and I'm sure they honestly believe that. But what does respect actually mean? What does it actually involve?

Literally, respect means to look again. Spect- to see or to look. Re- again. Respect- see again, take another look. And, if we are truly going to take that second look, if we are truly going to be respectful, we must do so with open eyes, with open minds, and with open hearts.

The first lesson on respect I can recall I received from Mr. Cassidy. It was 1968 and I was in eighth grade. The prior-year, we boys had Mr. Cassidy as our gym teacher. We had all heard stories about him and they were scary. We were told he would walk around the gym with a pool cue and would brook no disobedience. We were told he would make problem students run around the gym in their underwear. In seventh grade we found almost all the stories to be true. (Not the underwear story.) One day we weren't behaving and Mr. Cassidy made us stand in our places for 40 minutes while he walked around the gym banging his pool cue on the wood floor and lecturing us. "You're not human, you're a herd!" is all I remember from that lecture. Our class became much more compliant.

When we got to homeroom on the first day of eighth grade, we not only found Mr. Bookman, who was to be our science teacher in our half of the room, we saw Mr. Cassidy with a class in the other half of the room. With great trepidation, a number of us boys went up to Mr. Bookman,

"Mr. Bookman, do we have Cassidy for gym again?"

Bookman smiied, "Oh no. You have him for social studies."

We were mortified. It was bad enough having him two days a week in gym the previous year; now we were going to have him five days a week! We were beside ourselves. We frantically got with the girls in our class and told them what we were in for. We told them to be quiet and do exactly as he said for he was the most frightening teacher we had ever seen.

Frightening as he was as a gym teacher, he turned out to be one of the very best teachers I have had in my schooling from kindergarten through my graduate work at UCLA. He was edgy, funny, and engaged us in new ways, a number of which he would be fired for in a heartbeat in today's milieu.

I don't know if it remains part of the curriculum, but back in the late 60s when I was in junior high school, eighth grade social studies classes did a 10 week unit on "New York City - the Melting Pot." In this unit students were to learn about the many ethnic groups that made up our city. In our class, Mr. Cassidy covered one ethnic group a week and Monday of each week was dedicated to ethnic jokes for the group of the week. We all certainly laughed a lot, and after we got through all the jokes on the sheets of paper he handed out, we created a list of stereotypes and prejudices that people held for each group. Then we dissected them. We discussed how those stereotypes came to be and who kept them alive. Most importantly we analyzed their accuracy. Mr. Cassidy provided us with an opportunity to take another look at each ethnic group, face our own prejudices, and develop our understanding. The rest of the week we would focus on each groups contributions to New York City in particular and our nation in general.

Today, if a teacher tried to do something like this they would likely be attacked mercilessly. More's the pity. For in those weeks I began to understand some of my own prejudices and some of those of my family. I also began to understand how disconnected our prejudices and stereotypes are from what is actually true.

Mr. Cassidy provided me with my first opportunity to look again. I have had untold opportunities since. Some opportunities I have passed on and others I have taken advantage of. As I began my work in Portland's African-American community those opportunities were presented almost daily. Fortunately, I had a number of very forgiving teachers.

Taking Another Look at Ourselves

Many of us have prejudices and biases. Some of these were passed down by our families; some of these were inculcated by our schools, some the daily news. Still others by the movies and television shows we watch, music we listen to, and literature we read. Many of them are strengthened regularly by our friends and close associates. It is important to note that most of us remain unaware of many of our prejudices and biases, and don't often have the opportunity to take another look at ourselves.

I invite you to do so. What was your family like? What did your parents pass down? What might you and your friends have grown up believing about other ethnic groups in America and around the world? What prejudices might you have passed down to your children? What stereotypes of others might you be keeping alive today? These can be difficult questions as bringing answers to our consciousness is not necessarily easy, nor may it be comfortable exploring aspects of ourselves that may belie our self-image.

I have memories of my father, who was a great man in so many respects, letting go racial epithets particularly aimed at African-Americans and Puerto Ricans when he would listen to the news on the radio or watch the news on television. I have memories of my mother, who was a wonderful mom, talk about others in terms of the derogatory 'them' and 'those people.' Both were fiercely proud of their Jewish background. Both treated others fairly and were generous of spirit. Both also clearly held prejudices, particularly when it came to people of color and especially when they believed one of them might be my girlfriend.

During my freshman year in college in upstate New York I met a most stunning young woman. Her mother was Japanese, her father Native and African American. She had almond shaped eyes, long dark hair that was somewhat kinky, an African-American nose, and beautiful reddish brown skin. And . . . wait for it . . . She was Jewish. One weekend we were both back in the City and I brought her to meet my parents. Both my mother and father were their typical gracious selves. We had lunch together and they showed much interest in my friend and her future plans.

Later that day, after taking her to the train and returning to my parents' home, my mother and I sat down for a talk I knew was coming. You see, ever since I started bringing girls home in middle school, it seemed to me that my mother would look at them in terms of their marriage potential. So, I was not surprised when she started grilling me about my friend.

"Who is she?" "Where does she live?" "Have you met her parents?" "What do they do?" "How interested in her are you?"

While all these questions were from her usual repertoire, she asked them with an edge that had been reserved for the girls of color that I'd brought home since my freshman year in high school. I answered all of my mom's questions, saving the best for last.

"Mom, she's Jewish."

"Don't give me that, Jay."

"No, she really is Jewish, mom."

At the time, my mother was not able to accept this.

When I was 14 years old, my 88-year-old grandmother, one of the toughest women I have known, was hit by a car. Her femur was broken in two places, she had ribs in her lungs, and a host of other internal injuries. The doctors didn't give her a great chance to live, and if she did manage to survive, they gave her no chance to walk again. (Two months later all of her internal injuries had healed; a year later we had to try repeatedly to get her to walk with a cane as she was a fiercely proud and independent woman.) At the time of the accident, she was living independently in her own apartment just down the block. After the accident, Grandma spent most of her convalescence in our little apartment.

My mother's side of the family is fairly large and very close. We all attribute our closeness to our grandparents. Grandpa, unfortunately died before I was born. All who knew him sang his praises. I have been told he was one of the warmest, most loving, and gentlest men to have graced this earth. Grandpa was the soft one, Grandma – the hard. She was the family disciplinarian. She was the matriarch. For months and months as she convalesced, relatives would come and go. They came from all over the country. During all this coming and going, I would get to see relatives for whom I only had a name; I had heard of them all; now I would have faces.

One afternoon, the phone rang and on the other end was a man who claimed to be my cousin Dennis. I never knew I had a cousin Dennis, no one in the family had ever spoke of him. They spoke of all our other cousins. Why not him? I handed the phone to my mother and listened to the conversation from one side. I heard my mother tell him,

"Grandma would love to see you, just please don't bring the rest of your family."

"What!?" I thought to myself.

I had never heard my mother say anything like that before. When mom got off the phone she sat me down and told me about cousin Dennis.

"When he was a boy, he was Grandma's favorite. He went to college and became a teacher." *'So far, so good,'* I thought to myself. *'Nothing here.'*

My mom continued, "Then he married a girl who was not Jewish and was currently living on a commune in New Hampshire with his wife and two children."

Now at this moment, Dennis became my favorite cousin. I was a budding young wanna be hippie, he sounded too good to be true. He was also at first family member that I knew of to marry out of the faith. I was so excited! But I still didn't understand why my mom didn't want him to bring his family. *'There must be something else.'*

At this point, I could see my mother was clearly struggling with something. She got quiet, and almost in a whisper, she said,

"His wife is black."

"So why don't you want him to bring his family?"

"You see, Jay, Grandma was told he married a non-Jew; she was never told she was black, and if she finds out, it might kill her."

'Kill grandma,' I thought. *No way! She's the toughest person I know.'*

To Dennis's credit he brought the whole mishpuchah (family) and Grandma did what I learned grandma always did - accept them like she accepted all of us. With that first meeting between Grandma, her new granddaughter, and her new great grandchildren, Grandma signaled to the family that no matter what, family always comes first. In her way she told our entire family to 'look again.' Since that time, I'm happy to say, the rest of the extended family began to accept Dennis and his family.

I'm pretty sure the real issue was my mother's discomfort rather than her fear for Grandma. So, as I have memories of being raised in a home with parents who had their prejudices, I also have memories of my parents being very gracious and inviting to all those I brought to our small one-bedroom apartment in the Bronx. Other than potential girlfriends, my parents never, ever suggested there were people I should or should not hang out with. This is all part of my background.

Have you heard of the DeWolfe family? Between 1769 and 1820 in Rhode Island, the family trafficked in slaves, bringing more than 10,000 captives from West Africa, and becoming one of the wealthiest families in America. In their hometown, statues have been built, streets named, and buildings erected in their honor, and up until fairly recently the family's sordid past remained unknown. It wasn't until one of the family's descendants, Tom DeWolfe began researching his family's history did the full story come to light. His ancestors were one of, if not the largest slave traders in America; a business they pursued long after it was outlawed. I have had the pleasure of attending one of Tom's presentations.

Once he unearthed his family's past, he sent out an invitation to all of their descendants inviting them to take a journey of understanding that would follow the triangular route the family's slave ships would take from their home port in Bristol Rhode Island, to the site of slave forts in West Africa, to the site of sugar plantations in Cuba. Of the hundreds invited, ten accepted. I highly recommend reading Tom's book, *Inheriting the Trade*,[92] and/or viewing the documentary, *Traces of the Trade: A Story From the Deep North*,[93] by another DeWolfe ancestor who accepted Tom's invitation, Katrina Browne. After taking their journey, each of the ten, in their own way began working for social justice here in America and around the world.

I had a woman friend who, while attending Portland Community College met a fellow student who claimed to be a Neo-Nazi. I'm pretty sure the young man had some intimate interest in my friend and so when she suggested they go see *Schindler's List*, and he agreed. After seeing the movie my friend told me her guy was shaken. He had had no idea with whom and what he was allying himself. He immediately ended his association, got rid of anything he had connected with that group, and worked to have his tattoos either removed or covered.

These are certainly more extreme examples. Few of us come from families of wealth and power who amassed their fortunes through human trafficking, though I do know a number of people whose ancestors were slaveholders. I'm pretty sure that few people who claim white supremacy in any form will be reading this book, though there are some readers who will have hailed from extremely racist families.

Likely, the majority of us grew up in families in which one or both of our parents exhibited prejudices every now and then, or grew up communities in which racial/ethnic biases were readily expressed. Some of us may have adopted our parents viewpoints and some of us may have accepted them without much critical examination. Similarly, some of us may have accepted the biases of those with whom we closely associate.

Here is a more typical example. I have a dear Jewish friend whom I love very much. We have been close friends for going on 30 years. He is one of the best men I know, beloved by many. He has been there for me through thick and thin and I'm confident he will always have my back. He is one of the truly good guys. He cares deeply for others and the plight of the oppressed. Like many Jewish men and women he is a strong supporter of Israel.

However, in my opinion, he does have a blind spot. He dislikes Palestinians and sometimes, it seems to me, his dislike borders on hate. He speaks of Palestinians in terms of "them" and paints Palestinians with a broad stereotypical brush.

One day, I was visiting him after he had just returned from one of his visits to Israel and he told me about his journey. He explained that people in America who have never been there have no idea what it's really like, for all we see is the conflict and violence the American media portrays. He said having been there numerous times that he has come to know Israel as a safe and wonderful place to visit, and he has come to know the Israeli people as full of joy and life.

Now, I know my friend has never spent time on the West Bank, nor much time in the company of Palestinians outside of his business interactions. It seems that it hasn't dawned on him that, like Americans who see only a sliver of the whole picture of Israeli life, he too, only knows Palestinians through the lens of his business engagements, the American media, or the eyes of other Jews who have little to no personal experience with Palestinians and their culture. When I attempted to point this out to him, he simply rejected this out of hand.

Please understand, we often need help to see ourselves with fresh eyes. My mentor used to say, "We are always the last to know." Typically, it is much easier for others to see our weaknesses and strengths then it is for us to accurately see our own. Over the years I have learned much more from others pointing out my shortcomings than I have working to find them on my own. I have also found that when I have accepted such criticism with some grace, it has helped our relationship to grow.

If we do take another look at ourselves and become more aware of our own history, prejudices, and biases, what do we do then? I would say the first thing to do is simply accept what you find. Then, decide how to move forward. If you find, you have made mistakes that have put others at disadvantage, you may be able to correct them. If they can't be corrected, you can always commit to doing better in the future. While there is nothing we can do to change our past, our future is yet to be written.

Taking Another Look at Others

Growing up as a boy in the 1960s in New York City, we took the 'Ye Olde Melting Pot' approach to ethnicity. We were taught where the different groups came from, and how and why they got here. Ethnic jokes aside, we were taught how each group contributed to the ethnic soup that is America, an America in which each group slowly lost their unique cultural identity and became American. (Both my parents were first generation Americans and bought into this ethos. One way they did so was to ensure their children would be 'American,' by not teaching us to speak their family's native tongue, Yiddish. Looking back, I so wish they did. In those days the advantages of raising children in multilingual homes were not common knowledge.)

A couple of decades later the soup morphed into a stew in which each group contributed and maintained their identity. In schools across the country the fruit and festival understanding of diversity dominated our education. Students would take part in events in which they ate ethnic foods and learned of each group's holidays, observances, and celebrations. Tolerance remained the byword.

A word here about tolerance. Tolerate: 1.to allow the existence, presence, practice, or act of without prohibition or hindrance; permit. 2. to endure without repugnance; put up with. Tolerance: a fair, objective, and permissive attitude toward those whose opinions, beliefs, practices, racial or ethnic origins, etc., differ from one's own; freedom from bigotry. Maybe it's just me, but to my ear the word tolerance suggests a power dynamic in which the tolerator allows something to exist that they may or may not like, or may or may not find somewhat repugnant. Maybe we need to find a better word. Just a thought.

Moving on. In the 1990s, we moved beyond the fruit and festival approach to diversity. For the past 20 years or so, governmental and corporate organizations have been sponsoring diversity trainings for their managers and their staffs. Overall, these have proven to be a great improvement over what passed for addressing cultural difference through the 1980s. They encouraged the participants to become aware of others' different approaches to the world and the different lenses through which they looked. They provided the participants with opportunities to understand the privileges that come part and parcel with being white in American society.

The best of these helped participants become aware of the many facets of life for which we assume a singular way of understanding, and how these assumptions limit our ability to work successfully with others. For example, how we relate with each other – how we greet people and the expectations we have in return – the concept of time and the expectations we have of people adhering to our concept – how we view our fellow man and our place in society – what friendship is and how it is expressed. So, so much of what we assume and therefore do not ordinarily examine turns out to be quite different across cultures.

Axiology – The Study of the Evolution of Values
The first presentation of Joy's I attended back in 1990 during my first day at SEI was on the axiological approach to the topic

of cultural difference based on the theoretical framework of Dr. Edwin Nichols.[94] I will do my best to describe it briefly. Dr. Nichols postulated that a group's values, understanding of time, epistemology, and view of an individual's place in the world evolved differentially over centuries as a result of the survival demands placed on them by the geography and environment in which they lived.

For example, Nichols' posited, Northern Europeans, were predominantly farmers living in colder climates with shorter growing seasons. How people maintained their food supply became the single most critical factor determining the likelihood and quality of their survival. Crops had to be planted on time, harvested on time, stored, and protected in order to ensure one's future and that of one's family. The preeminent relationship that would determine one's likelihood of survival was the relationship between that individual and their food. Over time, this preeminent relationship evolved into the relationship between an individual and all manner of material objects that would increase one's chance of survival. Developing a precise understanding of time and the ability to measure it became critical to the process, for one's survival depended on timely planting, timely harvesting, and timely distribution of food throughout the year. Measurement of time and the development of tools to do so accurately became priorities.

Let's take another example: sub-Saharan Africans and other nomadic and semi-nomadic peoples living in warm climates in which food was plentiful and the growing season year-round. The acquiring of food and other objects of material value were not emphasized, as these did not necessarily ensure survival. What evolved to ensure survival was how well you were able to relate with those around you. The preeminent relationship that would determine one's likelihood of surviving well was the person to person relationship between an individual and the other individuals in their community. Due to the almost year-round food supply, the need for precise timekeeping didn't evolve. Time became viewed as more fluid, more infinite, a thing not to be thought of as rigid.

Back in Northern Europe, as structures both physical and political were developing, ostensibly for the management and protection of material resources, those who served the wealthy were looked upon as relatively inconsequential. They themselves became objectified; if one person breaks, we will just replace them with another. We can see how this objectification manifested itself during the Industrial Revolution. Workers were for the most part viewed as cogs in a machine; one goes down, put another one in.

In places like sub-Saharan Africa, in which the preeminent relationship was that of person-to-person, individuals grew to matter more. Everyone in the tribe, men, women, and children have value to the tribe and had his or her place in it. Add or remove even one person and the tribe changes.

Nichols argued that we can readily see the effects of these differences in modern society. Almost all wars fought by Europeans have been fought over material wealth, primarily over land and the resources thereupon. Historically, most of the wars fought in Africa have been of a tribal nature, at times instigated by some personal affront. Often the gaining of material possessions, was secondary.

Those who have traveled to places like Germany, have experienced the impressively precise German transit system. If a train is to leave at 11:04, it will be leaving at that time exactly. Show up at 11:05, and you will be too late. For those who have traveled in Africa, it is not unusual for the bus to leave on Tuesday. It can be the arrogance of some tourists to get upset that buses do not 'run on time.' Of course they run on time; they just don't run on the time in the tourists' mind.

There have been those who have challenged Nichols construct, especially on its particulars. However, I believe, that is missing the point, for the true value of his work is the way in which it explains so much of the unexamined cultural differences we can see daily when we open our eyes. His work serves to give us pause before we attribute motivations about the behaviors of others, draw conclusions, and close our minds.

If I can draw an analogy, it's not unlike the concepts in the book, *Men are from Mars. Women are from Venus.* Whether or not the author has the particulars exactly right is arguable. Like axiology, such argument truly misses the point. The value of the book is not in the particulars. The value is in the pause it allows us before we make an attribution and draw a conclusion about the behavior of a member of the opposite sex. 'Perhaps my girlfriend is not a ditz; perhaps she just has a different approach. Perhaps my boyfriend isn't a Neanderthal; perhaps his brain is wired differently.'

In the African-American community, and many other communities of color, relationships rule. Of course, relationships are important in all communities, it's just that in white society they do not typically rise to the state of primacy that they do in some others. It is not unusual for a black man or woman to quit his or her job when they feel their boss has disrespected them once too often, i.e.: has violated the relationship. White folks might also leave their job under similar circumstances. The difference is where a white person would almost always line up a new job before they leave, a black person might leave on the spot.

White coworkers and black coworkers will likely have very different assessments when a fellow black coworker ups and quits her job so abruptly. Black coworkers are much more likely to have seen this coming, and when it goes down, they might nod knowingly to each other with that look that indicated it was only a matter of time and that they might have done the same thing under similar circumstances. It is very likely white coworkers would shake their heads and wonder what was wrong with their coworker.

In schools across the country this difference in relationship primacy can be seen every day. In elementary school white students will usually be motivated by material rewards: stars, smiley faces, grades, etc., much longer than their black classmates. Black students are motivated much more so by the relationship their teacher establishes with them. Once again, of course it is good practice for teachers to build strong relationships with all their students, it's just that with their students of color the quality of their relationships will be the single, most important factor influencing the quality of learning.

How many times have we heard children tell us, "I don't like Mr. Johnson," or "I hate Ms. Smith," when attempting to explain why they're not doing well in a particular class? Would it surprise you to learn that a black child attempting to explain similar poor performance is more likely to tell their parent, "Mr. Johnson hates me," or "Ms. Smith doesn't like me."? For black students it is often so much about the relationship.

This difference is also clearly evident in the home. I have yet to be in the home of one of my African-American friends where their children do not greet me. If their children are playing in another room when I arrive, my friends call them out to come and say hello, most often with a hug. When I am in the home and the children come in from outside, they almost always greet me when they enter. In the rare instances when they don't, mom or dad reminds them. Certainly, I am not special. My friends' children interact this way with everyone that is considered part of their family's extended village.

Such behavior may or may not take place in the homes of my white friends. Some of my white friends make a point of this with their children, others do not. This, of course, is neither bad nor good, wrong nor right. It is simply a difference in the manner in which people approach relationships.

Keeping Our Hearts and Minds Open

Keeping our hearts and minds open is critical in order to be truly respectful. For those of us who have a drive to, an urge for, or a habit of drawing conclusions, this will require us to work to suspend this particular faculty. Far too many people of all stripe are too ready to label others, and far too often our labels fall into dichotomous categories: good-bad, black-white, right-wrong, etc. Such labeling hampers our ability to more fully understand and address the complexities of our world and our fellow inhabitants.

Moving From Simplex to Complex Thinking

Perhaps being bilateral organisms, mostly equal left and right sides around an axis, it makes sense that it is natural for us to think in terms of dichotomies. Certainly, at a young age we are wired to do so. Dichotomous thinking is simplex thinking – either something is this or it's that. Such thinking can be very powerful as it tends to promote a kind of certainty. Those who believe they have a very clear sense of right and wrong can more readily act sans doubt. This is important as doubt can short-circuit our power. When we believe we understand a situation and our responses are correct, action becomes easier.

On the other hand, our actions based upon simplex thinking have a much greater likelihood to generate unintended consequences because such thinking is extremely limited. Simplex thinking is rarely up to the task of interacting well with others. Simplex thinking is the kind of thinking that underlies our prejudices. "Women are only good for one thing." "Men only want one thing." These are powerful statements. They can guide us in all our interactions with the opposite sex. Once we draw these conclusions we no longer have to think about them, and for many this can be comforting. But what happens when you run across a woman who is good for five things . . . and none of them are that one thing? What happens when you run across a man who wants three things? A simplex thinker will likely never even notice and potentially miss great opportunities.

Where simplex thinking is characterized by the word 'or,' complex thinking is characterized by the word 'and.' 'This or that' becomes 'this and that.' People are good and bad, right and wrong. All of us fall on a continuum. So many of our actions have both downsides and upsides. There are disadvantages and advantages in every event. There is bad and good in all of us.

I'm sure this seems pretty obvious to you, "There is really nothing deep here," you might think. However, when I listen to people talk, when I watch pundits comment, I notice how often people express themselves in dichotomous terms. I notice how often we are presented with dichotomous choices. I notice how ready we are to come to conclusions based upon dichotomies. The rapidity with which many condemned Muslims after 9/11, the rapidity with which Republican Congressmen decided to oppose our first black president even when he sent them their own proposals, the rapidity with which Donald Trump ascended from reality game show host to the presidency, all serve to demonstrate such close minded, simplex approaches to making sense of our world.

Complexity can be hard; it can hurt our brains. Refraining from drawing simple conclusions may go against our nature. Yet doing so will be to our advantage. The good news is that doing so is relatively straightforward. In Piagetian in terms it's the graduation from the concrete operational stage of cognitive development to the formal operational stage of cognitive development. One way to ensure you're keeping your mind open, is thinking and speaking in terms of probabilities, using words such as, 'likely,' 'probable,' 'usually,' 'mostly,' 'frequently,' 'generally,' etc. These will serve to give you and your mind greater perspective. It will also give you room to move when you are wrong, so you will have less of an urge to defend positions in which you might not even actually believe.

Complex thinking works to keep our minds open to greater understanding and our eyes open to greater possibilities. Where simplex thinking promotes prejudice, complex thinking allows for the potential of greater understanding and respect.

Listening and Learning: Developing Empathy

As I began interacting with the black community here in Portland I diligently worked to understand the lenses through which members of the community viewed the world as best as I could. I treated my experience as if I was entering a foreign land, not understanding the mores of the culture nor the rules of engagement. I went in watching and listening in order to figure out how best to interact. Everybody I met, from the youngest child to the most senior elder, I viewed as my teachers; a practice

I continue to this day whenever I engage with a group of people with whom I am unfamiliar.

I read books by black authors, watched films by black filmmakers, and listened to music by black artists to try to gain greater insight into the community. My work with Joy, began my study of African American history. All in an attempt to develop what understanding of their reference points I could. I listened to conversations in an effort to understand what my friends and coworkers found to be important. I listened to the way they used language so I could begin to gain a greater understanding of the meaning behind their words.

Some years ago, I was meeting with a white DHS caseworker and her client, an African-American father. As our conversation moved to his methods for disciplining his six-year-old son, he talked about timeouts, taking away privileges, and whuppin'. At his mention of whuppin' I could see the caseworker tense up. I looked at him and said,

"If you mean 'spanking' say spanking. Whuppin' to a white person means something very different. To them it means an abusive beating."

Even though we use the same words, their meaning can vary not only from culture to culture, but from person-to-person. It is not unusual for people to lay their meaning over other people's words, often resulting in misunderstandings. Listening carefully to what a person actually means can go a long way towards increasing our understanding, furthering our connection, and building our relationships.

Mostly, I showed up and observed. Over time I had opportunities to watch other white folks attempt to engage with the African American community in Portland. All too often they arrived arrogantly, believing they knew what was best for the community and how best to achieve those ends. Rarely did they ask those whom they believed themselves to be serving what their needs were, what their goals were, what their hopes and dreams were. Little respect.

I learned what many of 'them' thought of many of 'us.' I saw how white privilege was experienced from their point of view. I asked question upon question in an effort to learn. When I thought I could be of service, I made suggestions and asked them how they thought I could best further their vision. I made no judgments, for whom I to judge another community, especially a community I do not truly understand? As I understood more, the quality of my interactions improved, and as the quality of my interactions improved so did my relationships. Eventually, co-workers became friends, then friends considered me part of their families; organizations considered me a part of their tribe. Remember, relationships rule.

As a result of my work and my way of interacting, I came to have great empathy for, and a fair understanding of their community. I was with the staff and residents at the House of Umoja when O.J. was acquitted and saw the celebration. Most of the white folks I know were appalled at the decision. Me too. However, I was more interested in their take take than my own, so I asked them, "Why the celebration?"

"We won one!" they explained. "We all know he did it, but we got this one." For a community that regularly experiences rampant injustices at the hands of the criminal justice system, I understood. For a person who has witnessed the differential treatment the families of my African-American friends, coworkers, students, and clients receive, I fully understand their sentiments.

Knowing what I know of African-American history I was able to appreciate my first encounter with my new partner H. V., at the school we created at the House of Umoja. We met in the office of Umoja's Executive Director. H.V. was a young, highly educated black man who had recently graduated from Lewis and Clark college here in Portland. He was militant and deeply committed to furthering his community. It was decided that I would put a school in the House and that H.V. would work with me to do so. As the meeting concluded, I looked at H. and said,

"Let's get out of here and figure out what we want to do."

We got up and as we got out the door he spoke his first words to me,

"I hate white people."

"Me too." I knew exactly what he meant. We became a great team and good friends.

Disrespect

We all know what it feels like. And everyone I know has a fairly strong response when they have felt they have been disrespected. Those of us who are whole and who do not have these experiences regularly, can often put them in their place; even though we may experience an initial surge of anger, we can decide responding in kind simply isn't worth it. In the case of strangers, often we will process the event in such a way as to come out the other side unharmed. 'That guy didn't know any better.' 'She was having a bad day.' are explanations we may tell ourselves in order to keep our perspective. When we feel we have been disrespected by someone we interact with on a daily basis, (e.g., a family member, friend, coworker, or employer) once we calm down we are likely to talk with that person and come to a satisfactory resolution. That all said, if we receive a large enough dose of disrespect, there is a good chance we will strike back.

Now, imagine what it must be like to be disrespected 5, 10, 20, 50 times a day. Imagine getting into an elevator in your apartment building, offering a friendly smile and hello to your fellow passengers, and getting no response in return . . . every day. Imagine standing in line at your local supermarket, watching the cashier smile and chat up those in front of you, and when it's your turn seeing the smiling and chatty cashier turn stern. Imagine working at your job knowing your fellow employees believe you're there only because of your color rather than your competence. And these are only some the personal slights our brothers and sisters of color experience on a regular basis. These do not take into account the many times they are disrespected at the hands of our society's institutions. A steady diet of this, day after day, week after week, year after year can beat a person down, can have the most able of people wondering about their self-efficacy.

What do you think it might do to you? For many of us, this may be a difficult question to answer as we don't experience such a daily barrage of insults. For some of us, a single insult of significance might rock us. I have a white friend who is an exceptional man with a great story. He is a recovering drug addict who has been clean and sober since 2011, who has worked his tail off to have his three younger children returned to his care. (His older set of children are full-grown with families of their own.) He even went so far as to get custody of his younger daughter's baby sister who is not biologically his so the girls could grow up together.

About a year ago he and his children moved into an apartment building in which most of the residents were African and Latino American. Recently, he called me quite troubled. He told me some of the children in the building pointed to him and called him a racist. Now my friend is the farthest thing from that. He is one of the kindest, most generous, easiest going men I know. One of his older daughters is married to an African-American man and my friend is close with his son-in-law and his son-in-law's family. My friend has an amazing reputation in the recovery community here in Portland. He is an exceptional man.

It is highly likely that those children heard this from their parents. What did my friend do, or not do, for those parents to come to that conclusion? Were they basing their judgment upon his looks? As of this writing, it's hard to know. I have my suspicions which I will address later. For now, the important point is that some folks reached the conclusion without a second look and this single event rocked to my friend to his core.

Today, my friend is a respected man in his community, rarely having to experience such events. Once again, I ask what must it be like to have dozens of experiences like these on a daily basis? What must the impact be on people who are broken? What must the impact be on children?

Signs of Respect

There are many ways we show our respect for others. Whatever form our respect for others takes, keeping our hearts and minds open is the guiding principle. I knew H. V.'s statement wasn't personal; he could not have hated me, he'd never met me before. What he was referring to was his hatred for the white folks' prejudicial and racist mistreatment of black folks – something he had experienced throughout his young life.

I'm pretty sure many of us would have been put off by H.V.'s statement, and if that were the case, would likely never have established a good working relationship with him. And, my God, was he great to work with! We had a great time for the two years the school was active. That we were able to work so well together was in part due to the motive I attributed to H.V. when he made that statement.

Positive Attributions:
Giving Others the Benefit of the Doubt

Giving others the benefit of the doubt is one true sign of respect. In the work I am currently doing in support of Department of Human Services' (DHS) clients this is huge. Over and over again I am witness to caseworkers, lawyers, and judges attributing the worst of motives to the clients we all serve. To be fair, I understand how this happens. Caseworkers, in an effort to protect children and reunite families, which is their mission, experience so many disappointments, frustrations, and losses. As they work to get children home to parents who are under extreme duress, caseworkers repeatedly see their clients continue to make poor decisions. A drug affected mom in recovery ready to have her child come home, relapses. A father on probation coming close to having his child returned, violates that probation and goes back to prison. Enough of these events and it's no wonder it's difficult for caseworkers to look at their clients with fresh eyes each day.

So, when a client misses a meeting or shows up late to a visit with their child, it is understandable when a caseworker assumes the worst. When there is a report of an altercation in the home, it is understandable if a caseworker assumes that it is the father who was the aggressor. In a very real sense, they have seen too much. Unfortunately, such assumptions often become far more negative when families of color are involved.

It has been one of our great challenges to view each family as they should be viewed, separate and distinct. When Guiding Light first started contracting with DHS, I was working with a drug affected mother in recovery and her 11-year-old daughter. I found out that the daughter was very interested in music and highly motivated to study music in her school. She wanted to play the violin and her mother could not afford the rental fee. I sent out an email to everyone I knew asking if anyone had a violin lying around that they would be willing to give to this child. Someone did and I was able to give the girl her violin. She excitedly began her music class that week. A few months later, mother relapsed and sold the violin for drugs. I guess it would be easy for me to throw up my hands, take it personally, and 'never do that again.' Believe me, I've thought of it. A similar opportunity hasn't yet arisen again. If it does, I hope I will make the same choice.

On a lighter note, there's Johnny's Pastrami. About 15 years ago, I was getting ready to fly down to Los Angeles and I was hoping to arrange a ride back to my apartment from the airport upon my return. This day, I was working with Joy and asked if she could help.

"I'd be happy to," she said, "I just have one small request. Would you bring me back a pastrami sandwich?"

"Sure, no problem. I know a number of good Jewish delis in LA." (I lived there for three years while doing my graduate work at UCLA.)

"No, no, it has to come from Johnny's."

"Johnny's?" I asked. "I've never heard of it."

"It's in the hood." Joy was raised in South Central, Los Angeles.

"Joy, let me get you some real pastrami."

"No Jay, Johnny's is the best."

"Joy, pastrami is my people's food. I know pastrami. If I was looking for a good gumbo or jambalaya, trust me I'd be asking you. Let me get you the real stuff."

Joy was adamant, "Johnny's is the best. See if you could bring me back some Johnny's."

I agreed to try. "Okay Joy, where is it?"

"Adams and Crenshaw." For those of you unfamiliar with Los Angeles, it's the hood.

So midnight, a few nights later as my friend and I were driving home from a gathering, we found Johnny's Pastrami. It was a little 24/7 operation with only limited outdoor seating. You order at a window. I ordered four pastrami sandwiches to go, wrapped tightly. They came on a French dip role, which right away made them suspect. The next morning, I brought them on the plane and boy, did they wreak up the aircraft. (I love the smell, though I can't speak for the other passengers.) Joy picked me up at the airport, brought me back home, and offered to share a sandwich with me. I bit into my half dubiously. It was the best pastrami I've ever eaten! Who knew black folks could make pastrami? All in all, a wonderful reward for having an open mind . . . and mouth.

I have subsequently brought some of my Jewish friends there, and they too, agree it's amazing pastrami! (For those interested, there's another Johnny's Pastrami somewhere in Venice, LA. They are not connected to the one in the hood in any way. I've never been there and cannot speak to the quality of their product.) Also, I too have no connection with Johnny's other than a very satisfied customer.

What's In a Name?

One simple sign of respect is taking the time to learn how to pronounce names correctly. C'mon, we all like hearing our names pronounced correctly, especially those of us with names a little more unusual. People who take the time to pronounce our names signal us that they care and are interested enough in us to take the time. It's a sign of respect. Even with very difficult names to pronounce, people appreciate the effort. My first name, of course, is rarely ever mistaken. My surname, Klusky, is mispronounced regularly. Some people seem to want to make me Scottish by adding a Mc or a Mac to the front, others want to insert a 't' after the 's' to make it Klutsky. There are other variations. There are many names it takes me quite a while to get right. Some I never quite do, but I always keep trying. To borrow from a Monty Python skit. "My name is spelled, Arthur Luxury Yacht, but it's pronounced Throat Warbler Mangrove."

Equally as important as personal names, can be names of places. Pronouncing names as we choose rather than pronouncing names as the inhabitants choose is one small manifestation of white privilege. The two that come immediately to mind are Iraq and Iran. Iraq is not pronounced 'eye-rack.' Iran is not pronounced 'eye-ran.' Iraq is more properly pronounced 'i-rock' with the initial 'I' pronounced like the 'i' in the word bit. Iran is more properly pronounced 'i-'ron' with the same initial 'I' pronunciation.

There was a wonderful little exchange on the 'Colbert Report' a number of years ago as Stephen Colbert was interviewing

Christiane Amanpour, a very well respected international jour-nalist. He asked her, and I am paraphrasing slightly,

"So what's going on in Iraq? (eye-rack)

"It's pronounced Iraq." ('i-rock',) she told him gently.

"That's what I said. What's going on in Iraq? (eye-rack)

"That's Iraq." ('i-rock',) she corrected him again.

"I'm not hearing it," he said, looking a bit confused.

Americanizing names of foreign places indicates to the inhab-itants and those from there that we don't care. In a way it indi-cates that we believe we can do anything we want to you. True or not, that is how it is often taken.

Honoring the Ways of Others

Some time ago, I was told the story of a white teacher work-ing with Native American kindergarten students. The teacher was presenting a lesson on grouping and the children had nine objects comprised of three different shapes (square, circle, trian-gle) in three different colors (red, brown, yellow). He instructed the students to arrange them into groups of three. They ar-ranged them by color. He told them they were wrong. They tried to tell him they were right. This went back and forth for a short while until an elder came in and helped the teacher see his mistake. In the teacher's mind, he was working with shapes while the students were working with color.

One of my most dear friends, who recently passed, Ron, was a professor of math and science pedagogy. Soon after he completed his graduate work in education he took a position teaching at a university in Fiji. He told me of an experience he had while working with a teacher on the island. Ron's big thing was coop-erative education. He believed that students learn better when they have the opportunity to cooperatively solve problems with their peers and discuss the methods they used to come up with their answers. Ron was brilliant at helping people do this.

While in Fiji, he was demonstrating this method to a middle school teacher who had a classroom of about 20 students. He had the students pair up, gave them a problem, then had them begin talking amongst themselves to come up with a solution. The students were highly engaged. After about 15 minutes, two students raised their hand with a solution. Both Ron the teacher went over to see what the students came up with and congratulated them for getting it right. At this point, to Ron's great surprise, all the students got up and left.

You see, Fijians are a communal people. Once the problem is solved by one member of the community there's no need for other members of the community to solve the same problem. To Ron's credit, he had no trouble flowing with the ways of the Fijians. Rather than attempt to make the students sit and do things 'his way', he figured out ways to adapt his teaching to the Fijian culture. The next time he just gave everyone different problems to solve.

The Rules of the Road

I tend to be an aggressive driver. My father was, his younger brother was, my older brother still is, so is my younger brother. It must be some combination of genetics and growing up in New York City. I'm also very disciplined about being on time. This all changes when I drive through communities that are clearly not my own. For myself, when I'm driving in an African-American, Latino, Asian, or Native American community, I drive as if I am in a foreign land. I do not drive as if I own the roads or as if I am in a hurry to get someplace. I drive as politely and respectfully as I can manage. To me, this is simply the appropriate way to drive. (Yes, I know I should probably drive like this everywhere I go, but that is more of a challenge.)

Driving as if we own the road is reasonable through much of America, as we pretty much do own the roads. However, while we still pretty much own the roads wherever we go in America, it's a sign of respect in some communities to drive as if in some communities the roads are not ours.

I've had the pleasure of driving in Rome; one of the wonderful times in my life. They certainly have different ways there. In the early 1990s, I had the opportunity to travel to Rome for the Vatican's Sacred Music Festival. My good friend, Christopher Caliendo, had been asked by the Vatican to compose a piece for the event. (At the time, Christopher was the youngest person and first American to be given such an honor.) Upon my arrival, Giorgio, his business manager in Rome asked me if I wouldn't mind taking his car and driving Christopher and his family around for the next four days as he had business to transact in Tunisia. "Wow!" I thought to myself. "This is going to be fun!"

The next morning I was with Giorgio and his assistant as we were going to the airport. Giorgio was in a rush and was driving. We approached a stoplight and there was a long line of cars in front of us. Giorgio proceeded to go into the oncoming traffic lane, drive right up to the light, and when the light turned green cut in front of the first driver in line and continued. We did this two more times before we arrived at the airport. His maneuvers prompted me to ask him,

"Giorgio do they give traffic tickets for anything in Rome?"

"There are a few major intersections at which they do not like motorists running through red lights," he happily replied.

I later found out they will also give tickets for having too many people in a car. I spent the next four days having a great

217

time driving around the city. I remember there was a lot of almost bumper-to-bumper traffic moving at 30 miles an hour. It was exhilarating!

What must it be like driving in Tehran, Beijing, Mumbai, Bangkok? If you were to drive there, I'm sure you would take the time to learn their rules of the road. Believe it or not the unwritten rules of the road for foreigners (most of us) driving in the South Bronx are different than the rules most of us are accustomed to.

A Different Take on the Japanese Internment

A number of years ago I was talking with my mentor about respecting those from other cultures and eventually we got to the treatment of Japanese Americans during World War II. We both agreed that the way our government treated them was heinous. Imprisoning and dispossessing people who had done nothing wrong was itself criminal and likely unconstitutional. Certainly it was inhumane. While I held the viewpoint that we never should've done this, my mentor posited a view that I found to be quite unique.

He suggested that, given the environment at the time, he understood how people could come to the conclusion that we needed to separate Japanese Americans from the larger population. However, he went on, if we were going to separate them, we should have provided much better living conditions and made sure their possessions were safe and secure, to be returned to them at the end of the war. Then at the war's end we should have given each of them medals in acknowledgment of their service to their nation. Imagine what a different story those citizens would've had to tell to their children and grandchildren. There

are always ways we can find to be respectful even in the most trying of circumstances.

Appreciating Our Different Lived Experiences

My father would never, ever buy anything made in Germany. Both my parents lost large swaths of family to the Holocaust.
All four of my grandparents immigrated from Poland before
World War I and left many brothers and sisters, aunts, uncles,
and cousins to come to America. Though I'm not sure how many
siblings my grandparents on my father's side left behind, my
grandparents on my mother's side left behind 19 between them.
As for my father's relatives, suffice it to say that today the only
Klusky's in America are my relatives. A number of years ago, we
found one other Klusky living in Italy. That is all. My father
was not alone in his personal proscription against purchasing
German products. Tens of thousands, perhaps hundreds of thousands of Jews felt and continue to feel this way even until today.

My father also rarely, if ever, bought anything made in Japan.
During World War II, my father served in the U.S. Army in the
Pacific, I'm sure bearing witness to the death and suffering of a
number of his comrades in arms. He never did speak of those
times. Again, he was not alone. Though Japan became known
for the quality of their automobiles and Germany for the quality
of almost everything they produced, no one ever suggested my
father 'get over' these sensibilities. Certainly, many Germans and
Japanese are just as proud of their countries as most of us are of
ours. However, many Jews, and others have a quite different personal experience of Germany than many German citizens. Similarly, many Allied soldiers fighting in the Pacific theater have a
quite different personal experience of Japan than many Japanese
citizens.

I believe it was in the early 1970s when Joy, her older brother, and a number of friends were driving back to Los Angeles from a concert one evening when their car was pulled over by the police, for what turned out to be no other reason than that they were black. The police demanded that they get out of the car and ordered her brother to position himself spread eagle against his vehicle. Her brother did not immediately follow the officer's order, so the officer took out his side arm, put it in her brother's mouth, and began shouting threats. I can only imagine how frightening this must've been. Fortunately, her brother's girlfriend kept her wits about her and fell to the ground faking an epileptic seizure, taking the officer's attention away from her boyfriend. Soon after, the officer got in his car and drove away.

This is only one among many traumatic events in which they, their families, and their friends were mistreated and differentially treated by the powers that be in this country. And as traumatic as it must have been, it pales in comparison to what Samaria Rice must have experienced when a Cleveland police officer shot and killed her unarmed 12-year-old son. And the killing of Tamir did not only effect his mother. He had a father, grandparents, aunts, uncles, cousins, and friends. Given our nation's history of abuse and maltreatment of so many of our Native American African-American, Latino American, Asian and Islander American sisters and brothers, we can understand the rancor many of them feel when someone, usually white, suggests they just 'get over it.'

We might want to forgive them if their hackles get raised a bit when they hear people assert that America is a great country or the greatest country in the world, then, when they attempt to have an honest discussion about some of America's failings, receive the suggestion that they could always leave, or once again, 'get over it.'

Helping White America Join the Village

Now, it is important that we approach this from a complex thinking perspective. This is not a love it or leave it situation, nor is it a best or worst analysis. I believe it's fair to say that all my African-American friends view our country as a good country with significant flaws. For many it remains their preferred country in which to reside, though given the explosion of hate crimes perpetrated since November 2016, some of my friends are having second thoughts.

Whatever a person's views, whether they are about our country's, our country's institutions, or our country's inhabitants, I am clear they have been informed by their experiences, and I am certain that their experiences are likely different from my own. It is a sign of respect to be interested in understanding and honoring the way people see the world and the experiences that got them to where they are.

Being respectful is instrumental to being accepted by other communities. Further developing our capacities to withhold judgment, to suspend our urge to draw conclusions, and to keep ourselves open to new understandings is crucial. Culturally, people can be quite different in profoundly fundamental ways. And as people can vary at a cultural level, they can also vary from family to family. There are many aspects of being human that are similar across all cultures and connect us all, yet there are differences amongst ethnic, and cultural groups. Family units can have their own micro-cultures.

Striving to understand and respect the mores and sensibilities of the groups with whom you interact will speak volumes and are the first steps towards integration. There are so many small, yet powerful, ways we can show our respect for others. A simple smile and hello in an elevator, attributing good intentions to another's actions, and being genuinely interested in another's story are things we can all do that will help us better connect with our sisters and brothers and ultimately lay the groundwork for expanding our communities.

Chapter 9

Lessons Learned:

The Power of Humility

The irony of writing a chapter on humility has not escaped me, for I'm not sure that endeavoring to write a book such as this is not an act of arrogance. So, if some accuse me of such, I will certainly understand. I might even agree. That said, humility plays a significant role in our ability to connect with others. So, here goes.

Through the years, white folks in general and white Americans in particular have been viewed by many around the world as being arrogant. Who can blame them? Since the days of European exploration and conquest that began in the late 15th century, those of European descent have behaved as if we owned the world. Europeans would sail to the Americas, Africa, East Asia, the Asian subcontinent, the Middle East, and the Pacific Islands, and when they arrived would take what resources they would, and where possible, subjugate or enslave the indigenous peoples to work their will.

Today, much has changed. Nations of the 'First World' no longer directly colonize 'Third World' nations. Many nations that were once considered 'Third World' have grown to be industrialized and are working their way to 'First World' status. The United States remains the largest economy in the world, but China is closing the gap, and India is not far behind. Seemingly, most European nations have diminished interests in world domination.

And some things haven't changed so much here in the United States. There are those in this country who continue to believe our ways are the best ways and should be the ways of the world. We have arrogantly believed this since our earliest forays into global expansion in the late 19th century. Remember the example of our efforts to bring democracy to the Philippines at the turn of the 20th Century?

In our arrogance, not only do a number of us believe our ways are best for everybody, we believe that it is our duty to impose them on others. Hence, our misadventures in Korea, Vietnam, Iraq, Afghanistan, Libya, and Syria. As a result of our arrogance, approximately 85,000 U.S. soldiers have lost their lives and another 300,000 have been wounded in these escapades. Enemy soldiers and civilians killed and wounded in these engagements number in the millions. These adventures have cost our country trillions of dollars.

Of course, instilling our way of life around the world is only one of a number of motivations for our military involvement in world affairs. It seems as if chief amongst our motivations has been to protect what our leaders perceive are our national interests, and by national, they seem to mean mostly, business, and by interests they seem to mean, mostly, resources.

Now the world is a complex place, and geopolitics can be quite involved. I do not see the security briefings that make it to the president's desk first thing every morning, so there is much I do not know. Most assuredly, our government has to take steps to protect our way of life and our national interests, business and otherwise. It just seems troubling though, that some of those in power have also wanted to spread democracy and capitalism throughout the world with missionary zeal.

While I am not certain how best to protect our way of life, I am fairly certain that our way of life is not for everybody. It is proving to be unrealistic to bring our version of democracy to people who either do not want it or are not ready for it. It is proving to be unrealistic to instill an economy in which all have equal opportunity to flourish in societies in which the wealthy are committed to growing their wealth at the expense of the general populace. It may be proving increasingly unrealistic to protect our way of life here at home.

In fact, I wonder if our idealized way of life may even be for us. Do you think it might be hypocritical, even arrogant, to attempt to spread democracy while concerted efforts are being made to disenfranchise millions of our own? Do you think promoting equal economic opportunity around the world when we have created an economy that ranks in the bottom 25% of industrialized nations in terms of upward economic mobility might be a little arrogant? Today, people living in 75% of the industrialized nations in the world have a better chance of achieving the American dream than we Americans have.[95] Might it be arrogant to promote the American way of life when our citizens of color, as well as those on the lower rungs of the socioeconomic ladder, receive differential treatment in terms of education, justice, employment, and finance to name just a few?

Our national arrogance manifests itself in a myriad of ways amongst many of us white folks. The seemingly innate belief some of us have in our 'exceptionalism' as Americans. The manner in which many of us assume, perhaps unconsciously, our way of seeing the world is the way all others see it. The way a number of us have traveled through the world earning us the sobriquet – 'ugly Americans.'

In my work, I regularly witness caseworkers, court appointed advocates, lawyers, and judges, almost all of whom are white and middle and upper-middle class, impose their views of child rearing on families of color and white families on the lower rungs of the socioeconomic ladder. Far too often children have been kept from their parents simply because the family does not live up to one or another of these professional's standards.

One of the more insidious ways being arrogant is made manifest is in the attributions successful people make as to the causes of their success. It is common for successful people to attribute their successes almost solely to their own drive, discipline, and intelligence. A few may acknowledge the contributions of their families and perhaps even their genetics. These all certainly play a significant role. Yet, here in America, white folks rarely include another significant factor - the color of our skin.

Due to our being unaware of the natural advantages we have as white folks in a white dominated society, many of us have failed to realize that we would likely not have had many of the opportunities we have had were we otherwise. Whether it's finance, manufacturing, information technology, marketing, management, the list goes on, we would be much less likely to have had the jobs, careers, and opportunities that we have had were we other than white. The opportunities for advancement would have been more limited; fewer doors would have opened.

If we are to connect to others and join the global village, it would serve us well to shed the cloak of arrogance and replace it with the mantle of humility. Please be aware, because of the perceived arrogance of white people by those of color, we will more than likely have to go out of our way to be extra humble. This is akin to people of color in this country having to be smarter and work harder than their white counterparts in order for white society to view them simply as competent.

There But For the Grace of God

I arise every Sunday morning before dawn to take a walk and watch the sunrise along the Willamette River that flows through downtown Portland. Along my walk I see dozens of homeless men, women, and even a few children sleeping in tents, or in sleeping bags, or in their clothes on a piece of cardboard. I see them and I think to myself, *'There but for the grace of God.'*

You see, on two separate occasions I have been on food stamps. Not long ago, I was homeless for eight months, and only thanks to the generosity of my friends, did I not have to spend any time on the streets. I understand what it's like to be down to your last few dollars.

When I was 17, my low back issues began. Twice in the past 12 years I have had to be taken to the hospital by ambulance. I understand what it's like to barely be able to walk. Between the ages of 21 and 58 I only had health insurance for three years. It is in large part thanks to the Affordable Care Act that I have been able to afford health insurance these last four. Throughout my life I have had to work daily to keep my back healthy enough to enjoy the outdoor physical activities I love. I couldn't have done so without the help of some great chiropractors, massage therapists, and a particular Chinese physician.

Thank God, all the powers that be, and the Green genes (my mother's side of the family, whom I seem to take after) that other than my muscular-skeletal issues, I have been extremely healthy. So many of us are only an illness or accident away from being in dire straits. So many of us are living paycheck to paycheck and the loss of our job would put our financial lives and those of our family in serious jeopardy. I believe those who have a tendency to look down upon our less fortunate brothers and sisters would do well to keep this in mind.

Certainly, my struggles pale in comparison to those of many, many others. I now consider myself more than fortunate to have been raised by two good parents in a harmonious home. I now consider myself more than fortunate to have found amazing mentors and guides, and to have been in enough need and had enough wisdom to take advantage of what they had, and continue to have, to offer. I now consider myself more than fortunate to have wonderful friends and loved ones. It wasn't always this way. I wasn't always so grateful. It really wasn't until I began working in Portland's African-American community that I began to gain a greater appreciation for my life.

My Introduction to Portland's
African American Community

I had no idea what I was getting myself into. It was the second week in July, 1990, and I was about to meet my students for the first time. Two weeks before I had sat in a classroom with thirty black men and women, mostly college athletes, and listened to a lecture on the cultural differences between white folks and black folks presented by Joy DeGruy. A month before that I had sat in the office of the founders of Self Enhancement, Inc. (SEI), a program aimed at providing healthy options and support for predominantly African American youth, and presented them with my proposal for a learning skills program I wanted to see implemented throughout the Portland Public School system. When asked if I wanted to try out some of my ideas, I was so eager I volunteered my services for their summer program.

So, on a warm summer morning I walked into a room at Tubman Middle School to meet my class. The space itself was nothing special, just your typical classroom. I found the requisite thirty odd chair-desks neatly ordered in rows, a blackboard and a teacher's desk. It was painted in that ubiquitous institutional beige with all-weather carpet to match. The windows were big and the view was small; you could see only a small courtyard and the surrounding buildings. There were a few maps on the walls, as well as posters urging the students to work hard, and examples of some of the students' work from the recently completed school year.

While the room was as I expected, my students were not. Fouteen black middle school students were in their seats scattered about the room. As I walked in, they eyed me suspiciously. They had seen many well intentioned white people try to work them, only to leave when the going got tough.

It was my job to teach them about learning skills. I would have them three hours a day, twice a week for six weeks. Up until this moment I thought nothing of their age, color, or backgrounds. Like many who came before me and have come since, I believed I was colorblind. Race doesn't matter. *'Under the skin we are all the same,'* I told myself. In my eyes they were like any other students. I was excited to impart my 'great' wisdom to these open and fresh young minds.

I had taught before. I was fresh from completing my graduate work at UCLA where I taught research methods, and assisted with numerous other psychology courses. As an undergraduate at Portland State University, I developed and taught my own study skills course. Since 1977, I had assisted with, and later led, communication skills trainings for people of all ages, from young children to older adults.

Up to now almost all my students were white, though I was certain that it made no difference. I was a teacher. I was engaging. I was entertaining. I egotistically believed I had a chance to mold the lives of young men and women. And I was about to find out I was deluding myself.

Most of that first day was a blur. What I remember I remember through a haze of pain. It was a nightmare. I had planned to spend the day discussing goal setting, problem solving, and planning. I tried everything I could think of. I lectured. I tried to get them to talk about themselves, their goals and dreams. I told jokes. I told stories. Within 20 minutes they were bored out of their minds. They seemingly didn't care about me or anything I had to say. After about 40 minutes they began to do what most normal 12 to 14 year old kids do – they began to make their own entertainment.

Some of them got up and went to stare out of the windows. Playful banter started. Small practical jokes followed. Laughter bubbled up. Paper flew. Keeping some modicum of order now became my primary task. For the better part of the remaining 2 hours and 20 minutes it was all I could do to keep them in the room. They played me as well as Wynton Marsalis ever played his horn. I then knew first-hand what the substitute teachers had felt like when they came into my junior high school classes in the Bronx.

When that long, long afternoon was finally over, I was a beaten man. I hadn't reached them. I didn't even scratch the surface. Now, it's never been my nature to blame others for my failures, and I didn't do so then. To the contrary, the students had been more than gracious. It wasn't their fault the teacher was out of his depth. They had given me many chances to grab their attention, every so often when they would quiet down and listen up. I suspect in the hope that I would say or do something worthy of their attention, they would give me a chance to redeem myself. With these chances I could do nothing. As we headed towards the auditorium/cafeteria to end the day with the rest of the SEI staff and students, Ray Leary, one of the co-founders asked me,

"How did it go?"

"I was terrible. I'll be back in two days and I'll try to do better."

I was humbled. I had no memory of something like that ever happening to me in a classroom. I had to get their attention. Of all my failures, my inability to grab them was my worst, and the most important to remedy. I did a lot of soul searching that night. What could I do? I had heard somewhere that black kids are motivated by money. Most of the kids in my class came from relatively poor households, so maybe that would work. I had the beginning of plan.

Little did I know the next day would be one of the most moving in my life, and the money would have precious little to do with it.

I decided to focus the next class on mnemonics (memory training) and our memory system. I walked into class and saw the same expectant faces I had let down two days before. It was a new day and they seemed to be hoping this time it might go better.

Before I got down to the topic du jour, I tried something that was taught to me by my mentor. At the beginning of every class Dr. Samuels would ask for everyone's agreement to be a student. I gave it a shot. We discussed what it meant to be a student and what it meant to be a teacher and made a list of each one's responsibilities. We decided a student's job is to pay attention, cooperate, and work to understand what is being taught. A teacher's job is to present the best information they can and make learning as interesting and fun as possible. I then asked each student if they would agree to do their job to the best of their ability. They all did. I then promised them I would do the same. We agreed to help each other hold up our respective ends of the bargain.

Now to put my plan into action. I began by telling them we were going to look at how our memory system worked. I got three volunteers to come up to the front of the room and pulled out a dollar bill. I used the dollar to represent a piece of information moving through the memory, letting each volunteer be one part of the system. I had their attention . . . for the moment.

After some discussion, in which many of them participated, I asked them if they wanted to learn how to improve their memory.

They said they did. So for the next hour I showed them how it's done and had them practice. (If you're interested, go get a copy of *The Memory Book* by Harry Lorayne and Jerry Lucas.) All was going well. When a student started to lose focus I reminded them of their agreement and they readily went back to work. Soon it was time to see how well they were doing.

"OK. Listen up. Now we're going to have a little test to see how you're all doing."

The groans echoed around the room.

"OK. I'll make you a deal. I'll give a dollar to the student who scores the highest!"

"C'mon, let's do this."

"Shhh."

"Be quiet!"

It took them less than a minute to quiet each other down. I gave them a list of 15 items to memorize and they began. I could barely believe it. They were working! And one of the most moving hours in my life was about to commence. They were about to teach me a most important lesson.

As the students began to write, one of the young ladies looked up and said,

"I can't do it."

"Try." I encouraged her.

"I can't."

"Yes you can. Go on and try."

"I can't." This was coming from a young girl who the day before said she wanted to be an OB-GYN when she grew up.

"Yes, you can. You can do it."

"I can't."

"Why?"

"I just can't."

She gave no other reason. This was the first time as a teacher I had ever had a student quit before she even tried. I had never seen anything like it. I could not know I would be seeing it on almost a daily basis; so many talented and gifted young men and women thinking so little of their abilities.

What to do? I certainly wasn't going to let her fail without trying. I slowly walked over to her desk and the class stopped work to see what would happen next. When I reached her desk I leaned over until our noses were almost touching. I looked directly into her eyes and quietly said,

"If you don't try you will never, ever become a doctor. It's OK to try and fail, but if you don't try you will never, ever be what you want to be."

As I moved away she began to work. She missed a perfect score by one. Four students got perfect scores on the exam. I gave each of them a dollar and we took a break. I was glad they had learned how to do basic mnemonics. They were glad to learn that I seemed to care about them.

After the break they were eager to come back to class. Something was happening. As they came back from their break I stood at the door, gave them each high-fives and words of encouragement. They were taking their seats when I noticed one of the boys, Ronnie, a thoughtful, heavy set boy with a ready smile, looking glum. He was one of those who had gotten a perfect score. Ronnie was also the dominant male in the class – a born leader. The one all the kids took their cues from. Two days before he had been the one with whom I had had the most trouble. I went over and asked him,

"What's up? You're not lookin' so good. Is something on your mind?"

"You know," he began, his eyes looking down at his desk. "I don't like it when teachers give kids their money."

"Why?"

"Because it's their money. They earned it. Besides, we could have cheated. You didn't have to give us each a dollar. You promised the highest score a dollar. Since four of us tied you could've given us each a quarter."

"I know some of you could have cheated." He looked up and saw I knew and wasn't going to make it an issue. I continued. "If you were a teacher I think you would be one that would do anything for his students. right?" He nodded agreement. "I just wanted to do whatever I could to motivate my students to learn. Four dollars is a small price to pay. You would've done the same thing, wouldn't you?"

"Yeah." I could see he was thinking about it.

"I was just doing whatever I could to help the class"

He lightened up a little and we started class again. We continued talking about mnemonics and their experience of the last ninety minutes. Hands were going up. They were almost jumping out of their seats to participate. They were actually engaged!

After some time I decided to take them to a swimming pool in the neighborhood as a reward for their cooperation and good work. On the way to the pool they wanted to stop off for some candy. As we left the store Ronnie came up to me, held out his hand with two pieces of candy, looked me right in the eye and said:

"Take one."

I didn't get it. Thinking that he was a poor kid and I didn't want take food out of his mouth. Politely, I refused.

"No thanks, you earned it."

Without taking his eyes off of me and his hand still held out, he raised himself to his full height, narrowed his eyes slightly and with a dignity that I had rarely witnessed, he held my gaze and said again,

"Take one."

I knew something important was going on but I couldn't put my finger on it. I took a piece and thanked him. He nodded and we walked in silence together to the pool. Later that night I realized it had been his way of balancing the books, and his way of showing respect. In that one hour I had made my first real connection with a person very different from myself. I would never be the same.

Beginning With an Empty Cup

Professor Leonard Trigg (my chief martial arts instructor) would often encourage us to come to class with our cup empty, for you cannot add another drop to a cup that is full. He was encouraging us to be humble. A student who knows everything cannot learn anything. There is no room for new knowledge. Not only is there no room for new knowledge, a person who knows everything will not even notice that there is anything to learn.

Being genuinely interested in the cultures and traditions of others, and by culture I mean the familial as well as the ethnic prerogatives, is one way to begin to connect. Being genuinely interested in how a person sees the world, asking questions, learning about their families, their history, their dreams, all lead to building trust. Learning about a culture's etiquette: Does their family have rituals before dining? Are they religious people, and if so, how do they practice? How should certain people be addressed? All can serve as the foundation for relationship.

There is great power in being a humble student. We expect people who are learning, to make mistakes; it is the nature of "studenting." We more readily forgive a student's trespasses. On the flipside, when a person presents him or herself as knowledgeable, perhaps even expert, and they make a mistake, we call that arrogance and it puts many of us off. Perhaps most importantly, by taking the viewpoint of a student, there is less of a need to be defensive. As a student, we should expect ourselves to make mistakes, and therefore more readily accept criticism and instruction.

Over the years, after more than my share of mistakes, I learned the value of humility. Now, whenever I enter into a new situation, I let everyone know I am new and that I have much to learn. I asked them to help me. If I say or do anything that is inappropriate or disrespectful, I ask them to please let me know. I have found that people are usually very willing to become my teachers.

I have also found most people to be more than happy to talk about their family and their culture. A genuine interest in learning will usually encourage a reciprocal interest in teaching. Speaking for myself, I have always enjoyed introducing people to the Jewish traditions with which I grew up. As a teenager I regularly invited my non-Jewish friends to Seders at my family's home, a custom which my parents never discouraged. I do not believe I am unusual. I have found many, many people excited to tell me about their family's and their culture's customs.

One important caveat. Please do not accept any individual's perspective as representative of their entire cultural group. Time and again, mostly on television, I see individual African-Americans, Latino Americans, Native Americans, Asian Americans put forward as speakers for their group . . . as if one person can speak for millions. During the 2016 presidential campaign, I was hiking with my Latina friend and asked her what her Latino friends and family thought of Trump and Hillary. I was surprised to learn that some of her Latino friends and family were either pro-Trump, anti-Hillary, or both. She, too, was surprised.

In my work with families, I have learned to find out as soon as possible who runs the home? Is it the mother, the father, grandmother, or grandfather? In some cases it may be the elder son or daughter. For all involved to get the most out of our interaction, I learned the importance of getting the blessing of the head of the household.

I am much closer in age to my friend and business partner Aaron's father then I am to Aaron. Yet, to me, Aaron's father is Mr. Bell or Mr. B. Whenever I arrive at a family gathering, I make it a point to find Mr. B, shake his hand, say hello, and ask him how he is doing. Then I will find the hosts and do the same. I'll then go around and greet everyone else. I do not wait for people to greet me. I go to as many people as I can. I hug, handshake, fist bump, whatever the person is comfortable with. Remember Axiology. Greeting is one way to reaffirm our relationship. This can be so important, given the primacy of relationships in African American culture.

We would do well to notice as much as we can about how people interact. How they greet each other. Who are the people that are accorded the most deference. We could try to notice the physical distances people maintain when they're talking with each other. We can do our best to be sponges. We can do our best to be aware of any prejudices, preconceptions, and biases we may have and work to see the world as they see it. We can work to keep our hearts and minds open, learn as much as we can, invite criticism, and work to correct our mistakes.

On a number of occasions, when I started hanging out with Joy, she would invite me to her home. Always, she would offer me food. Always, I would graciously decline. At the time, she was a single mother with three children. After about the fifth or sixth visit to her home she asked me,

"Why don't you eat in my home? Is it not clean enough for you?"

I was shocked at the inference. Of course her home was clean enough, Joy's home was almost always spotless!

I replied, "Joy, I don't eat in your home because I don't want to take food off of your children's table." I knew she didn't make much money at the time.

Now it was her turn to be kind of shocked. "Jay, when someone offers you food, eat. You don't have to eat a lot, but eat something. Not doing so, offends the host."

I have not refused food in a non-white home since.

Getting Comfortable: Being Yourself

As important as it is to get to know and understand others, it is equally as important to allow others the opportunity to get to know and understand us. So, it would serve us well to present ourselves as we actually are . . . no more, no less. It starts with accepting ourselves, the bad and the good, the low and the high, our weaknesses and our strengths. It is human nature to want to present ourselves in the best light possible. Fair enough. However, going too far, presenting ourselves as more than what we actually are, can have unfortunate consequences. It's not unlike a courtship in which one partner works to assume an idealized version of himself, only to marry and not be able to maintain that version, with the predictable results.

It is human nature to care what others think about us, especially when we are young. I forgot who said it, but a number of years ago a wise person talking about caring what other people think said,

"When we're in our 20's we care so much about what other people think of us. We care about our clothes, our hair, our job our career. We really want others to think well about us. When we get into our 40's we stop caring so much about what others think of us. Then we get into our 60's and realize no one was thinking about us in the first place."

We would do well to just be ourselves and allow others to see us. Be open about our past, our families, our hopes, our goals, and our dreams. If, we are not happy with who and what we are, we can work to become the people we want to be. That said, the more knowable we are, the greater the likelihood we will be able to build real connections with others.

Get comfortable being on the visiting team. Most white folks I know are uncomfortable to one degree or another when they are in the minority. Most of us are comfortable enough when we have the home-field advantage, where we believe we are in control, like in our homes or offices; where we make it incumbent upon others to be comfortable in our surroundings.

Many of us may be comfortable enough when we believe we are on neutral ground, like at a concert, a ballgame, or local park. This can be somewhat misleading because in our white dominated society, there are a few neutral grounds. Believing that neutral ground exists is actually an aspect of white privilege. From the viewpoint of others, no ground is neutral. Concerts, ball-games, school functions are almost always home fields for white people in America.

So many of my white friends would tell me how they tend to be uncomfortable when they are in the minority. How many of us have been at ease at an African-American backyard barbecue. How many of us have been at ease at a Quinceañera? How many of us have been at ease at a potlatch? How many of us have ever been to any of these? How many of us have simply been to a graduation celebration at the home of one of our friends of color?

How does it feel to be in a place where you're not sure how to act? Where you're not sure what is appropriate? Where we are unfamiliar with the culture and etiquette? I have been in such places many times and what has seen me through was my willingness to make mistakes and my interest in learning. I did my best to get comfortable being wrong, being embarrassed, and being out of place. Eventually, I was able to get quite comfortable embarrassing myself, and as a result my friends viewed many of my faux pas as endearing rather than offensive. And, I often came away with some fun stories.

In the summer of 2004 my mother passed. Her funeral was a graveside affair attended by about 30 of my relatives. (The story of my mother's passing and the funeral is one for another time. Suffice it to say, a rabbi's behavior was highly inappropriate, offending all in attendance.) I returned home from my mother's funeral only to find out that Joy's mother-in-law had just passed. I asked Joy if it would be appropriate for me to attend the funeral. "Of course," she said.

I showed up at the church on the appointed day and time. When I arrived, Joy, her family, and her husband's family were outside the church. I went up to each of them and gave them my condolences. The group was similar in size to that of my mom's service. After a time, we began to move towards the church entryway and I respectfully took my position in the back of the group.

Once inside the main hall I was mortified. I had assumed the group outside with the family were those that would be attending the funeral. Oh how wrong I was. Inside were 400 friends and family of Joy's mother-in-law packing the church. The only places open to sit were with the immediate family in the first two rows. Now I was nowhere near being part of the immediate family, yet I was now sitting with them.

This was my first experience attending a funeral in a black church. Suffice to say, it was very different from any funeral I had attended. There were women dressed all in white, a little like nurses, walking around the church with boxes of tissues for the mourners. Joy's mother-in-law was much beloved and a member of three or four different churches in her life. Pastors from each church were to speak at her service.

The service lasted more than two hours. At one point I needed to use the restroom and while in the lobby I met one of Joy's nephew's. I actually should've been sitting with him, so I asked if there was any room – there wasn't, so back to the second row I went.

As the service neared its conclusion, I noticed my blood sugar was low and I was pretty dehydrated. I likely looked a little pale. The service concluded with the entire congregation filing by the casket and paying respects to Joy's husband and his siblings. Now, the line flowed passed where I was sitting and I began to notice everyone looking at me as they walked by. It's likely they were wondering who I was and how I was connected to the dearly departed, since many, if not most, of them had never seen me before. I imagined they were wondering, *Who is this white guy?*

Probably due to my low blood sugar and dehydration I found this very funny and began to laugh somewhat uncontrollably. Of course laughing at a funeral is really inappropriate, so I bent over with my head in my hands to cover it up. Immediately, one of the women in white came over offering me a tissue and consolation. I laughed harder. I was sitting next to a nephew of the departed who put his arms around me in an attempt to comfort me. "I know, we all loved her," he said. It was too much.

I eventually got myself under control and I don't think anyone particularly noticed me laughing. At least no one mentioned it. Thank God.

About six months later I found myself back in church. Joy's book had just been released and Joy was on her first speaking tour in New York City. I was part of her small support group. She had spoken to a packed house in Westchester, the night before and tonight, Sunday, she would be speaking in Brooklyn. To help promote the event, the pastor of the largest African-American church in Brooklyn invited her to Sunday morning service where she would announce that evening's event.

Seven or eight of us arrived at the church that morning believing that Joy would go to the pulpit, invite the congregation to her lecture that evening, and be on her way. We expected we would all stand in the back of the church and let Joy do her thing. No such luck. The pastor invited us all down to the front of the church to take seats and join in the Sunday celebration. This time I was in the first row.

Whenever I am in a place of worship that I am unfamiliar with, I do my best to follow everyone's lead. I stand when people stand, kneel when people kneel, and sit when people sit. If the congregation is singing, I try to join in. Being in the front row made this a little more challenging, but I was still doing a good job, until . . .

As the pastor was talking I noticed out of the corner of my eye that the folks in back of me were standing up. So I, automatically, stood up too. As it turns out, the folks in back of me, all of whom were white, were visiting from a sister church in New England, The pastor was acknowledging them and introducing them to the congregation. And for a brief time I was one of their crew.

Once I realized my mistake, I didn't think there was much to do other than just stand there until it was over. When my people in the first row saw me, their reactions ranged from just shaking their heads to mouthing, "What are you doing?" to silently laughing. They clowned me for quite a while once we left the church.

I believe because I am at ease with myself, willing to make mistakes and learn from them, and comfortable with embarrassing myself, folks of color, once they have gotten to know me a little, have been willing to give me so much room to grow. I cannot thank them enough because I've needed all that room and more.

Lessons in Humility

Making Agreements

There is power in humility. It can help us become wiser. It can be disarming. It can be inviting. It can protect us. One way it can protect us is helping us avoid making promises we can't keep, and here in lies a cautionary tale.

It was my first day of graduate school at UCLA and early that morning I went to the gym for a workout. In the weight room was a guy wearing a New York Mets T-shirt. "Yo! New York!" I called out. And thus began my lifelong friendship with my composer friend, Chris. This was also Chris's first day as a graduate student at UCLA, studying music composition. (Five years later he would be asked by the Vatican to compose music for their Sacred Music Festival.) As we got to know each other, I learned that Chris aspired to compose for film.

Now, Chris had only been in Los Angeles a short time and he did not yet have an agent, so I offered him my services with the understanding that I would do my best to help him until he found real representation. After all, it is usually better to have someone talk about you than doing it yourself. In an effort to learn the business I began talking with everyone I knew who had any connection to the music world. As it turned out, one of my fellow students studying with my mentor back in Oregon was a singer who performed around the world. She introduced me to her manager, Stan, who worked out of Los Angeles. He invited me to his office.

Stan was an unassuming, easy-going, older man. He looked to be about 75-years-old and he been in the business almost 50 years. He proved to be a wealth of information and very generous. One exchange during that meeting more than 30 years ago still stands out in my memory.

"Always get it in writing." he sagely advised.

"Do you?" I asked.

"Never."

I was soon to find out why. During our meeting, in an effort to impress him, I agreed to do something for him. I have no recollection what it was, but whatever it was it was beyond my capacity. When I didn't deliver, he told me something to the effect that I was not a serious man and that he no longer wished to have anything to do with me. I never saw or heard from him again. Though it felt harsh at the time, it was one of the best lessons I have had. I wrote him a letter of apology, which I have no idea if he ever read, then apologized to Chris, my singer friend, and my mentor. Who knows, if I had been more humble and not made an agreement I was not able to keep, perhaps he would've helped my composer friend. Perhaps, he would've mentored me in the business. Perhaps we would've become friends. I will never know.

Feeling Others

Humility can help us to become more human. People who are humble do not believe they are better people than others. I may be better at some things than you are and you are very likely better at some things than I am, but we do not believe this makes us better people. I'm sure we all know people who believe they're better than. They may make more money. They may be highly educated. They may be consummate artists. They may be consummate athletes. They may be consummate recyclers. They may believe they are closer to God. They may believe they are more enlightened.

It hardly matters. The drive to identify oneself as 'better than,' is typically an effort to make up for some insecurity, real or imagined. By acquiescing to their drive, people become less likable and so less able to connect. And to the degree that they are unable to connect they become less human. Rarely do they see it, and rarely are they able to feel their loss of humanity. I have been a not so shining example of this. Remember those kids in school who seemingly did little work and got very high grades? I was one of them, and because of this particular aptitude I believed I was smart, smarter than most. And being smarter, I believed myself to be better. Until . . .

Back in 2002, I was working towards my Black Belt in a tactical fighting martial art system. It was one of the most challenging and rewarding endeavors of my life. It took me more time, cost me more money, and was exponentially more difficult than obtaining my PhD. You see, most of my classmates were 20+ years younger than I (I was 47) and much, much more athletic. (A number of my peers played ball in college and almost all of them were on one or another of their varsity high school teams.) With one or two exceptions, they were also much bigger. (And if anyone tells you size does not matter in combat sports, they have little experience with such activities. There is a reason boxing, wrestling, and mixed martial arts all have weight classes.) In my class, I was like the kid who wasn't big enough to go on the rides at Disneyland. I swear my instructor had a mark at the entrance to his school at about 6 feet, for there were only three of us that didn't reach that height. (One was a boxer, the other, the best athlete and best fighter at the school)

I held my own, though I was often overmatched and at times outclassed. I remember two nights in particular when I got so frustrated that when I got home all I could do was flop down into my chair and cry. The day after the second of these nights I went to speak to my instructor. I told him how frustrated I was and how difficult a time I was having. To which he responded,

"Dr. Klusky, now you know how we all felt in school."

I was stunned. I honestly never thought of that before. In all my years of working with teens, I never truly understood what many of them experienced, until that moment. I had always believed all one had to do was sit in class, listen, take some notes, crush the tests, turn in your assignments, and then get your 'A'. The only reason for not getting 'A's was simply lack of effort.

How wrong I was. I had heard of people struggling in school, I just had no real connection with the experience. It was almost as if I never quite believed it.

Since that event, I have come to understand that those of us who find school easy and do well are more lucky than we are smart. We are lucky that when we were young our brains and our chemistry were set up to sit for relatively long periods of time and process information in a manner that meets the demands of academia. Whether it's academics, athletics, music, the arts, construction, mechanics, or any other endeavor, if something comes easy to us it is evidence of our gifts. We are simply lucky to have them. What we do with them, is what makes us smart.

Listening –
You Never Know With Whom You May Be Talking

Many who work for the government and the social services are tasked with almost impossible jobs. At the Department of Human Services here in Portland Oregon, doing a good job is not almost impossible . . . it is impossible. Early in 2017, I was talking with a caseworker who was telling me of a study the department commissioned the previous year to determine how many new cases a Child Protective Services worker can adequately handle per month. She told me the study found that workers should be able to do a good job with six new cases per month. She went on to tell me that she had received eight new cases in the last week! Social workers, teachers, public defenders, and others who work in the service of those at the lower rungs of our socioeconomic ladder have some of the most difficult jobs in our society. It is no wonder many of them rarely get to truly connect with those they are serving.

One of my families in particular comes to mind. The DHS caseworker referred this particular father to us because he presented as belligerent and actually, a little frightening. He had just gotten out of prison and was seeking to have his young son returned to his care. This man was rather large, as he had lifted a lot of weights in prison, and I could see how he could've been intimidating. The caseworker told me he would get frustrated at Family Decision Meetings (meetings to help move cases forward) and this was of a concern to the people, all women in this case, who were at these meetings. The caseworker had also voiced concerns about his mother, as she too was combative and not easy to work with. The folks at DHS had put dad and his mother in the box labeled lower-class, poor, and maybe high school educated.

So, I went to meet dad to see how I could help. At the time, dad was living with his mother in a small, immaculate, well-appointed ranch style home. Dad and his mom greeted me at the door. While dad was a big guy, mom was a smallish woman with a big beehive hairdo. She looked to be in her 60s and had a kind of Okie accent. At first blush, I could see how the folks at DHS might have categorized this family, though I must say their home belied DHS's categorization.

It took about 15 or 20 minutes to discover how different both of them were. Yes, dad lifted a lot of weights in prison. And when he wasn't lifting weights he was reading a book a day. Many of the books he read were mechanics manuals. It turns out the young man had 150 IQ and the ability to read a manual, then go build what the manual described. His frustration in meetings stemmed from his discomfort with all the women, whom he felt were not listening to him, as well as the 75% hearing loss he had developed as a child from meningitis. He had learned how to read lips to make up for the loss. He said he found it frustrating as he would try to read the lips of two or three or four people talking at a time.

His mother, the combative woman with the beehive hairdo and Okie accent, the woman that sounded like she maybe had a high school education . . . She had just retired the previous year from her position as an engineer. It seems she had a hand in designing the flat screen televisions we all watch. Of course, at first she wasn't designing televisions; she was working on the heads-up displays for our military aircraft, which were the precursors to our TV's. In many ways, she was brighter than all of us. Until I told them, DHS never knew.

I have found Portland to be rife with all manner of exceptional people who have lived fascinating lives – lives you would never know about by looking at the people who lived them. Some of the most accomplished people I have met have been some of the most unassuming. I'm sure it's little different throughout communities around the world.

Always Having to Say You're Sorry

I first met Professor Trigg at a workshop my mentor, Dr. Samuels, was presenting back in the 1980s. I had been hearing about him from my friend and martial arts instructor, Norvin Johnson. Norvin had told me what an accomplished martial artist Professor was, one of the most accomplished in the world. (Of course Professor Trigg would never claim such.) He told me he was also one of the most traditional. Our initial meeting was little more than my bowing, shaking his hand, and expressing my happiness in meeting him. Over the next 25 years or so our paths would cross sporadically. I would see him at some of Dr. Samuels' workshops, I would attend a seminar or two he was presenting, and I would run into him at Norvin's school. At first, each time I would see him the very brief interaction was the same. Sometime in the 90s, when I learned that his son was having some difficulty in school, I would add an offer of help to our brief interaction. He would be very appreciative of my offer and never take me up on it.

You can imagine my surprise when, about 25 years after first meeting him, he asked me if I would like to train. This was even more surprising given that Professor was only teaching privately, at his invitation only. By this time, I had enough experience to give what I found out to be was the perfect answer,

"Sir, I would very much like to train but first I have to check with Dr. Samuels."

You see, in the traditional world of martial arts, one does nothing without the permission of his or her teacher. As Professor and my mentor were very close, this was the best answer I could have given. Needless to say my mentor was thrilled that I had such an opportunity and simply told me to do everything he instructed me to do to the best of my ability. For five years my three training partners and I studied with him four or five days a week, 3 to 4 hours a day. In addition my partners and I would spend time practicing together and on our own..

As I mentioned earlier, Professor is very traditional. Among other things, this means that respect and humility are essential. Of course there are the traditional acts of obeisance – greetings, bowing, and titles, but in the old school it goes much deeper. And there is one of those traditions that has served me very well in my interactions in many other environments.

The tradition of which I speak is that of assuming instructors are never wrong. That if there is an error, it is the students'. The way this works is thus: Let's say we were in the midst of a lesson and Professor asked us to show him a technique he believed us to have learned. And, let's say he in fact hadn't taught it to us yet. In the world outside of the world of formal martial arts, it would be considered appropriate to say, "You did not teach that to us."

In the traditional world of formal martial arts, a student would never say that to his or her teacher. The student would say, "I don't remember learning that, sir." or some such statement that puts the onus for not knowing on the student. When this happened in our training group, Professor would then ask each one of us if we had learned the technique, and if we all had not yet learned it, he would begin to teach it.

Outside of this world, I have found it so very useful to take responsibility in this way, especially given the inconsequential nature of so many potential disagreements. Someone gets the timing of an appointment wrong. There is a disagreement about who was supposed to pick something up. Someone was supposed to make a phone call. In most cases, does it really matter who was at fault? If one has the humility to take ownership, it becomes so much easier to correct the mix-ups and move on amiably and successfully.

Pitching In

Recently, I was participating in one of Dr. Joy's conferences, something I hadn't done in a few years. As I was reminded, it is not unusual for her to make reference to me, a white guy who managed to fit into a black community. She tells her audience how unusual it was for a white guy to just show up and help out. She says I helped with much that needed to be done, even the small tasks, such as taking out the trash. Now, I don't remember taking the trash out, but I do remember helping folks set up for gatherings, helping children with their schoolwork, doing what I could for the good of the order.

It surprises me when I'm told this is not ordinary, especially for a man of my station - you know a PhD. (I suppose I shouldn't be. I worked as a waiter for many years and had experienced customers who looked upon me as a "lowly server".) As I was never one for sitting around and watching others put themselves out on my behalf, it has always felt natural for me to pitch in where I could.

In many regards, helping others was my father's life. Most nights after dinner, he would go down to the synagogue and help wherever he could. If he walked into your home and heard your door squeak, he would go back to his car, get the WD-40 and whatever else he needed, and fix it before you had a chance to tell him not to bother. My younger brother, is so much like our dad. In May 2017, I had the opportunity to travel to Italy with him. For the ten days we were together, I watched him stop to help dozens of people pick up something they dropped, pull a cart across a busy street, help a woman with her baby in a stroller down some stairs. I have found that pitching in, getting my hands dirty, helping others to do the simplest of tasks goes a long, long way towards being accepted.

Simply Being

At the end of the day, it all comes down to simply being. Being knowable, likable, honest, and trustworthy are the cornerstones of deep, long-lasting relationships. Humility promotes these, as does respect. Humility and respect are intimately bound with each other. Being respectful requires humility. Being humble encourages respect. Becoming part of a community requires both. The more readily we are able to know and accept ourselves, to be open to learning from others, and to be willing to share ourselves with others, the more easily we will be able to simply be in, and be of, other communities.

Chapter 10

Lessons Learned:

Applied Reverse Integration

So how do you know you are part of a community? Good question. One day, Joy and I were talking about religion and I said that while I was raised Jewish I don't claim Jewish.

"You can't not claim Jewish!" I can't not claim black!" she exclaimed. We discussed this for a while, then she asked, "How do you know you're Jewish?"

I wasn't certain, so I began calling some of my family and friends. Most gave the matrilineal party line answer,

"If your mother is Jewish, you are Jewish."

However, while birth can make one technically Jewish, being Jewish, to me requires something more. So, once again, how does one know they are Jewish? The most satisfying answer I received came from my Jewish friend Judy.

"You get all the jokes," she told me.

Of course getting the jokes is a metaphor. It means you understand the nuances of the community. It also means people are comfortable enough with you to be themselves, to speak their minds as if you are one of them. I can only claim to 'get the jokes' in three ethnic communities: I get most of them in White America and Jewish America, and I get many of them in Black America.

It takes time to learn the nuances of a new community, a community very different than our own. It takes engaging with respect and humility. At first, it takes becoming comfortable with being uncomfortable, with feeling out of place. Over the years, in part thanks to my parents who raised me, and my mentor, Dr. Samuels, who provided me opportunity upon opportunity to grow myself, in part thanks to Joy and my other African-American teachers, I can genuinely say I can be comfortable interacting with just about any group of people. I have learned that getting comfortable in most communities begins with building relationships.

The Preeminence of Relationship in Black America

Once again, relationships rule. It can be difficult for us to truly wrap our wits around this concept. In many cultures it is nigh impossible for folks to get quality work done with others when relationships have been violated. It is also difficult to get quality work done before the relationship has been established. And again, while relationships are also important in our community, (it is common for us to produce quality work with people we don't know, don't like, or may even despise — in our world it's called, "being professional") relationships can be preeminently important in others.

Early in my tenure at SEI, I was helping write a grant proposal. One morning as we were nearing the deadline, I came into the office, went up to one of the staff, all of whom were black, who was also working on the proposal, and asked her how she was coming on her part. Did I do anything unusual? Was this inappropriate? In our world, this is pretty standard. Not necessarily so in others. One of the senior staff, witnessed this, pulled me aside, put his arm around me, and said,

"Say hello first. Ask her how her family is doing. Take a few minutes to connect. You'll get much more work done."

Now I understand what he was suggesting I do was reaffirm the relationship. It's hard to overemphasize how important this is to do. Of course he was right. So much more is possible when relationships are established and reaffirmed at the outset of every interaction. Axiology at work.

Dr. Edwin Nichols, the author of Axiology, is Dr. Joy's mentor. For about 30 years, when Joy has lectured and presented trainings on the subject of cultural difference, Dr. Nichols' work has been her foundation. While she had seen axiological principles at work throughout America, Joy told me it was during her visit to Southern Africa that she was able to see the roots of these principles. Joy was traveling with a group of African-American women and tells the story of a business meeting they attended in Lesotho and how different it was from similar meetings she had attended regularly in the States.

Here in America, let's say you have a meeting with about 40 participants at work scheduled for 9 o'clock in the morning. For

most of us, the 9 o'clock meeting will begin at 9:00 or very shortly thereafter. Let's say traffic is backed up and you are 20
minutes late for the meeting. What do you do? Most of us would
walk in quietly with as little disturbance as possible, find a seat,
and work to catch up. Whispering, we might ask the person next
to us where we're at and what have we covered.

In many parts of Africa, Joy said, things can be very different.
The meeting she attended in Lesotho was scheduled to start at
8:00am. Forty to fifty people were to be in attendance. Folks began showing up at about 815, got caught up with each other as
the group slowly gathered, and the meeting began by about 9
o'clock. When another participant showed up after the meeting
had started, she didn't join the meeting unobtrusively. The meeting stopped for her and she went around the room greeting everybody.

"How have you been?" "Good to see you." "How are your
grandchildren?" So on and so forth.

As others arrived, this was repeated. This is simply one example of the cultural imperative that demands the relationship be
the prime consideration. Did this make for a long meeting? Did
the meeting drag on? Maybe, but only by our standards. By
their standards, the meeting went just the right length of time . . .
as long as was necessary.

(Parenthetically, as I was writing this, I initially had written
in the paragraph above, *'when another participant showed up **late**,'* a
nod to my own European axiological sensibilities. Upon identifying my sensibilities, I changed the phrase to *'when another participant showed up **after the meeting had started**.'* Just an example
of how ingrained and automatic our approach to our worlds can
be.)

Helping White America Join the Village

A few thousand years of evolution will have its impacts. If we are to become comfortable with others, and integrate into a community, it would be to our great advantage to understand and respect these imperatives. Please understand, just as we take our evolutionary imperatives for granted and are often not aware of them, so too is it not uncommon for people of other communities to do the same.

Remember my friend who was called a racist by some children in the apartment building in which he resides? I strongly suspect some of his neighbors drew that conclusion because he did not make an effort to introduce himself, to connect with them, when he first moved in. My friend has told me that for the first few months he was there he was focused on setting up his home and managing his four children. I know this was the first place he had lived in which he was the minority. No one informed him how important it was to connect with his neighbors and begin to build relationships.

Similarly, during the onset of gentrification in the North, Northeast Portland African-American community, a white woman bought a home. She too, did not understand the importance of connecting with the folks on her block. After she had been there a short time, her next-door neighbor was having a party one night and things got pretty loud. She felt uncomfortable, and maybe even a little unsafe, going over to talk with them. Instead, she called the police. You can imagine how that was received.

What my friend should've done as soon as he had moved in was start knocking on his neighbors doors and introducing himself, begin developing relationships. Once he felt comfortable, he could then have introduced his children. It is likely his children would've found many more playmates. The woman above also would've been much better served going to meet her neighbors.

She might've chosen to host a little block party or some gathering that would indicate her interest in being part of the community. Then, I'm sure she would've felt comfortable going to her neighbor and asking if they could tone things down a bit. I'm fairly confident events would have transpired quite differently.

You see, it is a common misconception among white folks that many neighborhoods of color are unsafe. While it's true that many neighborhoods are unsafe for those who do not belong, it is also true that they are particularly safe for those who do belong. More than safe, the former African-American community in Portland was protective. Folks looked out for their neighbors and their neighbors' children. Folks did what they could to help and support each other, regardless of color. This is the way it has been in ethnic communities around the country. Contrary to popular belief, as long as a person makes him or herself part of the community, living in a community like the African American neighborhood in Portland is actually safer than living in many white communities in the area. Since before my grandparents moved into their first apartment in the Jewish shtetl in Manhattan in the early 1900s, little in this regard has changed.

Developing Relationships: Getting to Know Folks

As relationship is so very important amongst a number of communities of color, becoming adept at establishing relationships is a critical skill to cultivate if we are going to be comfortable with, and integrate into, communities different than our own. As discussed earlier, it starts with asking questions. In our community, "What do you do?" "What is your line of work?" is the type of question we are quite likely to ask very early during our introductions. It is not uncommon to ask it right after we exchange names.

In many other communities in general, and the African-American community in particular, this can be a very poor way to begin to get to know people. This involves one of those imperatives I mentioned above. Whether we are aware of it or not, asking people what they do for work provides us an opportunity to size them up, to see how we fit in. At its core, it is a question rooted in measurement, often with a flavor of competition. Certainly, many of us ask this question out of interest, perhaps looking for commonality. However, in many circles it is received as a challenge.

Typically, I introduce myself as Jay. Every so often, someone pulls out their title. In such cases I am happy to pull out mine, and if they feel a need to measure whose is bigger, I can do that too. It's like the guy who grips your hand overly tight and shakes vigorously during a simple handshake. It's often an indicator of insecurity. It can also be seen as an effort to assert dominance.

My black friends have told me that their initial response to a question about their work being asked so early in an engagement is suspicion. They might think to themselves, *'Why does he want to get up in my business?'* *"What's her angle?"* *"Who's really asking and what's their agenda?"*

As we are working to establish relationships, it is much more productive and friendly to ask relationship oriented questions. "Do you have children?" "How old are they? "What are their interests? "Do you have any brothers or sisters?" "Where is your family from?" (Be a little careful with this one, particularly with Latin Americans as some may feel this is an intrusion.) Music, art, and sports interests are all fair game. Eventually, you can begin to talk about work and career.

The more interested we are in others, the easier it is to become comfortable. At the end of the day, most of us love talking about ourselves. Being genuinely interested will encourage others to warm up to you.

Greeting: Reaffirming the Relationship

If you've watched enough movies or hung out in the black community, you can't help but notice the many different forms of greeting they have. Whether it's hugs and/or one of the seemingly infinite variety of handshakes, their verbal and nonverbal greetings are the way they reaffirm their relationship, their connection.

Back in the late 1980s, Joy wrote up a series of six standards of behavior that everybody at SEI, from the founders to the youngest child had to memorize. With these standards, Joy codified the behavioral expectations of everyone associated with the organization. They also provided a framework that allowed everybody to hold each other accountable. The very first standard paid respect to the place relationship has in the community.

> "At SEI we greet everyone with a smile and a handshake to strengthen the relationship between us."

It actually was the cornerstone of the organization. It was where I developed the habit of doing so. It is good practice to do with everybody, young and old, black, brown, and white. It has proved to be amazingly powerful with my students of color. For the past 27 years, whenever I've given a presentation, taught a class, ran a seminar, led a group, I have made it a point to shake hands, give some dap, and/or hug as many students as I can before we start. This one small gesture can make a world of difference.

Some of My Best Friends are Black:
White and Black Concepts of Friendship

Believe it or not, white folks and black folks have different takes on friendship. Many of us believe we have black friends. They may not tell you, but many African-Americans who you consider your friends do not necessarily consider you theirs. I have a question for you. Have you been to their home? This does not mean as part of a group social function. Have you been to their home and simply hung out? Have you hung out with their family? Do you know their parents, their children, their sisters and brothers? It is very likely if you haven't been to their home or of hung out with their family, they do not consider you their friend.

Oh, they may like you. They may enjoy your company. They may find you really great to work with. You both may go out for beers after work, shoot hoops at the gym on Saturdays, or golf on Sundays. You may go to the occasional restaurant, movie, or concert. You both may get along famously. However, if you have not hung out at their home and gotten to know their family, it is very likely they will not number you amongst their friends.

I have been told the same dynamic is in play for Latino Americans. You see, going to someone's home puts you on their turf, and for many of us that could be uncomfortable. It is our discomfort that can put a limit on the depth of connection we can build. Once again, if we are willing and able to be humble and be open to learning, if we are willing to be respectful of others' ways, and if we are willing to set judgments aside and simply be ourselves, our comfort level will continue to rise.

The Inadequacy of "Professional Distance"

Educators, social workers, doctors, lawyers, professionals of all stripes are taught to keep their distance. 'We mustn't get too involved with our clients.' 'Our emotions should have no place in our work.' 'Every client should be treated equally.' 'It should never get personal.' At some point in our training, all professionals are taught this, either directly or through strong implication.

Of course education, social services, medicine, the legal profession, just about all institutions in this country were developed by white folks in order to serve white folks. In this context the idea of professional distance makes some sense. However, when it comes to serving many communities of color, keeping professional distance may severely limit our effectiveness.

Remember, relationships rule. In many communities we can only be as effective as the relationships we build. There's a line from *The Godfather*, in which Michael talking to his older brother says, "It's not personal. Sonny, it's strictly business." Later, I believe it was Michael talking to his brother Tom, "It's all personal, every bit of business." Whether we are doctors, social workers, teachers, law enforcement officers, it's all personal, and it has been folly to have been taught otherwise, much to the detriment of those we have chosen to serve.

In the early 1990s, I developed and taught a graduate class for educators at Portland State University, "Building Self-Esteem in the Classroom." During the same time I was helping run SEI's, "2 x 2 Program," aimed at helping gang affiliated young men disconnect from the life and get on more productive paths. I thought it might be beneficial for the educators in my class at PSU to have an opportunity to talk with one of these young men in an environment in which everyone could be readily be open.

My guy, James, agreed to participate. James was a 17-year-old African-American young man who had been gang affiliated since the age of 12. James came to class and told his story. James' father disappeared from the family when he was a very young boy. When he was nine he began running the streets, getting in with an older crowd, and by the time he was 11 knew he wanted to be a member of the local set. He participated in his first drive-by as a shooter at the age of 12. Around that time his school attendance became sporadic and he dropped out of high school during the 10th grade. It had been only in the past six months, having run afoul of the law, that James began to think of walking another path.

The educators listened to his story with rapt attention. Most had never sat down with a young man with James' history. Most were pretty stunned to hear his story. When he finished, we opened it up for questions.

"Is there anything a teacher could have done that might've kept you in school and out of gangs?" one of the educators asked.

"Put an arm around me and let me know he cared." James told them. And he literally meant, 'Put an arm around me.'

"We can't." another of the educators said. "We are taught not to do that and it could get us in trouble."

It was James' turn to be stunned. "Really?" he questioned incredulously.

"Really." came the response.

We continued with a discussion of the needs of students and the limits of teachers. It is a credit to the folks at SEI, Umoja, and other grassroots community groups, secular and non-secular, that they do not accept such limits, that they understand their need to build and respect the relationship.

Being Personal in an Objectified World

Harken back to our original discussion of Axiology. If you remember, the preeminent relationship in northern Europe, one that ensured survival was that between the individual and their food. Eventually, the centrality of that relationship with food (subsistence) would evolve into various other aspects of the material world. As a result of the high value placed on objects, it is no great surprise that this tendency has grown to the objectification of people. Nowhere is this truer than in the institutions created by those of northern European descent. With the onset of the industrial revolution, workers came to be viewed as simply replaceable parts in a greater machine. Our school system was originally intended to produce factory workers. Here, students also came to be viewed as future parts in the greater machine.

Prior to the industrial revolution came the scientific revolution during which we learned that we could rapidly expand our knowledge through experimentation. By counting and measuring the myriad aspects of our natural world our capacities would grow exponentially. Couple the Scientific Revolution with the Industrial Revolution and it's easy to imagine how testing and assessment became the dominant characteristics of our educational institutions. And with such a focus, is it any wonder students came to be viewed as numbers.

The same can be said for just about all of our social institutions. The belief that we can experiment, count, and measure our way to understanding and serving people has some serious flaws. While at UCLA in the late 1980s, the University received one of a handful of "Connection Machines," the equivalent of a few hundred PCs operating in unison with each other. This was a very big deal at the time. One of my colleagues was particularly excited, for he believed we would now be able to duplicate human brain function and understand all of human thought, emotion, and behavior. It didn't quite work out that way. You see, we humans are much more than the sum of our neurological processes. Yet, our northern European axiology (i.e.: our white way of approaching our world) pretty much demands we make the attempt.

This way of looking at the world does have its advantages. Science and the scientific method have allowed us to learn so much, do so much, and attain so much. With respect to people it has helped us become healthier and more comfortable. It has allowed our institutions to become more efficient. On the downside, all too often we have made these gains at the expense of our humanity, our ability to connect and be one with others.

So how does a teacher help his students thrive, particularly those of color, in a system that, by its very nature, objectifies its participants? How can a social worker help her clients meet their needs in a system in which the highest value is to gather objective data in a subjective environment? What is a corporate executive to do when seemingly all their superiors and their boards of directors are interested in is the bottom line? The simple answer, though not the easy answer, is to focus on relationships.

Teachers, it's all about building relationships with your students. Whether we're discussing classroom management, teaching pedagogy, or motivation, it's all about the connections you develop and how well you respect them based upon the students criteria for respect.

As I wrote earlier, I would greet each student every day at the door as they walked into class. Early on, I would work to find out a little bit about each of their families and their interests. Here's the hard part - I would do my best to connect with each student's parent or guardian beginning with those I believe might need extra attention, and I would do so in person whenever possible. When I would meet them, I would be careful to present myself as a teammate in support of their child, rather than an authority. I would readily acknowledge that they are much more of an authority on their children than anyone else could hope to be. Making a connection when all is going well will make it more likely issues can be resolved to the student's benefit should the caca hit the fan. At the same time, when a student knows you and their parent are in regular contact, they are likely to be more motivated to excel.

There's a school here in Portland, the Metropolitan Learning Center (MLC), that is an alternative K-12 school within the Portland Public School system. The MLC does not have a system for bussing students to school. As students attend from all over the city, parents have to bring their kids. Some years ago, I was talking with the new principal, a man with whom I worked at his previous placement, and asked him how he liked his new gig. He told me he liked it very much and was surprised to find the great advantages of not having bussing available – parents have to show up to school every day. He told me that in the act of dropping the kids off the parents got to see the teachers regularly, almost socially. As a result, when teachers saw a parent coming down the hall, teachers weren't expecting a confrontation, which is what teachers at most schools expect when they see a parent, for typically parents only show up when there's trouble. Teachers and parents at MLC have a regular connection that allows for a variety of interactions, almost all of which are positive. So in the event of trouble, they have a positive relationship from which to work towards a resolution that works for all involved.

Understanding the cultural imperatives of students of color can be particularly useful to educators. Successful teachers would rarely, if ever, call a student of color out in class. Even if they have a strong relationship with a student, they would only do so very carefully, if at all. If there was an issue with the student, they would do their best to handle it one-on-one outside of the class. That is why the more a teacher knows about a student and their family the better chance they have of understanding what might be the underlying causes of their behavior.

Doing any of this requires that educators be understanding, humble, and respectful of the ways of their students and their students' families. The more comfortable and at ease an educator can be, the more likely they will be able to help put their families at ease too, and to encourage everyone to work together. Reverse integration.

A few years ago, I had a meeting at our local high school in Portland's African American community. I was walking in the school to my meeting when I saw two young black students hanging out in the hall during class time. One of them I knew from SEI the other was a stranger to me. I went up to them

"What are you guys doing out here?" I asked affably. The student I didn't know began taking on a very angry and aggressive mien.

"Put away the scare the white people face." I smiled at him. The young man I knew started laughing and the one I didn't was completely disarmed.

"Now, what are you guys doing out here?"

"Man, we don't like Ms. White's class and she don't like us."

"Look guys, I got no juice here, I can't make you do anything, but I think your best move is to get back to class. Go on. It'll be cool."

They went back to class and I went to my meeting. When you are integrated well enough into a community, you have a much better chance of understanding how to have things go well. In this case, I knew black folks, young men in particular, believe that it's fairly easy to intimidate white folks with anger and aggression. Rarely is there a plan to turn their anger into physical aggression, especially when we're talking about a teen and an adult. The easier you are, the easier they will be.

One school day at the House of Umoja, it was just myself and my students, 12 African-American young men. We were out in the living room and all the guys were grouped up on couches on one side of the room and I was sitting in a reclining chair on the other when they stopped talking with each other, folded their arms, looked in my direction and said,

"I bet you we all can take you."

"I bet you all can." I easily replied with a smile. "But two of you are gonna die."

They all laughed and shook their heads. Challenge met and answered. What I've learned about seemingly aggressive teens of color is that most of them are hard on the outside and hurting on the inside. So many of them have had to adopt a hard outer shell simply to survive day to day. If you treat them with love and respect they will return that love and respect many times over.

Social service providers - pretty much the same thing. The more cognizant you are of the way those whom you serve view and move through the world, the better chance you have of helping them. The greater rapport and commonality you can establish, the better the chance they will engage. Once again, this is particularly true in communities of color. The relationship is critical. Time and again, I've seen caseworkers and other providers, go to a client's home, or sit down with their client in their office, and the first thing they do is take out a notepad or a computer and begin taking notes. Client upon client has told me how off-putting that is, how uncomfortable it makes them, and how belittling it feels. I do my best never to have any tools or implements between myself and my clients. The few times I must, I ask my clients for their permission; this is simply a sign of respect.

It also rarely works when social service providers are afraid of their clients. The social service field is dominated by white women. A number of the clients they serve are men, often the men are Black or Latino, sometimes Native or Islander. Far too often, my friends of color tell me the counselors they or their loved ones have worked with have been scared of them. My friends would go on to tell me it became incumbent upon them, my friends, to put their counselor at ease. It is an unfortunate state of affairs when the person in the midst of trauma has to be responsible for getting their counselor to a space where she can do her job.

These are only a few examples of why it is so important for us white folks to learn how to be with people different than ourselves. How can we truly hope to serve people with whom we are uncomfortable, in places at which we are uncomfortable? The more we get to understand different communities, the more time we spend hanging out, the more at ease we will be and the better service we will provide.

Executives, you want to improve your bottom line? Businesses spend millions of dollars on hiring and training every year. Businesses in which employees are happy experience considerably less turnover than others. The less turnover, the lower the training costs. Businesses in which employees feel respected experience considerably fewer antidiscrimination suits. Fewer lawsuits means fewer legal costs and penalties.

It is important to note that respect is measured by the individual employee. I have been involved in countless situations in which a person in power truly believes they are being respectful to those who work for them, only to be shocked to find out that their employees have quite the opposite experience.

Organizations are most successful when employers and employees alike feel connected, feel they are valued. Management would do well to connect, on somewhat of a personal level, with those for whom they are responsible, as well as connecting with each other. Striving to improve your relationships with all those with whom you work is an endeavor that can pay off in a myriad of ways. Regardless of race or ethnic background, learn who your employees are, get to know about their families, understand their goals and dreams, and help them be successful. While good practice with all those who work for you, this is especially important with your non-whites colleagues and employees in your organization.

Make an effort to understand their perspectives and their ways, and more than that, make an effort to understand the individual. Be genuinely interested in the person, not solely as an employee or peer, but as a living, breathing human being. Take an interest in their families, their goals, their interests. Be yourself. If you are uneducated as to a particular culture, be uneducated. From there you can seek to learn. Be as respectful as you can be. Like many of us who have traveled abroad have found out, just a little effort to try understand the community's language can go far. It is a small demonstration of humility and respect. Demonstrating such humility and respect in the workplace can go a long way towards building long-term relationships that bring stability to an organization, and stable organizations tend to be more profitable organizations.

The Extremes

My Worst Day

It was the Fall of 1996, my second year at Umoja. In hindsight, I arrived at school that day feeling a little off. Why was I off? Truthfully, I don't recall. Perhaps I slept wrong; perhaps it was something I ate. Whatever the cause, at the time I didn't notice I wasn't quite myself, but later that morning it would become painfully apparent. The young men were scheduled to take a test on early North American history, from the European invasion through the French-Indian war.

The morning began as it usually did. We all greeted each other and checked in, said a little something about how we were doing. The fellas seemed to be in good spirits. After about 15 or 20 minutes, H.V. and I asked them if they were ready for the test and they all gestured noncommittally.

"Sure," "Yeah.," and various sighs.

We handed out the tests and watched as they began to work. Three or four students spent a few minutes answering a question or two and said they were done. The rest didn't even do that. They looked at their papers, shrugged, and handed them back to us.

I think it's fair to say that we all have our triggers, buttons that when pushed provoke behaviors of which we are not proud. One of my biggest buttons as a teacher during that time in my life was lack of effort. I was fine, even inviting, of all manner of student behavior. Challenges, distractions, questions, misunderstandings, disrespects, attacks. Rarely did they phase me. I've had insults hurled my way and I've even had a chair thrown at me. (It's not as dangerous as it may sound; furniture is relatively easy to dodge.)

But when I saw the way the young men approached the test, a rage started to build inside. I was able to keep a lid on it for a time. Then, later that morning, one of the students did or said something, I don't remember what it was, and I snapped. (The first and only time I have really lost it professionally.)

"Fuck you all!" I shouted, jerked the door opened and stormed out of the room, slamming the door behind me.

Moments later, I kicked the door open, stormed back in the room, and angrily addressed them:

"If you don't become educated, if you don't figure this out, you will all grow up to be nothin' but some stupid, dumb, niggers." And I stormed back out of the room.

Once I had calmed down, I was mortified. I was embarrassed. I was ashamed. I quietly reentered the classroom, sat down, and began to apologize. They were as stunned at my behavior as I was horrified. To my surprise, and to their great credit, they accepted my apology and we began a serious discussion about our differing views of education.

The relationships we had built the previous months were strong enough to weather my most unfortunate outburst. Some months later, we were in school when a new resident began testing me. One of the young men who was present the day I lost it nudged the new resident,

"Man, back off. He really cares about us. He lost it and kicked in a door because we weren't learning."

And One of My Best

We taught a lot of history at Umoja through film and video. Of course, much of the history we taught was from an African-American perspective. *Amistad, Eyes on the Prize, Malcolm X*, are just a small sampling. H.V. and I also felt it was also important to expose our students to the history of other cultures.

A couple of months after the worst day of my professional life, our students were going to watch *Schindler's List*. H. V. did a brief introduction to the film and we let it roll. Just a few minutes into the movie some of the guys began clowning around. I stopped the film.

"For the last few months, we have been watching movies about your people. This movie is about my people. Please be respectful."

Not a word was said, not a sound was made for the next three hours. No heads were down on desks, not an eye wandered. They were rapt . . . and moved. Whenever I see the movie, by the end I'm tore up. That day was no different. When the movie ended, one by one, each young man came up to me and hugged me. Not a word was spoken. None was needed. It was one of the more moving experiences of my life. In a small way, they showed me they had accepted me as one of their own.

Becoming Part of a Village

So how does one become a member of a village? More to the point, how does a white person in America connect with, and become part of, a community of color? I have come to believe that doing so can be rather straightforward and even simple. Now, being straightforward and simple does not necessarily mean it is easy, although it certainly can be. For those readers interested in doing so, connecting and becoming part of a community different from your own can be viewed as a simple three stage process: Showing up. Shutting up. Contributing.

Showing Up: Black? Like Me?

I'm pretty sure this is going to sound rather odd. It seems that in my early years working in Portland's African-American community, numerous times I was mistaken for being black.

Back in the Fall 1990, during the initial meeting of SEI's Family Literacy Program, I was introducing myself to the parents who would be participating in the program with their children. Most of the parents had seen me over the summer working with some of their children. Fifteen parents and myself were sitting at a round table in SEI's office. My purpose at this meeting was to find out what the parents needed and wanted, and how I might be able to contribute. I was doing my best to be as politically correct as possible. Three or four times during the first 45 minutes of this meeting I stated, "I am new to the community." I, of course, was meaning that I am new to working in the African-American community. Soon, I found out many parents thought I meant I was new to Portland. About 45 minutes into our meeting I mentioned something about being raised in a European household, to which one of the moms raised her hand and said,

"I know I'm not just speaking for myself, but a number of us around the table thought you were black. Now that we know you are white, what the fuck are you doing here?"

Without even being taken aback a little, I responded by talking about the opportunity SEI's founders had given me to be of service.

This turned out to be only the first of many. Sometime later I was being introduced to an older African-American grandmother, I'd say she was in her 80s. After we were introduced, she leaned towards me and asked me with a very cool southern accent and a twinkle in her eye, "What are you?"

Understanding what she was asking, I told her, "Mostly Polish, and a little Russian."

To which she responded, "You look awfully good for a white boy."

I was giving a presentation on learning skills at the local, predominantly African-American, high school, when one of the students asked me if I had ever been told I looked like Lenin. (That would be Vladimir Ilych) When I told him that was a new one on me, though I have been told I look black, jaws throughout the almost all black audience dropped; many just assumed I was.

These are just three examples of the many interactions of this kind that I have had while working in North, Northeast Portland. It happened with such regularity that Joy took to calling me the 'albino brother.' I must say that I have felt honored to be looked upon this way.

Why have a number of black folks mistaken me for being black? I do not believe I look black. I am unaware of any white person mistaking me for a black man. When I speak of this with white folks, they all have said that they don't see it. It happened so often that at one point I asked my mother if grandma had some family secret. (She said she wasn't aware of any.) Joy and I used to go round and round trying to figure this out. The best answer Joy came up with was that I simply showed up, consistently. And from an Portland African-American perspective, white folks simply showing up in the 'hood' with some regularity is a rarity.

Perhaps we white folks don't show up very often due to our discomfort with being in places where the rules of etiquette are unfamiliar to us, and the perceived costs of mistakes are high. Perhaps some of us are uncomfortable being the minority. Perhaps we simply have not been aware of opportunities to do so. Perhaps we just haven't made the time. Whatever the reason, I have found that continuing to show up is the most significant step towards eventually becoming part of a community.

Shutting Up: Bringing Our Respect and Humility

Of course, showing up in and of itself is not enough. How we show is critically important. All too often, when we do show up, we tend to bring our privilege and assumed dominance with us. I believe in most cases, we do this unawares. Time and again, I have witnessed well-meaning white folks with the best of intentions come into an African-American, Native American, or Latino American organization and attempt to run things. They give the paternal impression that they know what is best. Even if they do not mean to do so, their efforts are often received as such, to the chagrin and frustration of those they are trying to help.

If we are to become part of a community other than our own, we need to be aware of the messages we are sending. One of the best ways to begin to integrate with another culture is to initially be quiet, watch, and listen. We would do well to humbly check our egos, our values, and our approaches to the world at the door. The more we can learn about how others move through the world, about their moral and ethical value systems, about their needs and wants, hopes and dreams, the more readily and appropriately we will be able to contribute. We would do well to give all folks the respect we would like to receive. The more questions we ask and the more open we are to learning and understanding the cultures of others sans judgment, the sooner we will be able to find our place. And just to be clear, our place is rarely, if ever at the head of the table.

Contributing

Everyone has something to contribute. We all can provide some service that will add to the health and well-being of any community. My things have been education and mentoring. In just about every group of which I have been a part I have made myself available to help anyone who asks. I've written a book on parenting and another on learning skills. To date, I have given away many more books than I have sold. Folks know they can call me for help any time. I consider so many people part of my extended families.

At least as important, every community has so many organizations and individuals doing amazing work in support of their communities worthy of contribution. They do work that few of us ever hear about; positive news seemingly so much less 'interesting' than negative. The number of folks giving their lives in service to others every day are innumerable. In Portland, I had the great pleasure to work with some of them at Self-Enhancement, The House of Umoja, Friends of the Children, and numerous churches, among others. There are thousands of organizations, secular and non-secular, such as these throughout our country.

So, what do you have to contribute? Are you a professional, tradesperson, artisan, artist, or mechanic? Can you cook? Do you have a strong back? Do you have some wisdom? Everyone has something to contribute. And in every community there are needs, some of which you can help alleviate. The more you can be of value to a community, the more the community will appreciate your presence. Then, if you keep showing up and fitting in, in time you will become a member of that community.

I want to emphasize that it is the community that determines the value of the contribution. Providing something that a person neither needs nor wants, regardless of one's belief in its value, is often more a nuisance than a help. It has been my experience that such acts have usually been interpreted as an expression of privilege and paternalism.

One of the most valuable resources we have to contribute is our time. Not only can our time be valuable to the community, giving of our time can also be of great value to us. For it is during the times we are contributing that we will have some of the best opportunities to learn about the community's culture and build connections with its members.

Becoming part of a community can be as simple as showing up consistently, taking the time to understand the community's needs, and finding a way to contribute. If we do these genuinely with humility and respect, if we can learn to become comfortable with our discomfort, if we can learn to relish being in the minority, we will be able to fit in anywhere, at any time, with anyone.

Chapter 11

With Liberty and Justice for All

It was while listening to a discussion between my friend and his 15-year-old daughter that I came to understand one of the fundamental differences between Judaism and Christianity. My friend and I were sitting at his kitchen table one afternoon just after Christmas when his daughter came in to talk with him. She told him that in all good conscience she had to return the gift, a necklace with a Chai pendant, (Chai being the Hebrew word for "life") he had given her for Hanukkah.

(Just a brief bit of background - my friend was raised Jewish and his wife was raised Episcopalian. They both decided long ago that they would raise their children with aspects of both traditions. They made it clear to their son and daughter that their choice of religion, if any, would always be up to them.)

My friend, being an exceptionally wise man, a man full of questions and truly interested in how others looked at the world, asked his daughter what was her thinking was behind her decision. His daughter explained how she had a greater attraction to the way her mother acted towards a particular neighbor of theirs.

(This neighbor was not a particularly good guy. He was the type of person who often did what suited him regardless of its impact on others. During the almost 20 years my friend had been in his home this neighbor repeatedly caused trouble. From small slights, like his dog continuously defecating on my friends lawn, to more significant ones, such as when this neighbor built a shed from which rain water run-off drained directly down to the foundation of my friend's house, there was tension on and off on a regular basis.)

So, when this neighbor and his wife invited my friend and his family over to his home for a Christmas drink, my friend begged out while his wife and children accepted the invitation.

When my friend's daughter had asked him why he didn't go over to the neighbors for a drink, my friend had told his daughter that he didn't drink with people who consistently disrespected him. His daughter went on to say that while she respected her father's attitude, she more greatly appreciated her mother's more Christian approach, and as a result of seeing both approaches play out through the years, she had decided to choose Christianity. Of course, her father was very accepting of her decision.

While listening to this exchange a fundamental philosophical difference between Judaism and Christianity became clear to me. I saw that one of the foundational principles of Judaism was justice and two of the foundational principles of Christianity are love and forgiveness. All are required to be whole and healthy. The pursuit of justice without love and forgiveness can lead to self-righteousness, anger, and bitterness. Love and forgiveness without justice may lead one to feelings of impotence that can evolve into anger and violence.

Imagine someone steals your car. In the backseat you had a painting your grandfather painted for your grandmother, one you have always loved and one that was left to you upon your grandfather's passing. The person who stole your car was apprehended, but not before your car was totaled and the painting destroyed.

You go to this person's trial, a trial at which he seems to express genuine remorse. He is found guilty and sentenced to serve 18 months in prison. Justice? I'd say so. Would you? You lost something that is irreplaceable. If you cannot find a way to forgive him, an event such as this could eat at you for the rest of your life.

Now imagine the trial has a very different outcome. The car thief shows little remorse and is acquitted on a technicality. Justice? Let's say you can forgive him, choose not to pursue the case any further, and as a result of your forgiveness you feel much better. On the one hand this is good for you. On the other hand, there's a person out there who is likely to steal someone else's car.

Let's say, before the trial, this person contacts you, says he is sorry, and asks you not to press charges. Is just saying sorry enough for you to forgive and forget? Likely not. But let's say this person comes to you, expresses genuine remorse, and is truly willing to do what is in his power to pay for his crime and make you whole again. Under these circumstances, after some negotiation, you may feel that justice is being served and forgiveness is appropriate.

Of course, we have simply been considering the loss of material possessions. What happens when someone unjustly limits your opportunities to provide for yourself and your family, takes away your freedom, puts your health and the health of your family at risk, or takes the life of your child? These are all happening all too frequently. And the rate at which these are occurring is increasing. Yes, there needs be forgiveness and love . . . and there must be justice.

There must be justice as it pertains to the inequity of educational opportunity between the few at the top and the rest of us on the other rungs of the socioeconomic ladder. There must be justice as it pertains to the inequity of economic opportunities afforded to the affluent and the rest of us.. There must be justice as it pertains to the disproportional representation of our brothers and sisters of color in the criminal justice system. For in the presence of these inequities, striving and thriving are often replaced by struggling and suffering. And when people struggle and suffer for too long without being able to see a way through, the seeds for extremism and violence may be sown.

Make no mistake, we are at a tipping point. Will we work towards creating a society and a world that provides opportunities for the vast majority or the miniscule few? Will we work towards creating a society and a world in which all people are treated equitably by our social institutions?

Oh, matters might not seem dire to most of us today as many of us are getting by, though not nearly as well as those of recent generations, but forces are in motion. Similar to the effects of our changing climate which some of us have only recently been made aware of, and which a few of us continue to deny, but which have been in the works for more than half a century, the effects of the inequities in our society and the world are beginning to have impacts that are grabbing our attention.

The world is in crisis. Airports are being bombed, drinking water is becoming more scarce, our climate is changing and sea levels are rising. Religious extremism is once again rearing its ugly head. Here, in America, home-grown terrorism is on the rise as the disparity between rich and poor grows exponentially greater by the day. In the wealthiest nation the world has ever seen children are going hungry, people are still without medical care, and in some places our water is being poisoned. Now that it's become desirable to live near our city's centers, gentrification has taken hold throughout the country destroying what were once vibrant ethnic communities. Bearing the brunt of these ills are our citizens of color and their poorer white brethren.

As times get tougher, some have been adopting an us against them, circle the wagons mentality. Brexit in England and Trump in America are two recent examples. Throughout our country and much of Europe, blaming others for both our own failures and economic forces beyond our control has gained traction. This used to be called 'race baiting'. Neither immigrants, Latin Americans, African Americans, or Native Americans are responsible for our shrinking middle class, stagnant incomes, and rising cost of living. Nor are they responsible for the outrageous cost of education or the dearth of good paying jobs. They certainly are not responsible for our society's inequities. While I can understand how this approach has its appeal to some, I know it is clearly misguided and dangerous. It is the approach that brought us Nazi Germany, Fascist Italy, and more recently, Al Qaeda and ISIL.

Coming Together

Yes, we are presented with many great challenges. I believe the greatest of them is developing our ability to work together in order to create a just society in which all have equitable opportunities to strive and thrive. It is becoming increasingly difficult for white America to hold ourselves apart from the rest of the country with the expectation that the institutions and machinery of our society will provide us with the life to which we believe we are entitled. Every year, more and more of us are faced with uncertain futures. Every year, more and more of us fall into the ranks of the struggling and suffering. The American dream and the unalienable rights upon which that dream was founded are becoming more and more difficult to access.

I strongly believe it is no longer possible to raise ourselves up without raising up everyone. No longer is it possible to simply look out for number one and expect to be okay. No longer is it possible to separate our interests from those of the greater community. If we are to meet our challenges we must unite and work together. Rich and poor. Blue-collar and white-collar. Men and women. White, Black, Native, Latino, Asian, and Islander. It's going to take all of us.

If we are to meet all the challenges, large and small, with which we are faced, we must first meet this one, and to do so we need each other. We need each other's resources, both human and material. We need each other's ingenuity and creativity. We need each other's wisdom. We need each other's strength and perseverance. While every community has much to bring to the table to meet this challenge, there is one resource, unique to us, that it is imperative we share - our privilege.

We have done so in the past to great effect. I shudder to think where America would be today without the contributions of white Americans to the cause of abolishing slavery. It was partially through their efforts that the majority of Americans came to vote for men who ultimately would end the practice. The Civil Rights Movement of the 1950s and 60s would not have gotten nearly the attention if brave young white civil rights workers were not standing arm in arm with their courageous black sisters and brothers as they were beaten by police, attacked by their dogs, and brutalized by segregationist mobs. The anti-war movement that eventually lead to ending our involvement in Vietnam did not truly gain traction until white Americans made their voices heard. Today, like those who came before us, many of us are standing shoulder-to-shoulder with our brothers and sisters of color in the Black Lives Matter movement, in the renewed fight for voting rights for all, and other efforts promoting social justice. However, it still seems to remain one of the dynamics of our society that much national attention is not paid, nor outrage registered, until we are involved. Hence the need for us to stand up and show out.

Putting Our Privilege to Use Today

Using our privilege may be our singular, most important contribution we can make to the creation of a just society. We have a great advantage in that white people in power are more likely to genuinely consider what we say than they would consider similar information and sentiments expressed by people of color. We have greater opportunity to help others of us examine their thoughts, feelings, and actions that may put our brothers and sisters of color at disadvantage. As we establish genuine, personal relationships with folks different than ourselves, we can help our white friends and families look at the world through different lenses. In this way we can help them develop greater understanding, affinity, and empathy.

There is so much we can all do. All that is required is the willingness and courage to do so. I am well aware that for many this is easier said than done, yet as the saying goes, the journey of 1000 miles begins with the first step. For those new to this work here are some ideas.

Educate Ourselves

Discussions of race, ethnicity, inequality, injustice, and privilege are some of the most difficult discussions in which to engage, and some of the most important. They can be daunting as they can devolve into debates in which each side is more interested in winning their point rather than creating genuine understanding. Many of my friends intuitively know our criminal justice system is biased, know people of color receive differential treatment from social service providers, know many children of color are treated differently than their white peers in school. They intuitively know the institutions of our nation inherently disadvantage our citizens of color. However, many other of my friends do not.

When attempting to help our friends and family see injustice and understand its impacts, it is not enough to 'know.' We need facts and statistics to help make this more clear. Information has never been more easy to access than it is today. Take the time to arm yourself with the most accurate information you can. When you are doing so, make sure you're getting information from reliable sources. When someone sends you information that inflames your emotions, take a few moments to fact check that information. After a few times passing along such inflammatory emails to my friends list, then having friends get back to me telling me that what I sent was not true, and then having to send another email out in apology, I have learned to check for myself before I passed anything around. So, do your due diligence and you will establish the reputation of a person to be taken seriously.

Perhaps more important than facts and statistics are to our own education, is our capacity to see the world through the lenses of others. The larger portion of our education will come from talking with others, listening, and observing how they move through the world. The more we can do this without filtering other people's actions through our own cultural beliefs, opinions, and biases, the greater our understanding will be and the more able we will be to help others see events through different eyes.

Work to Increase Others' Awareness

Once we're comfortable with our knowledge base, we will be better prepared to have these discussions with our friends and families. We will be better prepared to help them become more aware of our society's inherent inequalities and their costs. With practice we can become better able to have these discussions in ways that may be more inviting and so promote greater understanding. As we become better able to see the world from the viewpoints of our friends and families of color, we will become better at helping our white friends and families see the world with different eyes and so become more empathetic.

This will all take practice. At first our efforts might come across as clumsy, perhaps a little off-putting. It took me some time to learn how to talk about these subjects in a manner that invited my loved ones to explore. It took me considerably more time to learn how to have these discussions with white people with whom I had little relationship. I am still learning and I believe I continue to have a ways to go. I'm fairly certain there are passages in this book that, in the future, I will see could have been written better. So, I suggest we be patient with ourselves, make our mistakes, do the best we can to correct them, and keep improving. As we do so, we will gain more and more ability and confidence.

Stand Up for Others

When we notice injustice, we can say something. We can point it out and see if we can help make things a little more right. Joy tells the story of being in line with her sister-in-law at a grocery store. Her sister-in-law is an African-American woman with very light skin and blue eyes. Often she is perceived as white. Her sister-in-law was first to check out, paying for her groceries with a check. The cashier readily accepted the check with a smile and moved onto Joy. When Joy wrote her check, the cashier asked Joy for two pieces of ID. Joy's sister-in-law called the cashier to account, asking her why the difference in treatment. A discussion ensued with the cashier and the store manager. We can be fairly certain that if Joy called the cashier to account, the cashier, and perhaps the manager would have been much less cordial.

This is one small example of how a person can bring their white privilege to bear. Whenever I hear people talk about others in a bigoted way, I do my best to help them become aware of the ignorance of their statements and understand their mistakes. Mind you, I do not take the approach that what that person said was offensive to me; in my world whether or not I am offended is not the issue. The issue is someone making statements that are ignorant and incorrect.

Actions very often speak louder than words. Sometimes we can stand up for others simply by physically positioning ourselves in a way that makes it known where, and for whom we stand. For those familiar with Jackie Robinson's story, Pee Wee Reese, his teammate, at a baseball game at which the fans were spewing venom at Jackie for his presence on the baseball field, famously walked up to Jackie on the field and put his arm around him, indicating that he had his back. Likewise, we can stand up for others simply by greeting them at gatherings in which they are in the minority and helping them to feel at home. I will do so whether or not I have a relationship with a person, or even know them.

Working for Economic Justice

We can also use our privilege to work for economic justice. We can make it a point to support businesses owned by our sisters and brothers of color, as well as those businesses that support their communities. If the choices are limited in our neighborhoods, we can shop online. An interesting project for an inner-city high school economics class might be to find out which community businesses are owned by local businessmen and women, and which businesses give back to the community. Then the class can publish the list of locally owned businesses and businesses which support the community. This way, community members will have a better idea which businesses to support.

If we are in positions to hire people, we can make it a point to give applicants of color a truly fair look. Sometimes this may mean looking beyond the words and numbers on a resume. This may mean getting to know the perspective applicant's story. How did that person get to be where she is? What challenges did he have to overcome? How tough might they be? Providing opportunities for others who wouldn't ordinarily be given a second look is a very important way we can take advantage of our privilege. Similarly, if we are in a position to decide on career advancement within our organization, we can move beyond what might seem the comfortable choices and give equal consideration to those different from us.

It is here that I must be careful. It is not sufficient to hire or promote just any person of color. Many times organizations, often without the conscious intention to do so, hire the person of color who is the least threatening, the person who sensibilities are closest to those doing the hiring or promoting. And in many, if not most cases, the men and women responsible for hiring or promoting are white. Time and again, I've seen many highly competent and effective people of color, who are deeply connected to their communities, get passed over in favor of those who have far less connection to their roots. So, my advice for those organizations looking to make a significant hire or promotion, is to seek guidance from community leaders and elders.

Perhaps of even greater value, we can work to develop real, personal connections with our brothers and sisters of color with whom we work and so become better able to support their efforts to move forward as professionals. This can be of particular consequence for those of those of us in senior positions. We can introduce them to our networks. We can help our friends and coworkers gain a greater understanding of, and appreciation for, those they have not yet come to know.

Working for Social Justice

We can do what we are able to promote fairness and accountability. As a number of states have been seeking to disenfranchise their citizens of color, we can, like many of us did in the 60s, renew the fight for voting rights. We can organize. We can protest. We can march. We can write letters and make phone calls to our representatives. We can use all the power of social media.

We can do any and all of the above any time racism and injustice rears their ugly heads.

Cell phones are doing for the social justice movement what television did for civil rights. We can make it a point to observe and record police activity, and so help to ensure fair treatment of our citizens and, when necessary, bear witness to acts of intimidation and brutality.

We can vote! In the 2016 election, less than half of the eligible voters between the ages of 18 and 45 voted, and only 43% of millennials did so.[96] Possibly, the single most lasting impact a president of the United States has is on his nominations to the Supreme Court, and it is the Supreme Court that has the greatest impact on our fight for justice and equality for all. As of this writing, if Donald Trump has an opportunity to replace one of the four progressive jurists on the court, our fight could be set back decades. Having a more progressive president in 2016 would have advanced our cause significantly. I know for many it doesn't seem to be the case, but voting does make a difference. Given our current climate, it should come as no surprise that in many parts of the country it is easier for white Americans to vote than Americans of color. So please, please vote and encourage your family and friends to do the same.

Eroding the Barriers of Institutional Racism

Those of us who work in institutions and organizations where our brothers and sisters of color receive differential treatment can be proactive in our efforts to change our organization from within. First, we can talk with those whom you believe may be receiving unjust treatment and come to understand their perspective. If they believe they are being so treated, together we can come up with strategies to affect change. We can help our white coworkers become more aware of these conditions in our organization and enlist their support. On behalf of our fellows, we can speak truth to power. If we do so respectfully and tactfully, beginning with the assumption that people are well-meaning, I believe we can improve our working environments. I may be naïve, but I would like to believe most people are fair-minded and would not intentionally treat others unjustly.

For those of us who work in organizations in service to others, we can also work to positively impact the lives of those we serve. Being cognizant of the prejudicial treatment many of those we serve receive at the hands of the various systems with which they engage, we can work to understand their experiences, pay particular attention to treating them with respect, and seek to ensure that at the very least they are treated more than fairly. Whether we work in the school system, the social services, or criminal justice, whether we work in healthcare, finance, or real estate, if enough of us change the way we engage with those we serve, our institutions will change with us.

I am well aware that the task of turning our society into a just and equitable one can at times can seem to be an overwhelming one, seemingly more so given the apparently deep divisions among the American people. To this I say, take heart and be courageous. We are still in the midst of the grandest of experiments in history. Never has such a diverse peoples created a truly egalitarian society. It has taken a long time, a lot of work, and much sacrifice to have come this far and even if we seem to be going backward in 2017, I know we are still progressing.

Yes, we still have a long way to go, but these things do take time. It took almost 250 years to end slavery in America and another hundred years to put Jim Crow to bed. Ninety-five years passed between the passing of the 15th amendment and the passing of the Voting Rights Act. So, I encourage all those who have been working for the cause of justice to continue to do so. More importantly, I encourage all those who have not yet done so to join the fight to whatever degree you are able.

Of course, it is easy to be cynical in today's America. It has become easier to turn a deaf ear and a blind eye to words of encouragement and optimistic visions. When producers of fiction pass themselves off as journalists, scientists, and educators it is understandable when people throw up their hands, say 'a pox on all your houses,' and tune out. And this is exactly what many of those who wield the vast majority of power in America would like. Sentiments such as these are what keep them in power. After all, the primary threats to their position are engaged, informed, motivated, and united people. We can be those people.

Though our demographics are shifting, the bulk of the power, for the time being, still lay in our hands. Sometimes it is not readily apparent, yet even those of us at the lowest rungs of the socioeconomic ladder have more privilege than all but a select few Americans of color. We will need to bring what power and privilege we have to bear if we are to join with others to create a society of which we will all be proud to be a part.

Beyond Using Our Privilege: Unity

However, using our power, privilege, and other resources as God gave us the wisdom to use them will not be enough. To be most effective we will need to be much more judicious in their application. To use our resources most strategically, we need to work as part of the larger community. And in order to work as part of the larger community, we need to be connected to it. Hence, reverse integration. The better we are able to look at the world through each other's eyes, to understand each other, to feel each other's sorrows and joys, to delight in each other's successes and come together in times of trouble, the stronger community we will build and the more powerful we will all be.

Doing our part to contribute to coming together means each of us being genuinely interested in how others move through the world, learning and respecting their ways, identifying with their needs, goals, and dreams. It means being able to comfortably talk about issues of race, ethnicity, and cultural difference. It means having the humility to listen and understand. At the same time it means having the courage to make mistakes, the willingness to acknowledge them, and the fortitude to correct them. It also means providing others with opportunities to see the world through our eyes, expressing our needs, goals, and dreams. It means truly connecting.

I believe that real connections, real relationships are the prerequisites for bringing the seemingly intractable issues of race, ethnicity, and cultural difference that have been like iron anvils draped around the neck of our society since our Nation's founding to resolution. I believe that real connections, real relationships are the prerequisites for folks coming together and helping each other to raise healthy, thriving families. I believe that real connections, real relationships are the prerequisites for building a community that is ready and able to meet the challenges facing us all.

Once again, it is not for us to take the lead in this grand endeavor, nor is it for us to show everyone else the way. Rather, it is for us to learn how best we can work with our sisters and brothers of color to reach our common goals. As White Americans, it is for us to learn how to integrate into the larger community, understand everyone's fears and concerns, needs and aspirations, and share our own. It is for us to learn how to become part of something greater than ourselves with others that we have thought to be different than ourselves. It is for us to become part of the greater village. We can do this. We move closer each time one of us opens our heart and mind, and extends our hand.

.
.
.

Epilogue

We Are All Connected

It was a bright spring Saturday morning at the church. Like every Saturday morning for the past six months, African-American parents and their children had gathered for the Family Literacy Program I was running for SEI. In the midst of a break, I was surprised when I heard one of the mothers singing a song to her young son that was very familiar to me. It was a song about the hierarchy of life. As I stood a respectful distance away, I listened to the English translation of a song I had sung in both Hebrew and Yiddish. The melody was the same, and with the exception of a couple of added stanzas, so were the words.

It was so surprising because I had never heard that song outside of the context of Passover. At every Passover Seder we would conclude with that song. For the entirety of my young life my parents would host the Seder in our small, one-bedroom apartment. Typically, we would have 20 or so relatives sitting at our table that stretched from the living room out to the foyer. Of all the Jewish traditions, Seder at my parent's home was my favorite.

I knew the song the mother was singing as both "Chad Gadya" and the "Der Her Utga Schicht," the former Hebrew the latter Yiddish. This was the song with which we concluded the Seder.

Towards the end of a very long service and wonderful meal we would all sing songs. (The evening would go on for about five hours.) For the last song, the song the mother was singing, half the people at the table would sing in Hebrew and the other half Yiddish, each joyfully attempting to out-sing the other. So, you could imagine my wonder when I heard the song in a vastly different context.

When the mother finished singing to her son I asked her, "What was that song you were singing?"

She smiled and said, "It's an old African folk song."

.
.
.

References

1. Kotkin, J. (2010, August). The changing demographics of America. Smithsonian Magazine. Retrieved from http://www.smithsonianmag.com/40th-anniversary/the-changing-demographics-of-america-538284/#CiqX6c3YylsdAMOy.99

2. Yen, H. (2013, June). Census: White majority in U.S. gone by 2043. Retrieved from http://usnews.nbcnews.com/_news/2013/06/13/18934111-census-white-majority-in-us-gone-by-204

3. Taylor, P. (2014, April 10). The Next America | Pew Research Center. Retrieved from http://www.pewresearch.org/next-america/#Two-Dramas-in-Slow-Motion

4. Kotkin, J. *op.cit.*

5. Cima, R. (2014, December 12). How diverse is your city? Retrieved from http://priceonomics.com/how-diverse-is-your-city/

6. Taylor, P. *op.cit.*

7. Gilson, D. & Perot, C. (2011, April). It's the inequality, stupid: Eleven charts that explain what's wrong with America. | Mother Jones. Retrieved from http://www.motherjones.com/politics/2011/02/income-inequality-in-america-chart-graph

8. Saez, E., & Zucman, G. (2014, October 19). The explosion in U.S. wealth inequality has been fuelled by stagnant wages, increasing debt, and a collapse in asset values for the middle classes. | USAPP. Retrieved from http://blogs.lse.ac.uk/usappblog/2014/10/29/the-explosion-in-u-s-wealth-inequality-has-been-fuelled-by-stagnant-wages-increasing-debt-and-a-collapse-in-asset-values-for-the-middle-classes/

9. Monaghan, A. (2014, November 13). US wealth inequality - top 0.1% worth as much as the bottom 90% | Business | The Guardian. Retrieved from https://www.theguardian.com/business/2014/nov/13/us-wealth-inequality-top-01-worth-as-much-as-the-bottom-90

10. American Institute for Economic Research
    https://www.aier.org/cost-living-calculator?utm_

11. Ross, H. J. (2011). Reinventing diversity. Alexandria, VA. Society
    for Human Resource Management. p. 20

12. Levit, J. (2007, November 9). The truth about voter fraud| The
    Brennan Center for Justice. Retrieved from
    https://www.brennancenter.org/publication/truth-about-voter-
    fraud

13. rPolitics (2015). Follow up on claims of voter fraud state by state.
    Retrieved from
    https://www.reddit.com/r/politics/comments/2jltnc/a_followup_
    on_claims_of_voter_fraud_state_by_state/

14. Mears, B. (2014, April 23). Michigan's ban on affirmative action up-
    held by Supreme Court | CNN Supreme Court Producer . Re-
    trieved from http://www.cnn.com/2014/04/22/justice/scotus-
    michigan-affirmative-action/

15. Germain, T. (2013, June 26). The anti-science climate denier caucus.
    | Think Progress. Retrieved from
    http://thinkprogress.org/climate-denier-caucus-114th-congress/

16. Ingraham, C. (2014, September 29). Our infant mortality rate is a
    national embarrassment. | Washington Post. Retrieved from
    https://www.washingtonpost.com/news/wonk/wp/2014/09/29/o
    ur-infant-mortality-rate-is-a-national-embarrassment/

17. Feeding America. (2014) Hunger and poverty facts and statistics. |
    Feeding America.org Retrieved from
    http://www.feedingamerica.org/hunger-in-america/impact-of-
    hunger/hunger-and-poverty/hunger-and-poverty-fact-
    sheet.html?gclid=CPmg24OI580CFcNlfgodbuAFOA

18. Poverty Program (2012). Poverty statistics: USA poverty. | Poverty
    Program. Retrieved from
    http://www.povertyprogram.com/usa.php

19. Ibid.

20. Ibid

21. Kliff, S. (2011, November 21). No, Congress did not declare pizza a
    vegetable. | Washington Post. Retrieved from

https://www.washingtonpost.com/blogs/wonkblog/post/did-congress-declare-pizza-as-a-vegetable-not-exactly/2011/11/20/gIQABXgmhN_blog.html

22. Wyler, G. (2013, May 22). All around the US, risks of a water crisis are much bigger than people realize.| The Business Insider. Retrieved from http://www.businessinsider.com/us-drought-water-scarcity-2013-5

23. Dimick, D. (2014, August 21). If you think the water crisis can't get worse, wait until the aquifers are drained. |National Geographic. Retrieved from http://news.nationalgeographic.com/news/2014/08/140819-groundwater-california-drought-aquifers-hidden-crisis/

24. *Sea level rise: Ocean levels are getting higher – can we do anything about it?.* (2012?). |National Geographic. Retrieved from http://ocean.nationalgeographic.com/ocean/critical-issues-sea-level-rise/

25. Water Aid. Retrieved from http://www.wateraid.org/us/what-we-do/the-crisis?gclid=CJSNjPD1680CFYqPfgodyC4JcQ#/water

26. Wong, E. (2015, December 8). Smog so thick, Beijing comes to a standstill. |New York Times. Retrieved from http://www.nytimes.com/2015/12/09/world/asia/beijing-smog-pollution.html?_r=0

27. Feistritzer, C. E. (2011, July 29). Profile of Teachers in the US 2011. |National Center for Educational Information. Education Week.

28. Maxwell, L. A. (2014, August 19). U.S. school enrollment hits majority-minority milestone. Retrieved from http://www.edweek.org/ew/articles/2014/08/20/01demographics.h34.html

29. *Labor Force Characteristics by Race and Ethnicity 2014* (2015). US Bureau of Labor Statistics.

30. Japsen B. (2012, September 12). U.S. Workforce illness costs $576B annually from sick days to workers compensation. Forbes. Retrieved from https://www.forbes.com/sites/brucejapsen/2012/09/12/u-s-

workforce-illness-costs-576b-annually-from-sick-days-to-workers-compensation/#5b7816fc5db0

31. Hunt, V., Layton, D., & Prince, S. (2015). Diversity matters. (PDF file) McKinsey & Company

32. McCambridge, R. (2017). Museums so white: Survey reveals deep lack of diversity. Nonprofit Quarterly. Retrieved from: https://nonprofitquarterly.org/2017/05/09/museum-boards-directors-whitest-getting-whiter

33. Hacker, A. (1992). *Two nations: Black and white, separate, hostile, unequal.* New York, NY. Scribner

34. Peterson, M. *The portable Thomas Jefferson: Notes on the State of Virginia, 1781.* New York: Viking Press. 1975. pp.192-193

35. Seifter, A. (2005, September 28). Media Matters exposes Bennett: "[Y]ou could abort every black baby in this country, and your crime rate would go down." | Media Matters.org. Retrieved from http://mediamatters.org/video/2005/09/28/media-matters-exposes-bennett-you-could-abort-e/133904

36. Haller, J. S. *Outcasts From Evolution.* Chicago, IL: Illinois Press. 1971. p. 4

37. Haller, J. S. Outcasts From Evolution. Chicago, IL: Illinois Press. 1971. p. 5

38. Cobb, T. R. R. *An Inquiry into the Law of Negro Slavery in the United States of America.* Savannah, GA: 1858. pp. 46-47.

39. DeGruy, J. (2005). *Post traumatic slave syndrome: America's legacy of enduring injury and healing.* Portland, OR. Uptone Press. pp. 80-81.

40. Rockmore, E. B. (2015, October 21). How Texas teaches history. | New York Times. Retrieved from http://www.nytimes.com/2015/10/22/opinion/how-texas-teaches-history.html?_r=0

41. Holzer, H.J., Whitmore-Schanzenbach, D., Duncan, G.J., & Ludwig, J. (2007, January 24). The economic costs of poverty. Center for American Progress. Retrieved from: https://www.americanprogress.org/issues/poverty/reports/2007/01/24/2450/the-economic-costs-of-poverty/

42. Brinkley-Badgett, C. (2016, September 30). Drug & alcohol addiction costs americans $276 billion a year. Atlanta Journal-Constitution. Retrieved from: http://www.ajc.com/business/personal-finance/drug-alcohol-addiction-costs-americans-276-billion-year/hnvrSvemEa1T5oIK1KZ9bI/

43. Coughlin, T.A., Holahan, J., Caswell, K., & McGrath, M. (2014, May 30). Uncompensated care for the uninsured in 2013: A detailed examination. Kaiser Family Foundation. Retrieved from: http://kff.org/uninsured/report/uncompensated-care-for-the-uninsured-in-2013-a-detailed-examination/

44. Van Sertima, I. (1976). *They came before Columbus: The African presence in ancient America.* New York, NY. Random House.

45. DeGruy, J. op.cit. pg. 75.

46. DeGruy, J. *op.cit.* pg. 79.

47. DeGruy, J. *op.cit.* pp. 79-80

48. Morris, T. (1996). *Southern slavery and the law, 1619-1860.* Chapel Hill, NC: The University of North Carolina Press. pp. 305-306.

49. State of Oregon Constitution, 1859. (repealed November 3, 1926)

50. State of Oregon Constitution, 1859. (Repealed June 28, 1927)

51. Berman, M. (2015, February 10). Even more black people were lynched in the U.S. than previously thought, study finds. | Mother Jones. Retrieved from https://www.washingtonpost.com/news/post-nation/wp/2015/02/10/even-more-black-people-were-lynched-in-the-u-s-than-previously-thought-study-finds/

52. Wells-Barnett, I. B. (1900). *Lynch Law in America.* The Arena 23.1: 15-24.

53. Bennett, L. J. (1966). *Before the Mayflower: A History of the Negro in America.* Chicago, IL: Johnson Publishing Co. p. 294.

54. Ginzburg, R. (1962). *100 Years of Lynching.* Baltimore, MD: Black Classic Press. p. 12

55. DeGruy, J. *op.cit.* pg. 96.

56. Flint Water Crisis Fast Facts (2016, May 22). CNN Library. Retrieved from http://www.cnn.com/2016/03/04/us/flint-water-crisis-fast-facts/

57. Kurtzleben, D. (2010, August 3). Data show racial disparity in crack sentencing. | US News and World Report. Retrieved from http://www.usnews.com/news/articles/2010/08/03/data-show-racial-disparity-in-crack-sentencing

58. Ibid.

59. United to End Genocide (2011). Atrocities Against Native Americans. Retrieved from http://endgenocide.org/learn/past-genocides/native-americans/

60. Ibid.

61. Ibid.

62. Hughes, V. (2014, March 5). Epigenetics: The sins of the father. Nature. Retrieved from: http://www.nature.com/news/epigenetics-the-sins-of-the-father-1.14816

63. Duba, U. (2004). How do young Germans deal with the legacy of the Holocaust and the third Reich?. Frontline. Retrieved from: http://www.pbs.org/wgbh/pages/frontline/shows/germans/germans/howdo.html

64. Sakala, L. (2010). Breaking down mass incarceration in the 2010 census: State-by-state incarceration rates by race/ethnicity. | Prison Policy Initiative. Retrieved from http://www.prisonpolicy.org/reports/rates.html

65. Johnston, L .D., O'Malley, P. M., Bachman, J. G. & Schulberg, J. E. (2004). *Monitoring the future: National survey results on drug use, 1975-2004.* National Institute on Drug Abuse. [PDF document]. (NIH. Publication No. 05-5727).

66. Jones, V. (2005). Are blacks a criminal race? Surprising statistics. | Huffington Post. Retrieved from http://www.huffingtonpost.com/van-jones/are-blacks-a-criminal-rac_b_8398.html

67. Ibid

68. Kindy, K., Fisher, M., and Tate, J. (2015, December 26). A year of reckoning: Police fatally shoot nearly 1,000. | Washington Post. Retrieved from http://www.washingtonpost.com/sf/investigative/2015/12/26/a-year-of-reckoning-police-fatally-shoot-nearly-1000/

69. Lee, J. (2014, August 15). Exactly how often do police shoot unarmed black men? | Mother Jones. Retrieved from http://www.motherjones.com/politics/2014/08/police-shootings-michael-brown-ferguson-black-men

70. Stamper, N. (2005). *Breaking rank: A top cop's exposé of the dark side of American policing.* New York, NY. Nation Books.

71. Ibid.

72. Hitt, J. "Does America Owe a Debt to the Descendants of Its Slaves?" in *Should America Pay? Slavery and the Raging Debate on Reparations.* Ed. R. A. Winbush. New York, NY: Harper Collins. 2003. p. 107.

73. Mapping Police Violence. (2016). Mapping Police Violence. Retrieved from: https://mappingpoliceviolence.org/unarmed/

73a Mooney, C. (2014, December 1). The science of why cops shoot young black men and how to reform our bigoted brains. Mother Jones. Retrieved from: http://www.motherjones.com/politics/2014/12/science-of-racism-prejudice/

73b Ibid.

74. Cook, L. (2015, January 28). U.S. education: still separate and unequal. | US News and World Report. Retrieved from http://www.usnews.com/news/blogs/data-mine/2015/01/28/us-education-still-separate-and-unequal

75. Hart, B. & Risley, T. R. (2003, Spring). The early catastrophe: The 30 million word gap by age 3. | American Educator. Retrieved from http://www.aft.org//sites/default/files/periodicals/TheEarlyCatastrophe.pdf

76. Deruy, E. (2016, August). Student diversity is up but teachers are mostly white. | American Association of Colleges for Teacher Education (AACTE). Retrieved from https://aacte.org/newsroom/aacte-in-the-news/347-student-diversity-is-up-but-teachers-are-mostly-white

76a Turner, C. (2016, September 28). Bias isn't just a police problem, it's a preschool problem. Heard on NPR's Morning Edition. Retrieved from:http://www.npr.org/sections/ed/2016/09/28/495488716/bias-isnt-just-a-police-problem-its-a-preschool-problem

77. DeGruy, J. *op.cit.* pp. 104-105.

78. Wilson, V. & Rodgers, W.M. (2016, Sep. 20). Black-white wage gaps expand with rising wage inequality. Economic Policy Institute. Retrieved from: http://www.epi.org/publication/black-white-wage-gaps-expand-with-rising-wage-inequality/

79. Li, W. (2014, June 5). How well do the GSEs serve minority borrowers? | The Urban Institute .Retrieved from http://www.urban.org/urban-wire/how-well-do-gses-serve-minority-borrowers

80. Lee, J. (2015, July 28). Getting a home loan is expensive —especially for black women. |Mother Jones. Retrieved from http://www.motherjones.com/mojo/2015/07/race-gender-interest-rates-mortgages

81. Effendi, S. (1938). Advent of Divine justice - an extended letter addressed to the Bahá'ís of the United States and Canada. Bahá'í Reference Library. Retrieved from: http://www.bahai.org/beliefs/life-spirit/character-conduct/articles-resources/extract-writings-shoghi-effendi-character-conduct

81a Sothern Poverty Law Center (2016). Retrieved from: https://www.splcenter.org/hate-map

82. DeGruy, J. *op.cit.* Pp. 80-81.

82. Dictionary.com Retrieved from http://www.dictionary.com/browse/racism?s=t

83. Ibid

84. Ibid

85. Gould, S. J. (1981). *The mismeasure of man.* New York, NY: Norton

86. Kendall, F. E. (2002). *Understanding white privilege* [PDF document].

87. McIntosh, P. (1989). *Unpacking the invisible knapsack.* [PDF document].

88. Hacker, A. *op. cit.* pp. 31-32

89. Wheeler, L. (2015, August 13). Poll shows bipartisan support for expanding background checks. | The Hill. Retrieved from http://thehill.com/regulation/251037-poll-shows-bipartisan-support-for-expanding-background-checks

90. Drake, B. (2014, March 4). Polls show strong support for minimum wage hike. | Pew Research Center. Retrieved from http://www.pewresearch.org/fact-tank/2014/03/04/polls-show-strong-support-for-minimum-wage-hike/

91. *Gallup Polling on Abortion.* (2015). Retrieved from http://www.gallup.com/poll/1576/abortion.aspx

92. DeWolf, T. N. (2007). *Inheriting the trade: A northern family confronts its legacy as the largest slave-trading dynasty in U.S. history.* Boston, MA. Beacon Press.

93. Browne, K. (Director). (2008). *Traces of the trade: Stories from the deep north* [DVD]. USA.

94. Nichols, E. J. (1976). *Introduction to the axiological model.* Paper presented to the World Psychiatric Association and the Nigerian Association of Psychiatrists. University of Ibadan, Nigeria.

95. Gould, E. (2012, October 10). U.S. lags behind peer countries in mobility. | Economic Policy Institute. Retrieved from http://www.epi.org/publication/usa-lags-peer-countries-mobility/

96. McDonald, M.P (2017). United States Election Project Retrieved from: http://www.electproject.org/home/voter-turnout/demographics

310

Index

Acknowledgements

First and foremost, I want to thank my good friend, guide, and confidant Joy DeGruy. The book would not, could not have been written if were not for her friendship, guidance, and encouragement these past 27 years.

This has been the most challenging work I have created. A number of friends read various drafts of the book and gave me wonderful, and much needed feedback. Discussions with Shirley Brown-Alleyne, Karen Abrams, Malik Bell, Jim Samuels, and Gilbert Witte all helped me believe I was able to meet the challenge of this work. Shirley and Karen read a number of rewrites and were instrumental in helping me focus my work.

Special thanks to Ebonee Bell, my editor for her great work helping to ensure this work is actually in English. If there are any mistakes left in the book, I assure you they are all mine.

Finally, thanks to all my guides, teachers, and mentors from the youngest child to the wisest elder of the African American Community of North-Northeast Portland. Their generosity of spirit, forbearance , and acceptance allowed me to grow and become a part of their community.

.
.
.

Made in the USA
San Bernardino, CA
18 September 2018